Athletic Scholarships

FOR

DUMMIES

by Patri___
Alexandra Powe All___

WILEY

Wiley Publishing, Inc.

Athletic Scholarships For Dummies®

Published by
Wiley Publishing, Inc.
111 River St.
Hoboken, NJ 07030-5774
www.wiley.com

WILEY

About the Authors

Patrick Britz: Pat Britz began his athletic career at a young age, playing youth league soccer. He continued to play soccer and earned a partial athletic scholarship to attend the University of North Carolina at Asheville. While there, he was a four-year starter and ended his playing career as the second all-time leading scorer in school history and the leading goal scorer since UNC Asheville went to Division I (1986). Britz has worked in the world of intercollegiate athletics for over 14 years, the majority of which he has been involved in NCAA rules and regulations. He began his professional career as the Assistant Commissioner for Championships and Compliance for the Southern Conference and then moved to East Tennessee State University as the Assistant Athletics Director for Compliance and Student Services. Britz spent five years working for the NCAA national office (1996–2001) and was primarily involved in the initial-eligibility and recruiting process. From there he went on to Texas Tech University, where he was the Senior Associate Athletics Director for Compliance and Administration. In August 2005, he followed his heart and never-ending passion for the game of soccer and accepted a position with the National Soccer Coaches Association of America as the Director of Division I Intercollegiate Programs. Although this is his first book, he has seen the need for *Athletic Scholarships For Dummies* throughout his professional career. Today, Britz lives in Lubbock, Texas, with his newlywed wife, Kim, their dog, Josie, and their cat, Shortstop. Even though age and lack of talent forced him to quit playing soccer, Britz is an avid golfer and sports a handicap of 10.

Alexandra Allred: Alex Allred earned two karate black belts and was honored Athlete of the Year by the United States Olympic Committee in 1994 when she was named to the first ever women's bobsled team. She went on to become a sports/adventure writer. Over the years, Allred has had a variety of unusual writing assignments. She test-drove and wrote about Volvo's Gravity Car, played as a professional female football player for *Sports Illustrated,* competed as a fighter (kickboxing), and took a rigorous firefighter physical — all for a good story. But when coaches began talking to Allred about her own daughter's soccer abilities, she began looking into athletic scholarships. As the author of over a dozen how-to and sports books, Allred saw the need for *Athletic Scholarships For Dummies.* Today, Allred lives in Midlothian, Texas, with her husband, Robb, their three children, and a variety of animals. Together, they try to balance soccer practices and games, horseback riding, tennis camps, karate, running, and volleyball.

Dedication

From Pat: I dedicate this book to Kim, who unfortunately learned how to be a book widow too early in our marriage; to my dad, who introduced me to sports and, for some reason, is still a die-hard Cubs fan; and to my co-author, Alex, who guided me through the process and showed tremendous patience while I got married and changed jobs during the writing of this book!

From Alex: I dedicate this book to my family, who endured countless phone calls and late-night sessions on the computer, and especially to Kerri and Katie, for opening my eyes to the book premise and for your amazing ability and agility on the field. You are so much fun to watch!

Authors' Acknowledgments

This book would have been impossible without the guidance and advice from Michelle Powe. You saved us. Thank you! Marc and Karen, your comments, suggestions, and constant input mean more than you can know.

We would like to thank all the athletes, parents, coaches, and trainers who took time to sit, talk, and share their own personal experiences with us. Oftentimes, these wonderful people held valuable information they did not know they had.

We would like to express our gratitude to Mikal Belicove who believed in the project from the beginning and fought to set it in motion. Thank you to Tere Stouffer for putting us on the right track. We knew what we wanted — we just didn't know how to begin. We would also like to thank many of the editors who weighed in, guided us, and moved the book forward. Thank you Jennifer Connolly (good luck with the baby!), Mike Lewis, and a big "thank you" to Elizabeth Kuball. You picked up the ball and ran with it. Thank you Joyce Pepple for your time, patience, and gift for scheduling. Whew! We made it.

Finally, thank you to all the parents and athletes who may read this book. This book was designed for the college-bound athlete and it is our sincerest hope that the information within these pages will help guide you toward a successful future. Thank you and good luck.

Publisher's Acknowledgments

We're proud of this book; please send us your comments through our Dummies online registration form located at www.dummies.com/register/.

Some of the people who helped bring this book to market include the following:

Acquisitions, Editorial, and Media Development

Project Editor: Elizabeth Kuball

Acquisitions Editor: Michael Lewis

Editorial Program Assistant: Courtney Allen

Technical Editor: Shane Lyons

Editorial Manager: Michelle Hacker

Editorial Supervisor: Carmen Krikorian

Editorial Assistant: Hanna Scott, Nadine Bell, David Lutton

Cover Photos:

Cartoons: Rich Tennant (www.the5thwave.com)

Composition Services

Project Coordinator: Adrienne Martinez

Layout and Graphics: Carl Byers, Joyce Haughey, Barry Offringa, Julie Trippetti, Erin Zeltner

Proofreaders: Joe Niesen, TECHBOOKS Production Services

Indexer: TECHBOOKS Production Services

Publishing and Editorial for Consumer Dummies

Diane Graves Steele, Vice President and Publisher, Consumer Dummies

Joyce Pepple, Acquisitions Director, Consumer Dummies

Kristin A. Cocks, Product Development Director, Consumer Dummies

Michael Spring, Vice President and Publisher, Travel

Kelly Regan, Editorial Director, Travel

Publishing for Technology Dummies

Andy Cummings, Vice President and Publisher, Dummies Technology/General User

Composition Services

Gerry Fahey, Vice President of Production Services

Debbie Stailey, Director of Composition Services

Contents at a Glance

Table of Contents

Introduction

When Navy came knocking on Ed Frawley's door to recruit his son, he wasn't at all nervous. He had done his homework. His son, Nick, had done his homework, too. As a nationally ranked pole-vaulter, Nick Frawley had been under the recruiters' microscopes for more than a year, receiving letters and phone calls from all over the nation. But rather than rest on Nick's laurels, the Frawleys went to work, researching schools (both academic and athletic programs) and scholarships; reading everything they could get their hands on; and talking to coaches, trainers, athletes, and parents from all different sports.

Ed Frawley admits that, despite the tremendous research the family has done, he learns something new each time he talks to another parent or attends a recruiting seminar. The world of athletic scholarships is a complicated one, with so many rules and regulations that it very well may seem daunting to you and your family. If so, you're not alone. Many families are so intimidated by the process that they rely on the wisdom of their high school coaches or guidance counselors.

But when Nick Frawley sat alone, talking to the Navy recruiter, his father had no worries. The entire Frawley family was familiar with recruiting terms, rules, and possible violations. Nick was well polished in what he needed to ask, what he was looking for in a college, and how he envisioned his own future.

What a wonderful way to enter one of the most important periods and one of the most important decision-making processes of your life. Yet Nick Frawley was unusual in this regard. Most college-bound student-athletes do not share this pleasant experience, although they could if they just had the knowledge.

You can. In *Athletic Scholarships For Dummies,* we provide you with the information to research your colleges so that you can enjoy this same sense of security and knowledge.

About This Book

This book was designed to be user-friendly. Each chapter should read as a miniature book on the topic at hand, making the information in these pages easy to access.

Athletic Scholarships For Dummies covers everything you, as a college-bound student-athlete, need to know about securing a college athletic scholarship. We fill you in on academic eligibility; combining academic with athletic scholarships; recruiting regulations; recruiting services; understanding the role of the college recruiter; the NCAA, NAIA, and NJCAA; self-promotion; working with high school coaches and guidance counselors; national signing day; scouting colleges yourself; campus visits; and parent and athlete do's and don'ts.

If you want an athletic scholarship, this book is the reference you need at your side as you try to make your dreams a reality.

Conventions Used in This Book

This book doesn't have many special conventions, but here are three you should be aware of:

- ✔ We introduce new terms in *italics,* with a definition that closely follows.
- ✔ Whenever we give you steps to follow in a particular order, we list them in a numbered list, with each step in **bold.**
- ✔ We put all Web addresses and e-mail addresses in monofont so you can spot them easily.

When this book was printed, some Web addresses may have needed to break across two lines of text. If that happened, rest assured that we haven't put in any extra characters (such as hyphens) to indicate the break. So, when using one of these Web addresses, just type exactly what you see in this book, pretending that the line break doesn't exist.

What You're Not to Read

This book is full of what you need to know and nothing that you don't. But occasionally we do go into more detail on a particular subject than you absolutely need, and when we do, we mark it with the Technical Stuff icon (see "Icons Used in This Book"). You can safely skip these paragraphs if you just want the bare-bones information.

You can also skip sidebars. Though you'll find interesting information in those gray boxes, they're not essential to your understanding of the topic at hand.

Foolish Assumptions

As we were writing this book, we made a few assumptions about our readers. For example, you may be

- A college-bound student-athlete who wants to know the ins and outs of the recruiting process because you want to attend college on a full or partial athletic scholarship.

- A college athlete who's already received an athletic scholarship but who needs help navigating issues like redshirting, dropped programs, and transferring to another college.

- A parent who believes your kid has a shot at receiving a full or partial college athletic scholarship, and who wants your kid (and you!) to be prepared.

- A high school guidance counselor or coach who advises students and parents about college athletic scholarships.

Other that that, we make no assumptions about what you do or don't know about college athletic scholarships.

How This Book Is Organized

This book has six parts, with several chapters in each part. The parts are organized based on how the recruiting process works. Here's the scoop on what each part contains.

Part 1: The World of College Sports

How can you possibly begin choosing a school you hope to attend if you don't fully understand what the NCAA Initial-Eligibility Clearinghouse does or what the differences between the NCAA, NAIA, and NJCAA are? This section of the book explains scholarship offers, how different scholarships may help you, and where scholarship offers come from.

Part II: Getting Recruited

Getting noticed among college recruiters is critical to getting an offer. You'll need to use effective communication strategies when you're dealing with different coaches and recruiters — in fact, communicating well is key to your ultimate success. You don't have to be on a nationally ranked team or break state records to garner attention. This part helps you come up with a strategy to get your talent recognized.

Part III: Making College Visits

Before you accept an offer from a specific college, you have all kinds of issues to consider. Your instinct may be to do back flips when you get an offer from a major university, but you have to know what that offer really entails and what it means for you. You need to know what kind of school is making the offer, what the school is like, where you would live and train, how the coaching staff deals with its athletes, and how your academics will fit in with this recruiting game. This part helps you ask the right questions, narrow down what it is you want for yourself, and create your own set of guidelines to go shopping for the best school for *you*.

Part IV: Committing to a School

Understanding the National Letter of Intent is only the beginning of your journey into the world of collegiate sports. When and how to make a verbal commitment to a school, what the long-term ramifications of a verbal commitment are, and how to negotiate a better scholarship offer for you and your family are very important steps. Before you go to college, you want to be sure that you're happy with your contract and that you understand what is expected of you. In this part, we show you how.

Part V: When You're in the Big Leagues: For Existing College Students

Not everything goes as planned. Despite your efforts to pick and choose the best coach, school, or degree, things beyond your control can change. This part of the book walks you through each step of the decision-making process. It also shows you how to transfer schools properly and maintain your eligibility status at the same time.

Part VI: The Part of Tens

As its final bow, *Athletic Scholarships For Dummies* offers some top-ten lists of recruiting information and questions you need to ask yourself before making a final decision on your college career. If you want a lot of information, but you don't have a lot of time, this part is for you.

Icons Used in This Book

To help you recognize certain kinds of information, we use different icons to draw your attention. Icons are those little pictures you see sprinkled throughout the margins of this book. Here's what they mean:

When we use this icon, we're flagging helpful morsels of information. These are tidbits that will give you special insights that will make the process easier for you.

We offer warnings for a reason: They can help you avoid anything from losing a scholarship or an opportunity to talk to a recruiter to missing a critical deadline.

This book is chock-full of important information, and some of it bears repeating. We use the Remember icon to remind you of a procedure, ruling, or idea that appeared in earlier chapters or that's important enough that you should never forget it. Think of the "Remember" paragraphs as your coach watching over your shoulder, reminding you of the rules and proper form.

When we get a little technical, providing more detail than you absolutely need, we flag that info with the Technical Stuff icon. You can skip these paragraphs if you want — or you can read them and get even more insight into the topic at hand.

Where to Go from Here

You can dive into this book anywhere you want, using the table of contents and the index to find exactly what you need. Or you can start with Chapter 1 and read straight through to the Part of Tens. How you use this book is up to you.

If you're early in your high school career, and you don't know much about athletic scholarships except that they're out there, Part I will be right up your alley. If you're starting to get recruited, and you're not sure how to handle the phone calls and letters, Part II is your ticket. And if you're already a college athlete, Part V is where you'll want to begin.

Although you'll never have a guarantee in the world of sports and academics, this book is your guide to making the right decisions. We hope that you and your family will read this book together, take notes, and begin the process today. Good luck!

Part I
The World of College Sports

The 5th Wave   By Rich Tennant

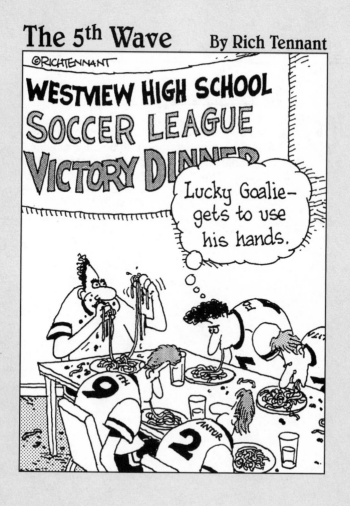

WESTVIEW HIGH SCHOOL SOCCER LEAGUE VICTORY DINNER

Lucky Goalie- gets to use his hands.

In this part . . .

We tell you everything you need to know about the NCAA, NJCAA, and NAIA; how to become eligible for college recruiting; and what you may expect from an athletic scholarship. This is your guide to getting started in the college recruiting game.

Chapter 1

Getting the Basics: Athletic Scholarships 101

*T*he world of college athletics — however seemingly vast and organized — is actually a relatively small community filled with confusing information, regulations, and rumors. There are myths — like the one that says billions of dollars of scholarship money are wasted because no one claims them, or the one that says every athlete who gets a scholarship gets a full ride — and there are dizzying real-life rules.

But don't worry. *Athletic Scholarships For Dummies* is designed to answer all your questions, address the persistent rumors, and ease your mind about how you should begin pursuing a scholarship.

In this chapter, we show you how to look at scholarships and how to think about where you want to play.

Don't worry about what other teammates are doing or how your cousin Joey got a full scholarship. We want you to begin thinking about *your* future, considering your assets, and making the moves that are best suited for you.

Sorting Through Scholarship Opportunities

If you know where to look, there is money to be found. The federal government is the largest source of funding, but you also can find all kinds of grants and scholarships available from major corporations and foundations as well as small mom-and-pop companies, all of which are committed to higher education.

Although your goal is to be awarded an athletic scholarship, you can't reach that goal without understanding where the scholarship money is coming from, what you have to do to get it, and what your responsibilities are when you've gotten it.

In an effort to raise the standard of education in this country, Uncle Sam has been a giving uncle, establishing loans, grants, scholarships, even work-study programs for students and student-athletes. State governments also award financial aid. And, of course, both the federal and state governments have vested interests in the money they award.

Colleges and universities are no different from the federal and state agencies in one important way: They expect something in return for the financial aid they offer, whether academic or athletic. Schools' academic or athletic departments will be interested in you only if they believe you have something to offer them in return. College athletic departments want athletes who will lift their programs, make boosters happy, and help ensure championships.

You need to understand what kind of scholarship is being offered to you before you sign anything. Chapter 2 shows you what a scholarship is and what the different types of scholarship are.

Finding the Right Program

Okay, so you're a top-rated soccer or volleyball player, you've broken state records in football or track, or you're a standout swimmer or diver. You show up to all your practices and games, have a great reputation among coaches and competitors, and are widely known and respected among recruiters. You don't need to worry about doing anything except playing the sport you play so well, right?

Wrong. Assuming that all they have to focus on is playing sports and that everything else will fall into place is probably the number-one mistake high school student-athletes make.

Think about approaching scholarship searches as you do the sport you play: In your sport, proper equipment is paramount to your success. Think about the money you and your family have invested in shoes, apparel, balls, and sport-specific gear for your practices and competitions. Think about the time and energy you've invested in practicing, perfecting your technique, and competing. Think about the time and money your parents have invested in getting you to your practices and games, getting you enrolled in club leagues, and allowing you to attend select camps. When you're going for a scholarship, you have to put in the same kind of time and effort.

Your educational choices are as wide and varied as are your choices in sport. But before you can make an informed decision about what school you want to attend, you have to decide what you want to achieve with your degree and what, if anything, you plan to do athletically after you graduate from college. You have to make this decision because different types of schools offer different advantages academically and athletically.

Universities are four-year institutions with a variety of colleges or professional schools (such as colleges of liberal arts, business, law, medicine, and theology) and several kinds of degrees in many areas of study. They offer bachelor's degrees in arts or sciences after four years of study; graduate degrees (master's degrees and doctoral degrees), which require additional years of study; and nursing, dental, and medical degrees, which also require additional years of study after completion of a bachelor's degree. Universities are usually much larger than colleges, carry out research, and offer on-campus housing.

Four-year colleges usually concentrate on one major area of education (such as colleges of liberal arts) and offer bachelor's degrees. Colleges generally do not support research or offer graduate programs, but they do have on-campus housing.

Within the category of four-year schools, there are large and small colleges and universities. Most large institutions participate in National Collegiate Athletic Association (NCAA) sports. The large, Division I universities and colleges are the schools that send the majority of football, basketball, and baseball players into the major leagues. So, if your dream is to be a professional football or basketball player, you should shoot for attending an NCAA Division I school.

Many small colleges and universities are superior schools with excellent academic reputations and prestigious faculty members. Many student-athletes who are interested in education first and athletics second attend small universities, which often participate in National Association of Intercollegiate Athletics (NAIA) or NCAA Division II or III athletics. Many student-athletes also attend NCAA Division III schools for the opportunities to play in multiple sports (which is usually not allowed by NCAA Division I schools).

Community colleges or junior colleges offer associate's degrees, which typically take two years to complete, and typically do not have on-campus housing. There are many reasons for attending two-year colleges:

✔ Some students are interested in obtaining an associate's degree to pursue specific technical careers.

✔ Some students begin at a community or junior college with plans to transfer to larger colleges or universities because they didn't qualify academically for admission into four-year schools. They plan to earn the grade point averages (GPAs) required for admission to four-year schools and then transfer.

✔ Some student-athletes start out at junior colleges when they haven't been accepted by the athletic program at the four-year school of their choice. They hope to maintain acceptable GPAs at the junior college, accrue playing time in the National Junior College Athletic Association (NJCAA), and attract the attention of recruiters from four-year schools.

To understand what the different types of schools mean for you academically and athletically, and what you need to do to be admitted to these different schools, check out Chapter 3.

The most difficult chore, of course, is narrowing down the list of schools in which you're most interested. You don't want to choose a school based on its team mascot, whether your dad went there, or because it's where your best friend is going. Finding the right program requires researching which colleges offer the programs you're most interested in, student graduation rates and transfer rates, academic and athletic success, athletic probation, recruiting methods, the coaching staff, and more.

For help with researching the right school for you, turn to Chapter 11.

Taking the Clearinghouse Seriously

"Nah, I don't have to mess with that. Coach tells me what I need, and he didn't say anything about the clearinghouse."

Unfortunately, this is an all-too-common response when student-athletes are asked about the NCAA Initial-Eligibility Clearinghouse. But if you want to play in the NCAA in Division I or II, and if you have visions of getting any kind of scholarship, you must register with and be certified by the clearinghouse. But what is the clearinghouse, and why — if it's so important — might your coach not stress that importance?

The NCAA Initial-Eligibility Clearinghouse is an agency that offers certification for prospective student-athletes to become eligible to play collegiate sports in Divisions I and II of the NCAA. Like everything you do as a student-athlete — the training, the competitions, the recruiting process, the letters and phone calls — you have to go through the clearinghouse if you hope to play in Division I or II of the NCAA.

The clearinghouse is not a recruiting service, nor does it guarantee that a college will take an interest in you. What it does is review your academic record to determine if you're eligible to participate in Division I or II schools as a freshman athlete (whether you've met the academic and athletic requirements of participating institutions) and then give colleges the green light to look at you after you've received your eligibility certification. When you understand and respect the process, you can be sure you've taken your first sure step into the big game: collegiate sports.

Your coach may not have mentioned the clearinghouse to you, because high school coaches — however wonderful, however nice, however gifted as coaches — can easily become overwhelmed by other responsibilities. Most high school coaches or club coaches hold other jobs. Most high school coaches also teach academic subjects in school. They're responsible for dozens of students, grading, testing, parent-teacher conferences, and school facility meetings, not to mention games, support staff, and all the other athletes on your team. The point? You can't rely on your coach for all the answers.

Going Through the Recruiting Process

Believe it or not (and you'd better believe it), just because you're the best on your team doesn't guarantee recruitment or a scholarship offer. Just because you set state records doesn't mean you'll go to the school of your dreams. And just because a college recruiter is telling you everything you want to hear doesn't means you'll get what's being promised.

Up until the point when you start getting recruited, all the running, lifting, straining, pushing, sweating, winning, and losing you've done has been the easy part. Again and again, we've heard parents share their dismay at the recruiting process. So many parents had no idea how exhausting and confusing it is. Many student-athletes never knew how cold and businesslike recruiting procedures are. Because they were unprepared, the experience was even more frustrating. Worse, that lack of preparedness can lead to devastating consequences.

But you can make your experience a positive one by knowing what to expect. In Part II of this book, we show you the ins and outs of college recruiting.

As you begin the recruiting process, you need to:

✔ **Carry a portfolio notebook.** This notebook should include 4-x-5-inch cards on which you can jot down questions you need to ask coaches and recruiters.

✔ **Have copies of your academic and medical records.** Your medical records should include a detailed medical history on injuries, allergies, and medical conditions that trainers should be aware of.

✔ **File and catalog questionnaires you receive from interested colleges, including the names of recruiters and coaching staff.**

✔ **Begin creating a list of things that are important to you — and continue to add to it as you go through the recruiting process.** When discussing potential schools, list things that are most important to you, such as school traditions, athletic facilities, winning records, graduation rate among athletes, or geographic location of a school. This list will help you remain focused as more schools show interest and you research individual schools.

✔ **Create a list of pros and cons for each school you make contact with.** Include the names of recruiters and coaching staff you meet, along with your impressions of them. After an aggressive recruiting period, the names and attitudes of different recruiters begin to blend together, and you may not clearly remember who you liked or disliked (and why).

Making College Visits

College visits come in two varieties: official and unofficial. *Official visits* are ones that are paid for in full or in part by the college that's invited you to visit, and you can make only five official visits during your senior year of high school. *Unofficial visits* are visits you pay for completely on your own, and you can make as many of them as you want.

For unofficial visits, be sure to make arrangements ahead of time to meet coaches and staff and to be able to view the sports facilities (and perhaps a practice). If you don't schedule these appointments ahead of time, you may get to campus and find everyone you wanted to meet with is away or busy.

Because the experience can be so overwhelming and exciting, many student-athletes later feel like they were in a haze as they walked across their first college campus. You can prevent that from happening by bringing a notebook with you on your visits, and writing down everything you see and hear. If you're able to have family members with you on your campus visits, ask them to do the same. (But don't take anyone with you on the official interview.) Your family's notes and your own notes will help you recall sites, sounds, conversations, and names of people and places that you may not remember later otherwise.

Talk to other college students — both athletes and nonathletes. What makes the school special to them? Ask about the campus issues that are most important to students. Find out how large the classes are, what classes are offered in your degree plan, what the professors are like. Find out what the athletic and dorm facilities are like and how the team members get along with one another and with the coach and staff.

Ask your parents or other family members who are with you to help you notice details like whether the dorms have adequate laundry facilities and what transportation will be available to you. Find out who will be sharing your living quarters. Seemingly minor details like these will make a big difference in how you feel about your college and your dorm room or apartment six months down the road.

While you're looking around and scrutinizing the college campus, you're being scrutinized by those you're visiting and those who are hosting you. How you conduct yourself can play a big part in how the coaching staff and your potential teammates remember you.

See Chapter 10 for tips on what to take, what to do, and what to ask on college visits.

Committing to a School

Committing to play sports at a school is a huge step — a life commitment. For this reason, you need to refer to your notes and prioritize your list when deciding on a school.

Rank the schools you're considering. If your first choice makes an offer, you've made your choice. But in most cases, the third or fourth school on your list will make the first offer, leaving you to agonize about what to do. ("Do I wait for a better offer and risk losing this one?")

The answer lies in your notes. Ask yourself the following questions:

- ✔ What is it you want and expect from this school?

- ✔ What did you like most about the team and coaching staff?

- ✔ What did you think of the academic department where you'll do the majority of your coursework?

- ✔ What can you offer this school?

- ✔ What do the academic and athletic departments expect from you? Are their expectations reasonable?

- ✔ How much you are willing to give to go to a specific school? Are you willing to ride the bench and see almost no playtime just to be able to say you went to a certain school? If not, and if you have no realistic chance of playing, pass on these schools. Take them out of your ranking.

If you've ranked a dream school because of its image or status, giving little consideration to what it may offer you academically or athletically, you've missed the entire purpose of the scholarship offer. When a school makes an offer to you, it's pledging money to you because it believes you'll be giving something back. You want this opportunity to improve your education and to give yourself a promising career, as well as to become a strong and positive force for the team you're joining.

As you wade through the very complex process of college recruiting, you'll begin to understand why your school ranking system and the research that has gone into it matter.

Part IV of this book outlines what to do when you're given an offer: reading a scholarship agreement, knowing whom to talk to, making a verbal commitment (and understanding how that verbal contract can be revoked), and signing the National Letter of Intent.

Staying Eligible After You're in College

What? You mean after everything you've been through, after all the hard work, the practice, the playtime, the recruiting, the research, and the signing, there are still *more* tests to come? You bet. Your scholarship is good for one year. Assuming you adhere to all the rules and regulations, keep up with your studies, maintain an acceptable GPA, and work hard and perform for the team, you should be offered a scholarship again for the following year. And the process repeats itself a year after that.

If you fall below the minimum scholastic level required for competition, your scholarship may be revoked — and poor grades are an easy mistake made by incoming freshman overwhelmed by new responsibilities.

In high school, you have everything under control. You may be very confident, popular, and organized. You're the big fish in a little pond. But in college, be prepared to be a little fish in a very big pond — at least for the first year or so. There are far bigger, faster, stronger fish in the college pond with more academic savvy and competition to their credit. Your absolute best defense to this kind of competition is to know all the rules and regulations of your school and its athletic association before setting foot on campus.

Transferring

After you've gone through all that work to choose the right school, you may find that it's not everything you thought it would be. Or maybe you've intentionally attended a particular school with the goal of transferring after a couple years.

Whatever the reason, as you consider the notion of transferring, remember that the college scholarship offered to you is a yearly gift from your college. This gift doesn't transfer with you.

Before you act, be aware of the following:

✔ **You cannot have direct or indirect contact with a coach or anyone from the athletic department from another four-year school without the permission of your current school.** You must receive a release — in writing — from the athletic director from the school you're currently attending.

✔ **You must voluntarily withdraw from your sport and relinquish your scholarship before moving forward.**

✔ **Talk with your coach, athletic director, and guidance counselor to discuss the option or penalties of transferring.** You'll have to meet certain legal and financial requirements.

✔ **You may want to request an official letter of withdrawal from your coach.**

✔ **If you're denied the opportunity to transfer, you may appeal this decision to a committee made up of members outside the athletic department.**

Transferring is a decision that should not be taken lightly. Be sure to research and compare the academics and athletics, location, cost, and personal needs. But also be aware of the different rules and regulations for moving from one division to another.

Chapter 18 is an excellent resource on the different rules and regulations of transferring.

Chapter 2

Defining a College Athletic Scholarship

*W*atch any Hollywood sports movie, and the sequence is always the same: Star athlete faced with a personal trauma or seemingly impossible living situation displays the grit and determination of a true champion and makes the winning shot/catch/kick/throw that wins a national championship, all before the unbelieving eyes of a college scout. The player is carried off the field by his teammates as the scout rushes forward, determined to have that athlete wear his school colors.

Only in Hollywood.

In the real world, most scholarships are far more complicated and much less rewarding than movie scripts would have you believe.

If you envision a university as a house, the athletic department of that university is often referred to as the front porch, or the first part of the house that people see or hear about. The academics, research departments, and other areas are then thought of as the rooms of that house. A successful athletic program can and does attract the interest of students who may want to apply to that university — even if they have no intention of playing sports. This is why many schools spend millions of dollars to attract the top athletes in the country (and around the world) in the major sports through athletic scholarships.

In this chapter, we tell you what a scholarship is and how it works. Think of this as the reality TV to a Hollywood sports script. Just because you're a superstar doesn't mean recruiters are standing in line to hand out scholarships. And when that scholarship does come to you, it's not for life — you have to know how to keep it.

Understanding the True Value of a Scholarship

The reality is, many students simply cannot afford college without some financial assistance. This is where scholarships come in. When you're offered an athletic scholarship, you'll have some or all of the following expenses covered: tuition, fees, room, board (meals), and books. An athletic scholarship is often worth more than the actual dollar figure that is attached to it. Therefore, the receipt of such a scholarship can be a major factor in a student's decision to attend a college.

Before we go into the variety of scholarships available, we want to make sure you know what a scholarship is and how it might serve you.

Show me the money!

Despite what you may have heard, scholarships do not grow on trees. They're difficult to come by. Not all four-year colleges offer athletic scholarships. Only NCAA Division I and II schools, NAIA schools, and junior colleges offer athletic scholarships. Plus, not all varsity sports at a particular NCAA Division I or II school may offer athletic scholarships. For example, Butler University (a Division I school) sponsors the sport of varsity football at the I-AA level, but the sport is considered nonscholarship, which means none of the players on the team is receiving an athletic scholarship.

No Ivy League school or NCAA Division III school offers athletic scholarships — these schools offer only need-based and academic awards. Many parents and student-athletes automatically eliminate these schools from consideration simply because they don't offer athletic scholarships.

Approximately 5 percent of the student body at large universities play varsity sports, whereas 40 percent play at smaller colleges. A large school doesn't automatically mean playtime or a better scholarship.

What it looks like on paper

The NCAA and NAIA mandate the *maximum* number of scholarships a school may offer in a particular sport, but how much a particular school offers is up to the discretion of that school. Table 2-1 provides the maximum number of scholarships for NCAA Division I sports and Table 2-2 provides the maximum number of scholarships for NCAA Division II sports.

Table 2-1	Maximum Number of Scholarships Allowed for NCAA Division I Schools
Head-Count Sport	*Number of Scholarships Allowed*
I-A football	85 overall and 25 initial (first year)
I-AA football	63 equivalencies spread out over no more than 85 student-athletes and 30 initial (first year)
Men's basketball	13
Men's and women's ice hockey	18 spread out over no more than 30 student-athletes
Women's basketball	15
Women's gymnastics	12[1]
Women's tennis	8
Women's volleyball	12[2]
Men's Equivalency Sport	*Number of Scholarships Allowed*
Baseball	11.7
Cross country/track and field	12.6
Fencing	4.5
Golf	4.5
Gymnastics	6.3
Lacrosse	12.6
Rifle	3.6
Skiing	6.3
Soccer	9.9

(continued)

Table 2-1 *(continued)*

Men's Equivalency Sport	Number of Scholarships Allowed
Swimming	9.9
Tennis	4.5
Volleyball	4.5
Water polo	4.5
Wrestling	9.9

Women's Equivalency Sport	Number of Scholarships Allowed
Archery	5
Badminton	6
Bowling	5
Cross country/track and field	18[3]
Equestrian	15
Fencing	5
Field hockey	12
Golf	6
Lacrosse	12
Rowing	20
Skiing	7
Soccer	12[4]
Softball	12
Squash	12
Swimming	14
Synchronized swimming	5
Team handball	10
Water polo	8

[1] Could be increased to 14.
[2] Could be increased to 13.
[3] Could be increased to 20.
[4] Could be increased to 14.

Table 2-2   Maximum Number of Scholarships Allowed for NCAA Division II Schools

Men's Sport (All Equivalencies)	Number of Scholarships Allowed
Baseball	9.0
Basketball	10.0
Cross country/track and field	12.6
Fencing	4.5
Football	36.0
Golf	3.6
Gymnastics	5.4
Lacrosse	10.8
Rifle	3.6
Skiing	6.3
Soccer	9.0
Swimming and diving	8.1
Tennis	4.5
Volleyball	4.5
Water polo	4.5
Wrestling	9.0
Women's Sports (All Equivalencies)	**Number of Scholarships Allowed**
Archery	9.0
Badminton	10.0
Basketball	10.0
Bowling	5.0
Cross country/track and field	12.6
Equestrian	15.0
Fencing	4.5
Field hockey	6.3
Golf	5.4

(continued)

Table 2-2 *(continued)*

Women's Sports (All Equivalencies)	Number of Scholarships Allowed
Gymnastics	6.0
Ice hockey	18.0
Lacrosse	9.9
Rowing	20.0
Skiing	6.3
Soccer	9.9
Softball	7.2
Squash	9.0
Swimming and diving	8.1
Synchronized swimming	5.0
Team handball	12.0
Tennis	6.0
Volleyball	8.0
Water polo	8.0

Note: An institution shall not provide more than an equivalent of 60 total awards in all men's sports other than football and basketball in any academic year.

Table 2-3 provides the maximum number of total scholarships allowed for NAIA sports. These limits pertain to all financial assistance that is funded, controlled, or allocated by the institution. This includes athletic grants or scholarships, academic scholarships, leadership and/or performance scholarships, outside scholarships administered by the institution, tuition waivers, benefits, room credits, meal credits, institutional loans, and work-study. What this means is that in baseball, for example, an NAIA school may not award more than 12 total scholarships (athletic and nonathletic) to the players on that team. There can be 25 guys on scholarship, but the total can't be more than 12 full scholarships.

Table 2-3   NAIA Financial Aid Limits (All Equivalencies)

Sport	Total Amount of Financial Aid Awards Allowed
Baseball	12
Basketball (Division I)	11
Basketball (Division II)	6
Cross country	5
Football	24
Golf	5
Soccer	12
Softball	10
Swimming and diving	8
Tennis	5
Track and field	12
Volleyball	8
Wrestling	8

The NCAA allows a Division I men's soccer program to award 9.9 scholarships per year. Not all schools that sponsor men's soccer, however, will offer 9.9 men's soccer scholarships due to budgetary restraints. The same can be said for several other Olympic sports, such as field hockey, volleyball, tennis, baseball, and so on. If the school has a successful football and/or basketball program and generates large amounts of revenue in these sports, it can allow the athletic department the opportunity to offer more scholarships in the Olympic sports, which normally don't operate in the black. This is why most Division I schools focus the majority of their budgets on the sports that produce the biggest revenues.

Using the soccer example, how does the coach distribute 9.9 scholarships to his team? *Remember:* The athletic scholarship can consist of tuition, fees, room, board, and/or books based on the cost of each of these items at a specific school. So, for example, if the cost of a full scholarship at a school is $12,000, and the school offers the full 9.9 scholarships in the sport of men's soccer, the coach could distribute $118,800 in scholarships to as many players as he deems appropriate.

Let's say a coach has $18,000 worth of new scholarships to offer for the next year. He could offer one really talented player a full scholarship ($12,000) and divide the remaining $6,000 among three other players. The coach could even decide not to offer the full allotment, saving it for one or two players who are not even on the market but will be in the future.

Very few coaches will use their entire allotment of scholarship; most leave some money available every year. During a particularly good recruiting year, a coach may use a large portion of his scholarship money, leaving little for the next recruiting class.

The competition for athletic scholarships is high, and parents and students must understand they are competing not only against other recruits, but also against other players who are currently on the team.

A lot of scholarship money is tied to returning players.

Asking the Big Question: What's a Full Scholarship?

While speaking to Ed and Shelley Frawley, parents of pole-vaulting phenomenon Nick Frawley, we asked about the *full ride*. Because Nick ranked third in the nation, placing first in the state of Texas, the Frawleys invested themselves fully in the world of athletic scholarships. As they began talking to other parents attending competitions, they learned that the myth of scholarship money is still alive and kicking. You know the rumor: There's millions of dollars in scholarship money just begging to be given away. The reality is that scholarship money is more difficult than ever to get. And the full ride? "It's rare," agree the Frawleys. "Very rare."

The full ride

A full-ride scholarship is a free ride, right? It is just as you might imagine, providing for the full tuition, fees, room, board, and course-related books in exchange for the athlete's performance for four or five years (as long as the athlete keeps up his end of the bargain and remains eligible).

The reality, however, is that full-ride scholarships are very rare and are becoming more so with the increased pressure from conferences around the country in favor of *one-year renewable scholarships*. As the number of full-ride scholarships declines, the renewable award is a viable way for recruiters to recognize and reward student-athletes with the promise of a full ride. It is a one-year award that is renewed at the end of each school year for the standard four-year academic/athlete career. The renewable award is a good-faith offer. In other words, student-athletes and their parents must go on faith that the award will be renewed at year's end.

We recommend that you talk to recruiters and other athletes from the schools you're considering, and investigate their record of renewing awards for athletes who comply with the academic and athletic standards set before them.

It is important to understand that athletic scholarships are awarded directly by each academic institution, not by the NCAA or NAIA. Within the NCAA, for example, approximately $1 billion in athletic scholarships is awarded each year. Although that dollar sum sounds high, the cost of awarding scholarships is even higher, mainly due to rising tuition costs. For this reason, schools favor partial or renewable one-year scholarships because they can offer more money to more athletes.

The numbers count

Some sports are known as *head-count sports;* they generate more revenue among boosters, fans, and the residual effects from major television deals. Some of the bigger head-count sports for Division I schools are

- ✔ Football (85)
- ✔ Men's basketball (13)
- ✔ Men's hockey (18 full scholarships spread out over no more than 30 players)
- ✔ Women's basketball (15)
- ✔ Women's volleyball (12)

Because they participate in head-count sports, most of these student-athletes are on a full scholarship because even if you're receiving only tuition and fees or books, you count as one of the "heads" toward the maximum limit. For example, if you're playing women's volleyball at a Division I school and receiving only a partial athletic scholarship, you still count as 1 of the 12. Obviously, the schools with deeper pockets will be able to offer more full scholarships in these head-count sports, but for a lot of Division I schools that do not sponsor football, basketball (and sometimes volleyball or hockey) are the money-makers so these student-athletes receive full scholarships with the hope of being more successful and, thus, earning more revenue for the entire athletic department.

Although the debate on commercialism rages on, the reality is, with scholarship costs increasing, schools need outside revenue to further their athletics programs. Again, people continue to debate which sports should benefit from such revenues and how. In the meantime, logos, sponsored halftime shows, tailgating events, and in-game and postgame entertainment promotions — as well as lucrative television deals partnered with big business such as Coca-Cola, General Motors, and Cingular — are on the rise. Think of sponsorship (the research and securing of) as a business deal for the student-athlete's future — the more revenue a school can generate, the more scholarships it may be able to offer.

Some people argue that activities such as these are exploiting student-athletes and that the school is making money off the talents and skills of young men and women. In the end, however, athletic scholarships are a wonderful privilege for student-athletes and an expensive proposition for any university. Therefore, athletic departments are becoming more and more creative about how to generate more revenue in order to allow student-athletes like you to earn a scholarship!

Can I keep the scholarship the church gave me?

If you get a scholarship from your church or the local Rotary Club or any other organization, you have to be careful. If the scholarship was awarded to you based on athletic merit, this may pose a problem with your potential school.

For example, a baseball player is given a scholarship from his church, but the number of baseball scholarships at his school is limited. Thus, this gift may be counted against the school.

It is not uncommon for a coach to give you a choice: Keep the money or play ball, but you can't do both.

Whether you're given money by your church or the local Rotary Club, talk to your high school counselor, or if you've already decided on the college you want to attend, talk to the financial-aid office. There is a cap on how much money a student can receive, and you must abide by the rules.

To avoid any trouble, always be open with your coaches and advisors about any monies you're offered. Many well-meaning gestures can land you in trouble if you aren't careful.

Riding the Full Four Years

The promise of four years doesn't always *mean* four years.

Athletic scholarships are renewed every year and may not be guaranteed (in writing) for more than one year. In other words, a coach may *tell* you that you will receive a scholarship for four (or even five) years, but that sort of promise may not be in writing. That said, it's unusual for a coach not to renew an award simply because someone isn't performing well. Coaches are keenly aware of the recruiting grapevine, and they don't want to earn a bad reputation among good athletes. Keep in mind, though, that coaches can lose their jobs if the team isn't doing well, so while you may keep your scholarship even if you aren't performing well, your playing time may suffer.

Coaches have the right to reduce or cancel your scholarship after the period of the award (usually during the summer). If this happens to you, and you feel it is unfair, you have the right to appeal. (See the following section for more information.)

Fortunately, Division I and Division II schools have guidelines that mandate that student-athletes must be notified by July 1 of each year whether their scholarships for the following year will be renewed, increased, decreased, or not renewed at all. If a scholarship is decreased or not renewed, the student-athlete must be given the opportunity to appeal this decision to a committee made up of members outside the athletic department. Again, although it is rare for a student-athlete's scholarship to be taken away based solely on performance, the revoking or reducing of a scholarship can happen for a variety of reasons.

How to keep your scholarship

If you talk to almost any coach in the country, he'll tell you that it isn't that difficult for a student to keep his or her athletic scholarship. Give your best effort each day at practice and in games, work hard in the classroom, and keep a positive attitude. Oh, yeah, and stay out of trouble!

Many student-athletes believe that, after they've been awarded a scholarship for the year, it can't be taken away regardless of behavior, performance, or outside circumstances. This is not true. In reality, a scholarship may be revoked during the period of award for a number of reasons, including:

✔ Ineligibility for intercollegiate competition

✔ Fraudulent misrepresentation on a school application, National Letter of Intent, and/or financial-aid statement

✔ Misconduct warranting substantial disciplinary penalty

✔ Voluntary withdrawal from the team

If your scholarship is reduced or cancelled for one of the preceding reasons, you're entitled to an appeal hearing. However, the chances of a committee overturning your coach's decision if you're engaged in one of these activities generally fall in the slim-to-none category — unless there are some strong mitigating circumstances. For example, you quit the team because you needed to focus on your academics so you wouldn't be suspended from the university — the coach allowed you to keep your scholarship for the remainder of the year but did not renew it for the next year.

You can't accept a scholarship, quit the team, and then continue to receive the scholarship. Your grades, behavior, and commitment to the team are all extremely important factors in whether or not you will receive a scholarship for four or five years — or be dropped after one.

Unfortunately, injuries are a part of athletics, and sometimes those injuries are severe enough to end a student-athlete's career. Be sure to ask your coach if you'll continue to receive your scholarship if you suffer a career-ending injury or illness. The scholarships that are awarded to student-athletes who will never play again due to injury do not count toward the team's maximum limitations we cover earlier in the chapter.

Who decides if you get to keep your scholarship?

Ultimately, the decision as to whether you'll keep your scholarship and for what amount is made by the head coach. Most coaches have individual meetings with players toward the end of the spring semester and let them know their status. This way, it isn't a surprise when you receive the financial-aid agreement (or a letter telling you that you aren't receiving a scholarship) in the summer.

Although the coach is the one who makes this decision, you have the power to make it a "no-brainer" decision. If you stay away from the four ways your scholarship can be immediately cancelled that we discussed in the preceding section and adhere to the following

tips, the chances of your keeping your scholarship for four or five years will increase to nearly 100 percent:

- ✔ **Go to every class unless you have an away game or are sick.** Take a schedule to your professors the first week of class, and let them know the days you'll be gone for away games.

- ✔ **Try to schedule your classes around your practice schedule as often as possible.** Just don't do this at the expense of your ultimate goal: to get your degree.

- ✔ **Show up on time (or early) for practices and games.**

- ✔ **Dress appropriately for practice.** Don't wear torn T-shirts and your hat on backward.

- ✔ **Dress appropriately to travel to away games.** When you're on the road, you're representing your team, your school, and yourself!

- ✔ **Work out on your own in the off season to try to improve your skills and get in better shape.** Talk to your coach to find out the areas in which you need to improve.

- ✔ **Stay focused and pay attention during practices and games.** Don't talk to your teammates about the frat party later that night. During games, avoid waving to your buddies and family in the crowd. If you're on the bench, stay ready to play at any time.

- ✔ **Keep a positive attitude even if you aren't playing a lot (or traveling) as a freshman or sophomore.** More than likely, there are juniors and seniors on the team who went through the same experience.

- ✔ **Be respectful of your coaches, teammates, and professors.** As corny as it sounds, treat them the way you want them to treat you!

Even though there are events that can happen beyond your control, in which you may have your scholarship reduced or cancelled (for example, your coach quits, or an unexpected star transfers to your school), following these tips will make a coach want to keep you on scholarship and as part of the team!

If your scholarship is reduced or cancelled, the school must notify you of this in writing and give you the chance to appeal the decision if you think it's unfair. If you want to appeal this decision, a committee made up of members outside the athletic department (for example, the director of financial aid, the dean of students, faculty members, and so on) will hear the appeal, and their decision is final. If you have specific questions about this, the director of compliance on campus should be able to help you.

Winning the scholarship

Vince Lombardi once said that winning isn't everything, it's the only thing. Somewhere along the line, this became a way of thinking in the sports world — a motto for young rising stars. But we wonder if Lombardi really meant the game. Although winning the game is wonderful, exciting, and seemingly fulfilling, earning a scholarship is the real win. Through your scholarship, you've been given the gift of an education, the opportunities that only higher education can offer, and the experience of a lifetime. Talk to any person who has been out of school 10 or 15 years and who's still paying student loans — you'll discover the value of a scholarship!

Defining the Term Half-and-Half: The Academic and Athletic Scholarship

Your chances of playing sports at the college level are far less than they were at the high school level — no big surprises there. According to the NCAA, high school men's basketball has close to 500,000 players (150,000 of whom are seniors). Approximately 4,500 freshman positions are available at the college level, which means about 3 percent of high school seniors will play college ball, and fewer than that will be offered scholarships.

The good news is these figures do not include the NAIA or NJCAA colleges, and they don't take into consideration the fact that a lot of those high school graduates will not attend college. The sport you play and the college you hope to attend are both factors when it comes to scholarship availability. For example, if your grades are not as high as you'd like, your chances of getting into and earning a scholarship at a top-notch academic school may be limited. Further, if you aren't starting on your high school or club team, you probably won't get offered an athletic scholarship at a program ranked in the top 20.

Half-and-half scholarships may be a fine alternative to the tradition full-ride scholarship. Textbooks alone can cost upward of $1,000 per year. Half-and-half or partial scholarships may offer financial aid for both athletic and academic purposes. Books are not the only costly expenses at college. Room, board, tuition, and computer fees can make higher education impossible — but a partial scholarship may absorb one or more of these costs.

Discovering the FAFSA

The scholarship you're offered may not be a full ride, which means you'll have to come up with some money on your own to pay for college. How are you going to cover the cost of tuition or room and board? Start by becoming familiar with the Free Application for Federal Student Aid (FAFSA). FAFSA is the form you fill out to apply for federal loans and grants.

If you want to qualify for financial aid, speak to your high school guidance counselor or go to the FAFSA Web site (www.fafsa.org). Applying for financial aid may sound daunting, but in reality, the form is short and painless. Don't let the idea of applying for financial aid scare you away. You may be surprised by everything financial aid may have to offer you.

Most important, after you've met the agreed-upon terms of your partial scholarship and played to the satisfaction of your coaches and specific sport departments, you may be able to negotiate for a full scholarship after your freshman year.

Scholarships cost money — often, more money than a school has. This is another reason why your grades are critically important. Although a school may be able to give you only a partial *athletic* scholarship, it may be more than happy to find *academic* monies for a second partial scholarship to help absorb the costs.

Chapter 3

College Alphabet Soup: NCAA, NJCAA, NAIA

In This Chapter

▶ Knowing the NCAA rules and divisions

▶ Deciding to play for the NJCAA

▶ Appreciating what the NAIA can do for student-athletes

*A*lthough football and basketball may dominate when it comes to television coverage, there are actually numerous sports for college athletes. Regardless of your sport, you have many options for where you can play.

There are three main organizations, and you'll find benefits in playing for each. But before you can choose, you have to understand what the different organizations and divisions are about. In this chapter, we help you start thinking about your goals for college and after college, which school is the best fit for you, and your chances of getting into the college you want to attend. All of these factors will help you figure out which organization to focus on.

Understanding the NCAA

The National Collegiate Athletic Association (NCAA) is made up of nearly 1,300 colleges and universities, athletic conferences, and sports organizations devoted to the fair and equal administration of intercollegiate athletics. The association's governance structure consists of divisionwide legislative bodies that govern within their specific levels; 125 committees that oversee sports rules and conduct championships; and the Executive Committee, which serves as the highest governing body of the NCAA.

More than 360,000 student-athletes compete each year in NCAA-sponsored sports. And more than 40,000 of these young men and

How it all began

You'll hear many students refer to scholarships as *free money* — something that doesn't have to be repaid — and for that reason alone, getting a scholarship is lucrative.

The idea of scholarships has appealed to people since the mid-1800s, when Harvard University created the first scholarship system. Lady Anne Radcliffe Mowlson provided the funds for a student-loan program in 1840. By 1878, Harvard had the best-funded scholarship program in the nation. But it wasn't until 1905 that colleges and universities seriously considered the health, welfare, and education of student-athletes.

The early years of football were violent ones — even by gridiron standards — and many athletes were killed during playtime. Because there were so few rules, plays such as "hurdle" plays were allowed: Teams would pick up their ball carriers and launch them over the opposing lines. Mass-momentum plays such as the "flying wedge" allowed players to link together in a high-speed play of mass momentum. In 1905, 18 players were killed in play, with another 140 injured. There was a call to ban the sport of football, and President Theodore Roosevelt came to the rescue. As a Harvard graduate, former student-athlete, and fan of the sport, he demanded that the game be reformed or be banned.

The Intercollegiate Athletic Association of the United States (IAAUS) was formed in 1906, but the rules were not rigid enough, and even greater numbers of players continued to be injured or worse. In the 1909 fall season, 33 players were killed. In 1910, the IAAUS reconfigured itself with clear rules and regulations. The new organization called itself the National Collegiate Athletic Association. The rest, as you know, is history.

women compete annually in the 88 championships in 23 sports held for NCAA member institutions.

Understanding the rules and who makes them

A major restructuring of the NCAA in 1973 led to the establishment of three new membership classifications for sports: Division I, Division II, and Division III. Further restructurings over the years have continued to diversify and decentralize the NCAA, adding not only more bureaucracy (with more people, more levels, and more money), but also more autonomy for different divisions.

For example, in 1978, NCAA Division I football divided itself into Division I-A and Division I-AA so that a Division I-AA football championship could be added. In 1981, 12 women's sports were added to the NCAA championship program, a number that has continued to grow over the years, thanks to *Title IX* (a law created to ensure that men and women are given equal athletic and academic opportunities). In 1997, the NCAA implemented a change in its governance structure that provided more control by the presidents of the member colleges and universities.

Grappling with the divisions

Each division has its own institutional mission and its own athletics philosophy. Each division also has its own criteria for membership. The more prominent of those criteria pertain to sports-sponsorship requirements and the amount of athletics-related financial aid that schools may provide to student-athletes.

Division 1: What it means for the athlete

Of the three major divisions, Division I requires its schools to make the largest financial-aid commitment and sponsor the most sports. Division I institutions compete at the major-college level. According to NCAA by-laws, these schools must sponsor at least seven sports for men and seven sports for women (or six for men and eight for women, but not the other way around), with two team sports for each gender and each playing season also represented by each gender. Each sport must meet certain contest and participant minimums, as well as scheduling criteria.

For sports other than football and basketball, Division I schools must play 100 percent of their minimum number of games against other Division I opponents. If a Division I team plays more than its minimum number of games, at least 50 percent of its remaining games must be against Division I opponents.

Men's and women's basketball teams have to play all but two games against Division I opponents, and the men must play one-third of their games in their home arena.

Division I schools that have football are classified as Division I-A or I-AA. Division I-A football schools are usually fairly elaborate programs and must meet minimum attendance requirements in one of the following ways:

✔ They must sponsor at least 16 varsity sports, including football. This must include at least six men's sports and at least eight women's teams.

✔ They must schedule at least 60 percent of their football games against other Division I-A schools.

✔ They must have an average of 15,000 spectators (in actual or paid attendance) per home football game once every two years.

✔ They must award at least 90 percent of the maximum 85 scholarships (76.5) each year (this can be averaged over a two-year period).

✔ They must offer at least 200 full scholarships or $4 million on athletic scholarships for all the varsity sports.

Unlike Division I-A schools, Division I-AA teams do not need to meet minimum attendance requirements. But all Division I schools — whether I-A or I-AA — must meet minimum financial-aid awards for their athletics program, and there are maximum financial-aid awards for each sport that a Division I school cannot exceed.

Playing for a Division I school is a big deal. It means playing on high-caliber teams with high-caliber student-athletes. It very often means playing a higher-profile sport, such as football or basketball, with a great deal of media exposure. Division I schools are *full-scholarship schools,* which means that all individual tuition, room and board, books, and other expenses can be paid for by the school. But, of course, this means that the standards for getting into these schools are also higher than those of non–Division I schools. (For more information on financial-aid or scholarship opportunities, see Chapter 2.)

Division II: A viable option

According to new NCAA by-laws, Division II institutions have to sponsor at least ten varsity sports: five sports for men and five for women (or four for men and six for women, but not the other way around), with two team sports for each gender and each playing season represented by each gender. As in Division I, each sport must meet contest and participant minimums, as well as scheduling criteria.

Division II football and men's and women's basketball teams must play at least 50 percent of their games against Division II or Division I-A or I-AA opponents. However, there are no attendance requirements for football or arena-game requirements for basketball. And there are no scheduling requirements for sports other than football and basketball.

As in Division I, there are maximum financial-aid awards for each sport that a Division II school must not exceed. According to Division II athletics philosophy, Division II member institutions believe they should provide athletic aid to student-athletes to increase the opportunity to participate in intercollegiate athletics. Division II athletics programs are financed in the institution's budget like other academic departments on campus. Many Division II student-athletes pay for school through a combination of scholarship money, grants, student loans, and employment or work-study earnings because there is not as much athletic-scholarship money available as in Division I.

However, there are some financial-aid requirements that all Division II schools must meet beginning with the 2005–2006 academic year. A Division II school must meet at least one of the following requirements each year:

- ✔ A minimum of 50 percent of the maximum allowable equivalencies (the maximum in men's basketball is 10.0, so at least 5.0 that sport and a minimum of 50 percent in three others) in four separate sports, at least two of which must be women's sports

- ✔ A minimum total expenditure of $250,000 in athletically related financial aid, with at least $125,000 in women's sports

- ✔ A minimum of 20 *total full-equivalency grants* (full scholarships), with at least ten total full-equivalency grants in women's sports

Division II schools are encouraged to offer as many participation opportunities as possible in regional competition against other Division II members. As a result, traditional rivalries with regional institutions dominate the schedules of many Division II athletic programs. Because most Division II schools have limited recruiting budgets and are sometimes not well known outside their region, Division II teams usually feature a number of local and/or in-state student-athletes.

More important, Division II members believe in promoting the academic success of their student-athletes and believe that participation in intercollegiate athletics benefits the educational experience.

Division III: Dispelling the myths

Division III institutions have to sponsor at least five sports for men and five for women, with at least two team sports for each gender and each playing season represented by each gender. There are very few minimum contest and participant minimums for each sport. Contest and participant minimums do apply to each sport used for sponsorship purposes (the minimum of five for men and five for women that the school has to offer).

Division III athletics features student-athletes who receive no financial aid related to their athletic ability. Their athletic departments are staffed and funded like any other departments in the university. Colleges and universities in Division III place the highest priority

---

Keeping up with NCAA rules changes

You've probably figured out by now that NCAA rules and regulations are lengthy, detailed, and often quite confusing. They also change frequently, which can be frustrating because you really do need to stay on top of the most current regulations that apply to you. So just how do all these rules and regulations come to be, and who is responsible for creating them?

All NCAA legislation is proposed and adopted by NCAA member institutions and conferences. Division II and Division III constituents vote on legislative proposals at the annual NCAA Convention (held in early January). Division I adopts its legislation through a yearly legislative system. New legislation or changes to existing legislation may occur only through this process; therefore, a rule cannot be changed without the proposed change going through the normal legislative process. (To better understand the Division I legislative process, go to `www2.ncaa.org/ legislation_and_governance/rules_and_bylaws/submitting_ legislative_proposals/d1_leg_cycle.ppt`.)

Next, proposals are submitted by the conference offices or by the committees of two different cabinets. The two cabinets are the Academic/Eligibility/Compliance Cabinet (A/E/C) and the Championships/Competition Cabinet (C/C). The A/E/C is responsible for reviewing and proposing legislation regarding amateurism, recruiting, eligibility, and financial aid. The C/C cabinet deals with playing seasons, awards/benefits, and any issues having to do with the national championships.

Proposals submitted by the A/E/C and C/C are then sent to the Management Council, which is made up of athletic administrators (usually athletic directors and senior administrators) and faculty athletic representatives. After the Management Council reviews and approves a proposal, it forwards the proposal to the Board of Directors, which is made up solely of university/college presidents. The Management Council and Board of Directors review proposals twice in order to give NCAA members the opportunity to offer comments and opinions over a three-month period.

---

on the overall quality of the athlete's educational experience and successful completion of academic programs. Division III institutions ultimately hope to graduate well-rounded individuals who have successfully integrated athletics with academics, who have integrated into the student body, and who have experienced the full range of college life.

Division III athletic departments place special importance on the impact of athletics on the participants rather than on the spectators. The student-athlete's experience is of paramount concern. Division III athletics encourage participation by maximizing the number and variety of athletics opportunities available to students, placing primary emphasis on regional in-season and conference competition.

The Division III athletics philosophy also strives to establish and maintain an environment that values cultural diversity and gender equity among their student-athletes and athletic staff.

Jumping In with the NJCAA

The NCAA (whether Division I, II, or III) is not your only option for playing college athletics, and it may not even be your best option. In fact, a junior college may be your best bet. Of the nearly 1,200 two-year colleges in the United States, 510 are members of the National Junior College Athletic Association (NJCAA), providing quality athletic opportunities along with valuable educational and career experiences.

Junior colleges have some excellent programs that may suit your career interests. There are two programs for students who are interested in higher education:

- **The transfer program** enables you to enter the school as a college freshman, complete one or two years at the school, and transfer your credits to a four-year school. As a student-athlete, you can compete in your sport while obtaining an education — whether you want to transfer to a four-year college in the hopes of playing for an NAIA or NCAA school or whether you just want to extend your education to a four-year degree (without playing sports at the NAIA or NCAA level).

- **The terminal program** results in graduation after two years with an associate's degree and provides you with the qualifications to find a job in your field of specialization.

What is the NJCAA?

The NJCAA is the governing body of intercollegiate athletics for two-year colleges. Its programs are designed to meet the unique needs of a diverse group of student-athletes who come from both traditional and nontraditional backgrounds and whose purposes in selecting a junior college may be as varied as their experiences before attending college. (If you're a home-schooled, learning-disabled, or international student, for example, Chapter 4 provides more information on eligibility rules.)

Like the NCAA, the NJCAA is divided into three divisions:

- **Division I** NJCAA schools award full or partial scholarships to their student-athletes. This may include transportation costs to and from the school once per academic year.

✔ **Division II** schools also award scholarships, but only for tuition, books, and fees.

✔ **Division III** schools are not allowed to award athletic scholarships.

Because a limited number of schools sponsor certain sports like women's golf and men's wrestling, they aren't divided by divisions. Therefore, it's common for Division III (nonscholarship) schools to compete against Division I and II (scholarship) schools. The sports that are divided up by divisions (such as basketball and soccer) compete only against other schools in the same division.

Founded in 1938, the NJCAA now comprises 510 two-year institutions, participating in 15 men's and 13 women's sports. The NJCAA sponsors 50 national championships for men and women throughout the United States, including nine football bowl games.

Playing a sport in a two-year school

Playing a sport while attending a junior college is really a win-win situation. Junior colleges generally have an open-door admissions policy, which means that you probably don't have to worry about getting in. So you're able to continue playing the sport you love while pursuing a higher education — two important opportunities and privileges that may have seemed out of the question when you left high school.

Because you're participating in structured conferences and maybe even national-championship games, as an NJCAA student-athlete you're getting increased exposure and publicity compared to what you may have received while competing in high school or at the club level.

The NJCAA is affiliated with a number of national organizations — the U.S. Olympic Committee, the American Association of Community and Junior Colleges, the Women's Sports Foundation, USA Basketball, USA Track and Field, and USA Swimming, to name a few. Not only do these affiliations allow member colleges the ability to remain actively involved in issues that concern athletic programs nationwide, but they also provide student-athletes even greater possibilities for exposure.

Playing in a two-year college is an excellent way to get the attention of four-year college recruiters. In fact, many NCAA coaches go after proven talent by raiding the junior-college ranks each year.

Being eligible to play later in the NCAA

The opportunities the NJCAA offers student-athletes for increased exposure and publicity are exactly what student-athletes who want to move to the NCAA need. If you failed to qualify academically for an NCAA institution, your dream of competing in the NCAA probably appeared to have died. But a junior college can offer you a critical second chance to improve your grade point average (GPA) while gaining college credits and continuing to play. It can ultimately allow you to transfer to a four-year school to earn a bachelor's degree and to compete on an NCAA team. (See Chapter 18 for much more information on transferring.)

Running with the NAIA

The third major national collegiate sports organization is the National Association of Intercollegiate Athletics (NAIA). The NAIA represents more than 300 four-year colleges and universities. Mostly comprised of smaller schools, the NAIA is divided into 32 districts and hosts 24 national championships in sports such as baseball, basketball, cross country, football, golf, soccer, swimming, tennis, track, and wrestling.

The philosophy of NAIA institutions is to view athletics as part of the overall educational process with emphasis on *student* in the term *student-athlete*.

The NAIA is dedicated to academic achievement above athletic excellence. It expects ethical behavior from its student-athletes, and it is committed to scholarship, sportsmanship, and leadership. The organization has been a trailblazer in providing equal opportunities for all student-athletes.

What is the NAIA?

Just as the NCAA was begun largely because of one sport (football), the NAIA was originally focused on one sport: basketball. Its original name — the National Association of Intercollegiate Basketball (NAIB) — says it all. In 1937, a men's basketball tournament (which, by the way, has become the longest continuous national collegiate tournament in any sport; see www.naia.org/campaign/history/history.html) tipped off in Kansas City, Missouri. That small-college basketball tournament, and the resulting formation of the

NAIB, were initially the brainchildren of a group of Kansas City businessmen who wanted to provide Kansas City–area fans with exciting amateur competition and to provide small colleges and universities with realistic opportunities to win a national basketball championship.

But the association's goals and achievements outgrew its founders' aspirations, and it became much, much more. In 1948, the NAIB affirmed its commitment to equality by becoming the first national organization to offer intercollegiate postseason opportunities to African American student-athletes. Five years later, in 1953, the NAIB — which had officially become the NAIA the year before — continued its trailblazing ideals and voted historically black institutions into its membership.

With the association's new name came the addition of national championships in several sports over the years. Then, in 1980, the NAIA moved into its second half-century by revolutionizing national collegiate athletics again with the establishment of athletics programs for women, becoming the first organization to offer collegiate athletics to both men and women. The championship calendar for women began that year with eight sports, and — of course — more were added later thanks to Title IX.

Defining how the NAIA serves athletes

In 2000, the NAIA reaffirmed its purpose — to enhance the character-building aspects of sport — by developing the Champions of Character initiative. Through this initiative, the NAIA seeks to create an environment in which every student-athlete, coach, official, and spectator is committed to the true spirit of competition through five tenets:

- ✔ Respect
- ✔ Integrity
- ✔ Responsibility
- ✔ Servant leadership
- ✔ Sportsmanship

The goal of this program is to "educate and create awareness of the positive character-building traits afforded by sports and return integrity to competition at the collegiate and youth levels while impacting all of society."

NAIA schools — among the most prestigious colleges and universities in the country — provide some of the best educational programs and some of the most successful placement opportunities in the nation after graduation, both for jobs and graduate school. Not only are NAIA schools competitive in academics, but they're also extremely competitive in athletics, boasting some of the finest athletes in the nation.

There are many advantages to competing in NAIA sports, including:

✔ Maximum opportunities to participate in regular-season contests and national championships

✔ Maximum opportunities for athletic scholarships (more than 90 percent of NAIA institutions offer athletic scholarships)

✔ Minimum recruiting restrictions (fewer than in the other collegiate sports organizations)

✔ Close-knit communities

✔ Small class sizes, which provide informal and personalized educations, allowing students more one-on-one time with their professors

The focus of NAIA schools is on the education and character development of the student-athlete. In fact, if you're playing sports for an NAIA school, and you feel that the school or team is not the right fit, you can transfer to another NAIA institution and compete the next season without sitting out a year, which is not always the case at the NCAA level.

Although the NAIA has strict academic requirements, the process of establishing eligibility is streamlined because there is no clearinghouse. Unlike the NCAA, each NAIA school certifies the eligibility of an incoming student-athlete on its own as long as he or she has graduated from high school and meets *two* of the following requirements:

✔ At least an 18 on the ACT or 860 on the SAT

✔ GPA of at least 2.0

✔ Graduation in the upper half of the high school class

Chapter 4

Clearing the Clearinghouse

· ·

In This Chapter

▶ Finding out about clearinghouse eligibility rules

▶ Qualifying for Division I, Division II, and Division III

▶ Looking at the NAIA and NJCAA requirements

▶ Knowing what to do if you're a home-schooled, international, or learning-disabled student-athlete

· ·

*N*ow that you're ready to begin the process of applying to college, you need to know the different eligibility requirements for the different athletic divisions or associations. Why? So you know where you may or may not qualify and where you should or should not apply.

Deciphering all this information is no small task. Just as each college has its own *academic* admissions requirements, you'll find different athletic eligibility requirements based on your GPA and ACT/SAT scores for each division in the NCAA, NAIA, or NJCAA.

You may also find different eligibility requirements if you were home-schooled, if you're an international student-athlete, or if you have a learning disability.

The bottom line is that, as a student-athlete, you need to know about and fulfill both the governing athletic organization's athletic eligibility requirements *and* the individual school's academic admissions requirements in order to be admitted to and compete at the college of your choice. So pay close attention to this chapter, take notes, and begin the arduous (but very worthwhile) process of applying for and being accepted to college. With the information you'll find in these pages, you'll already be miles ahead of the rest.

Discovering the NCAA Initial-Eligibility Clearinghouse

If you intend to participate in Division I or Division II athletics as a freshman, you must register with and be certified by the NCAA Initial-Eligibility Clearinghouse. And, of course, that means you must know all the requirements, fees, and due dates in order to register.

But before we get to the deadlines and rules, what is this clearinghouse? The *clearinghouse* is an agency that certifies prospective student-athletes as eligible to play collegiate sports in Divisions I and II of the NCAA. The clearinghouse determines your eligibility (based on grades, completed core course requirements, ACT/SAT scores, and so on). Then, when colleges request information on your eligibility, the clearinghouse makes a certification decision about you and reports that decision directly to the colleges. In short, the clearinghouse tells those colleges whether or not you're eligible to play Division I or II sports. If the clearinghouse says you're not eligible, the colleges won't spend any time considering you or trying to recruit you.

Three types of eligibility are possible:

✔ Certification of eligibility for expense-paid campus visits

✔ Preliminary certification of eligibility to participate in college sports (meaning you appear likely to meet all NCAA requirements, but you haven't yet graduated)

✔ Final certification, granted when proof of graduation is received

The clearinghouse does not work as a recruiting service, a placement agency, or an admissions office; it simply provides your eligibility certification results to any school that requests information about you as a prospective student-athlete. The clearinghouse stays on top of your grades, your SAT/ACT scores, and whether you've taken all the courses you're required to take for graduation. If you haven't fulfilled these requirements, you won't receive certification of eligibility from the clearinghouse, and you won't be allowed to play in Division I or II.

The clearinghouse is also an important source of information for prospective student-athletes. From the NCAA Initial-Eligibility Clearinghouse Web site (www.ncaaclearinghouse.net), you can

get information on Division I and Division II eligibility requirements, register with the clearinghouse, and access your individual
clearinghouse records.

Facts and figures

The clearinghouse reviews your academic record to determine if
you may participate in Division I or II schools as a freshman athlete.
Understanding this process and keeping up with the latest initial-
eligibility information are essential tools for making your move into
collegiate sports.

For example, the initial-eligibility requirements for Division I and
Division II incoming freshmen have recently changed, and you need
to be familiar with these changes as they apply to you. The new
requirements for 2005, 2006, and 2007 in Division I and Division II
increase the number of required core courses from 13 to 14. The
new requirements for incoming freshmen in 2008, Division I only,
will be 16 core courses. To understand what core courses are and
where the additional courses must come from, see "Core course
requirements," later in this chapter.

The SAT and ACT also have made changes to their tests, and one of
the most significant is the addition of a writing component, for
which you'll be asked to write an essay. (The SAT writing section is
mandatory, while the ACT writing section is optional.) As a result
of adding the writing section, the SAT now has three parts: critical
reading (formerly known as *verbal*), mathematics, and writing.
Because each section is worth 200 to 800 points, the SAT score will
now range from 600 to 2,400.

But the NCAA has determined that the writing component should
not be required at the present time. Therefore, the clearinghouse
continues to combine the sections of critical reading and mathematics for the total score. The writing section is not used.

Although the ACT is adding an optional writing component, the
scores on the ACT will remain the same. The writing section —
even if an essay is written — will not be used.

You can find more information about the new SAT at `www.college
board.com`. Read about the new ACT at `www.act.org`. Also, for
help with the SAT and ACT, check out *SAT I For Dummies,* 6th Edition,
by Geraldine Woods; and *ACT For Dummies,* 3rd Edition, by Suzie
Vlk, both published by Wiley.

Cost and contract information

To register with the NCAA Initial-Eligibility Clearinghouse, you must fill out and sign the Student Release Form (SRF) — which you can download from the clearinghouse Web site (www.ncaaclearing house.net — click Prospective Student-Athletes and then click Domestic Student Release Form or Foreign Student Release Form) — and send it to the clearinghouse, along with a $30 registration fee.

This SRF authorizes each high school you've attended to send the clearinghouse your transcripts, test scores, proof of graduation, and other necessary academic information. The SRF also authorizes the clearinghouse to send your academic information to all colleges that request your eligibility status.

Apply for certification with the clearinghouse after your junior year in high school if you're sure you want to participate in intercollegiate athletics as a freshman at a Division I or II institution. If you fail to submit all required documents, your incomplete file will be discarded after three years, requiring you to pay a new fee if certification is requested after that time.

The clearinghouse registration process is the beginning of your academic career, and if you mess up the clearinghouse application, it could nix your chances of competing as a freshman.

Most students prefer to register online. Get a credit card ready, because you'll need this to register online. If you complete the online Web application, be sure to print a copy of your completed registration form (see the instructions on the SRF submission screen), and be sure to keep your credit-card receipt with your files. When you print your registration form, you'll receive two copies: Copy 1 and Copy 2. Give both copies to a high school official (such as a guidance counselor); that person sends Copy 1, along with an official copy of your high school transcript, to the clearinghouse. (This way, the clearinghouse and, by extension, the colleges interested in you can make sure that you're staying on track academically not only for graduation, but also to meet the NCAA requirements.) Your high school should keep Copy 2 in its files. After graduation and before your school closes for the summer, your high school must send the clearinghouse a copy of your final transcript that confirms your graduation and contains final grades and credits, along with Copy 2 of the form.

If you prefer to register through the mail or by fax, download the SRF at www.ncaaclearinghouse.net or photocopy it from the *Guide for College-Bound Student-Athletes,* which you can get by calling 800-638-3731. Fill out the SRF by typing or clearly printing your information on the form. Mail or fax the top (white) copy of the form to the clearinghouse, along with the $30 registration fee. (The address is NCAA Clearinghouse, 301 ACT Dr., Box 4043, Iowa City, IA 52243-4043.) If you fax the copy, you must include your credit- or debit-card information; if you mail the copy, you may send a check or money order. Give the yellow and pink copies of the form to a high school official, who then sends the yellow copy (Copy 1), along with an official copy of your high school transcript, to the clearinghouse. Your high school should keep the pink copy (Copy 2) for its files. After graduation and before the school closes for the summer, your school also must send the clearinghouse a copy of your final transcript that confirms your graduation from high school.

When you give both Copy 1 and Copy 2 of the SRF to your high school guidance counselor or other official, that official will enter the proper code for the high school you attend (or you may use the code lookup at `www.ncaaclearinghouse.net`). If you've attended more than one high school (including summer school), your current counselor will enter the proper codes for each school in chronological order.

If you've attended more than one high school, you also must complete Section III of the SRF, listing in chronological order all schools you previously attended, starting with the most recent. If you attended ninth grade in a junior high school in the same school system where you later attended high school, do not list the ninth-grade school. (If you need to list more schools than space allows and you're registering by mail, use a separate sheet of paper. If you're registering online and need to enter more than six high schools, go to the clearinghouse Web site, click Prospective Student-Athletes, click Registered Student Login, and add information for the additional schools on your record.)

You cannot send your own transcript information to the clearinghouse. Only your school may send your transcripts to the clearinghouse. And, for reasons of security, the clearinghouse will not accept faxed transcripts.

When filling out the SRF, enter all information accurately, including your Social Security number (SSN) and date of birth. This information *must match exactly* other data the clearinghouse receives for you (like high school transcripts and requests from colleges seeking your eligibility status). Before you send it in, carefully examine the entire SRF to make sure you have completed it correctly, included your fee payment authorization, and signed it. If you're younger than 18 years old, your parent or legal guardian also must sign.

Print additional copies of the completed SRF for your records. Remember that in building your own portfolio, you want to have copies of all important paperwork in case something gets lost or is destroyed.

Create your own personal identification number of four digits (numbers between 0 and 9) for the SRF to register with the clearinghouse. Keep a record of that PIN in the file you've organized for college documents. Pick a number that you can easily remember, but not a number that might be easily guessed — such as a birthday or street address. Use the same common sense you would use in choosing a debit-card PIN on an online password. Whether you're online or sending hard copies, you'll need to have your own identification number, so make it something you'll remember but that you won't share with others.

After you've submitted your SRF and PIN, check your file status periodically. You may do this in one of three ways:

- ✔ Visit www.ncaaclearinghouse.net and, on the home page, click Prospective Student-Athletes, click Registered Student Login, and then enter your SSN and PIN.

- ✔ Call the clearinghouse's 24-hour, toll-free number (877-861-3003) from a touch-tone phone, and be sure to have your SSN and PIN available, because you'll be asked for them.

- ✔ Call the clearinghouse customer-service line at 877-262-1492. (Customer-service representatives are available from 8 a.m. to 5 p.m. Central time, Monday through Friday.)

If you've forgotten your PIN, fax or mail your new PIN choice to the clearinghouse, along with your name, address, SSN, date of birth, and signature.

The clearinghouse may communicate with you by e-mail or U.S. mail. E-mail correspondence will require that you've submitted a valid e-mail address in Section I of your SRF. You'll need to indicate the communication option you prefer. The clearinghouse prefers you to select the e-mail option because it's faster and easier for the clearinghouse, and it enables you to receive correspondence from the clearinghouse up to two weeks earlier than you would with snail mail. You may change your communication option or update your e-mail address at www.ncaaclearinghouse.net or by writing or faxing the clearinghouse.

Your SRF will be eligible for processing *only* with payment of the $30 application fee (or submission of a fee waiver if you've been granted a waiver). No documents can be processed by the clearinghouse until it receives the form and fee. You may pay by debit or credit card, check, or money order. Do not send cash. If you fax your form, you must pay by debit or credit card.

Economically disadvantaged students may be eligible for a waiver of the registration fee — *if* they have already received a waiver of the ACT or SAT fee. If this applies to you, the SRF fee-waiver section must be completed by an authorized high school official and include your high school's seal. If you're eligible for a fee waiver, and you registered online, an authorized high school official may validate the waiver online by following procedures on the clearinghouse Web site. If you haven't yet been granted a fee waiver by ACT or SAT, you're not yet eligible for a waiver of the registration fee, and your SRF will not be processed (meaning that you cannot be granted eligibility) until official verification arrives.

Remember that if your SRF has not been processed, any colleges that request information about you will be told you aren't yet eligible. Those colleges will very likely take you off their lists of prospective student-athletes — definitely not a risk you want to take. The bottom line: Register between your junior and senior years of high school, no matter what.

Becoming a Division 1 Qualifier

Of the three associations (NCAA, NJCAA, and NAIA), the NCAA has the most stringent academic requirements for athletic eligibility. At the Division I level, the NCAA categorizes each incoming athlete as either a qualifier or a nonqualifier based on the student-athlete's fulfillment of the NCAA's minimum academic requirements. (Division I no longer recognizes partial qualifiers unless a nonqualifier is given that status through the NCAA waiver process.)

These qualifying categories are also sometimes referred to as *certification status,* and each category dictates the privileges to which you're entitled. Your classification as a qualifier, partial qualifier, or nonqualifier is important because it determines what an athletic program can provide you.

Qualifier, obviously, is the classification you want, because it provides you with the best possible opportunity to compete and receive athletic-scholarship money. In Division I, as a qualifier, you're entitled to compete, practice, and receive an athletic scholarship in your freshman year. In addition, you're eligible for four seasons of competition.

After you've registered with the clearinghouse (allowing colleges to request information about your eligibility), you need to determine if you are, indeed, a Division I qualifier, and you need to decide if you want to play for a Division I school. So how do you go about becoming a Division I qualifier? In this section, we give you the answers you need.

Core course requirements

When you're on the path to becoming a Division I qualifier, you have to determine what the basic academic requirements for Division I are. You need to get this information early enough in your high school career (ninth grade is *not* too early) so that you have time to work toward and obtain those requirements. For example, if at the end of your junior year in high school, you realize that you need to take two more years of English to qualify for a Division I school, you're going to be in a bind.

The earlier you know what is expected of you and the more diligent you are about staying on top of your academic requirements, the better off you'll be.

The NCAA has what are called *core course requirements*. A *core course* is a regular academic course taken at a high school — not a vocational, remedial, or prep course. In order for the course to count, you must have taken the course only during grades 9 through 12.

Check with your school's guidance department for the listing of core courses offered by your high school (or go to the Initial-Eligibility Clearinghouse Web site at www.ncaaclearinghouse.net to obtain the same list).

Two different courses on the core courses list cannot be counted as two courses if they have the same content. And high school courses taken in eighth grade or earlier do not count toward your required core courses.

If you've taken a college course during high school, you may use that as a core course if it is accepted by your high school and if all the following apply:

✔ It meets the core course requirement.

✔ It would be accepted for any other student.

✔ It is on your high school transcript.

Also, independent-study, Internet, and correspondence courses may count as core courses as long as:

- ✔ The course meets core course requirements.

- ✔ You and the instructor have access to each other during the course so that the instructor can teach, evaluate, and provide assistance to you.

- ✔ Appropriate academic authorities evaluate your work according to the high school's academic policies.

- ✔ The course is acceptable and available for any student to take.

- ✔ The course is placed on your high school transcript.

Class of 2006 or 2007

If you're entering a Division I college or university in the fall of 2006 or 2007, your NCAA initial eligibility will be evaluated using the 14 core-course standard. To be classified under this standard, you'll need to graduate from high school and have successfully completed 14 core courses as listed here with a minimum grade point average of 2.0 out of 4.0.

The 14 core courses are as follows:

- ✔ Four years of English

- ✔ Two years of mathematics (Algebra I or higher)

- ✔ Two years of natural/physical science (one year of lab if offered by your high school)

- ✔ One year of additional English, mathematics, or natural/physical science

- ✔ Two years of social science

- ✔ Three years of additional core courses (from any area listed here or foreign language or nondoctrinal religion or philosophy)

Computer-science courses are not used for initial-eligibility purposes for students entering a collegiate institution on or after August 1, 2005. However, computer-science courses (such as programming) that are taught through the mathematics or natural/physical-science departments receive either math or science credits and are on the high school's list of approved core courses, because math or science may be used after August 1, 2005.

Class of 2008

If you're entering college in fall of 2008, the new requirement for Division I will be 16 core courses in the following breakdown:

- ✔ Four years of English

- ✔ Three years of mathematics (Algebra I or higher)

✔ Two years of natural/physical science (one must be a lab science)

✔ One year of additional English, mathematics, or natural/physical science

✔ Two years of social science

✔ Four years of additional core courses (from any area listed above or foreign language, nondoctrinal religion, or philosophy)

Again, computer-science courses can no longer be used for initial-eligibility purposes — except for those meeting the requirements mentioned earlier.

GPA and test-score requirements

As a Division I qualifier, you also — in addition to graduating from high school and successfully completing the core courses — must meet the SAT or ACT requirements for your grade point average (GPA). This is obtained from a sliding scale and decreases from a 1,010 on the SAT and an 86 on the ACT for a 2.0 GPA to a 400 on the SAT and a 37 on the ACT for a 3.55 GPA. If you have a higher GPA, you can get away with lower SAT or ACT scores to fulfill your academic requirements, and vice versa.

You must make sure that the clearinghouse receives your ACT Assessment and/or SAT I score reports. You can have score reports sent directly to the clearinghouse by entering a specific code (9999) printed in the ACT Assessment and SAT I registration packets.

Table 4-1 lists what is required of you as a student to meet the academic requirements. You can see what is expected for your grade point average and scores from the ACT and SAT tests. If you don't meet the academic requirements listed in this table, you'll be considered a nonqualifier for Division I. As a nonqualifier:

✔ **You are not eligible for regular-season competition or practice during your first year in college.**

✔ **You may not receive an athletic scholarship.** You *may* receive financial aid based only on need in your first year in college.

✔ **You are permitted only three seasons of competition.** To earn a fourth season, you must graduate before your fifth year of college.

Table 4-1	Core GPA, ACT, and SAT Scale for Division I	
Core GPA	**ACT Sum**	**SAT Sum**
3.550 or higher	37	400
3.525	38	410
3.500	39	420
3.475	40	430
3.450	41	440
3.425	41	450
3.400	42	460
3.375	42	470
3.350	43	480
3.325	44	490
3.300	44	500
3.325	44	490
3.300	44	500
3.275	45	510
3.250	46	520
3.225	46	530
3.200	47	540
3.175	47	550
3.150	48	560
3.125	49	570
3.100	49	580
3.075	50	590
3.050	50	600
3.025	51	610
3.000	52	620
2.975	52	630
2.950	53	640

(continued)

Table 4-1 *(continued)*

Core GPA	ACT Sum	SAT Sum
2.925	53	650
2.900	54	660
2.875	55	670
2.850	56	680
2.825	56	690
2.800	57	700
2.775	58	710
2.750	59	720
2.725	59	730
2.700	60	730
2.675	61	740–750
2.650	62	760
2.625	63	770
2.600	65	780
2.575	65	790
2.550	66	800
2.525	67	810
2.500	68	820
2.475	69	830
2.450	70	840–850
2.425	70	860
2.400	71	860
2.375	72	870
2.350	73	880
2.325	74	890
2.300	75	900
2.275	76	910
2.250	77	920

Core GPA	ACT Sum	SAT Sum
2.225	78	930
2.200	79	940
2.175	80	950
2.150	80	960
2.125	81	960
2.100	82	970
2.075	83	980
2.050	84	990
2.025	85	1000
2.000	86	1010

Division II and III Requirements

Although Division II and Division III are both held to NCAA standards and requirements, those standards are more lenient for Division II than they are for Division I — and even more lenient for Division III. But both of these divisions also offer athletes excellent opportunities to play for NCAA teams while obtaining top-notch educations.

Like Division I student-athletes, Division II student-athletes must graduate from high school, have successfully completed 14 core courses (see "Core course requirements," earlier in this chapter), and meet the SAT or ACT requirements for their grade point averages.

But Division II is a little bit more lenient in its academic requirements than Division I. The Division II sliding scale requirement for student athletes is a minimum of 2.0 (out of 4.0) with a sum of 820 on the SAT and 68 on the ACT. You may use the Division I sliding scale to determine your eligibility as long as you remember the minimum for Division II (of 2.0 with an 820 SAT/68 ACT). So if you have a 2.0 GPA and get an 800 on the SAT or a 66 on the ACT, you do *not* qualify for Division II.

If you've graduated from high school and have *either* successfully completed 14 core courses *or* have met the SAT/ACT requirement for your grade point average, you'll be considered a Division II *partial qualifier*. As a Division II partial qualifier, you may practice with the team and receive athletic scholarships during their first year,

Delaying enrollment for a semester or two

You may decide to delay enrollment in college for a semester or a year, but you need to know the pros and cons of this choice. Here are two reasons you might make that move:

✔ **The college that has been recruiting you and that you would like to attend may have already met its limit for new athletes for the semester and, therefore, cannot add you to its roster in the fall.** The coaches may be telling you that they really want to bring you onboard in the spring and that they really don't want to lose you. So they ask you to delay your enrollment until spring so that they can add you to their roster at that time. College athletics departments may add athletes coming into their program in the spring to either the previous year's scholarship award limits or to the following year's limit. So, assuming you had planned to enroll in August 2006 but put it off until January 2007, the school where you're headed could add you to its 2006–2007 roster or to its 2007–2008 roster, if necessary.

The risk with this arrangement is that what you have is a verbal agreement — nothing is in writing. Before January 2007 rolls around, those same coaches may find another athlete they want more than you. If so, you're out of luck.

✔ **You may not have qualified academically and, therefore, decide to delay enrollment in order to try to bring up your grades at a community college, for example.** This is a good idea, especially if you go to a school where you can continue to play (NCAA Division III or NJCAA, for example) while improving your academic record.

The problem with this plan is that the longer you delay enrolling in a Division I school, the more likely it is that the coaches at the university you initially planned to attend will lose interest in you — especially if you aren't able to play at the school you're temporarily attending.

but you may not compete your first year. After that, you're eligible for four seasons of competition.

If you have either not graduated from high school or have failed to meet the core-course GPA or the SAT/ACT score requirement, you will be considered a nonqualifier. As a Division II nonqualifier, you may not participate in competition or practice during your first year in college, and you may not receive an athletic scholarship as a freshman (but you may receive financial aid based on need). After your freshman year, you — as a Division II nonqualifier — are eligible for four seasons of competition.

Because NCAA Division III schools do not award athletic scholarships, their athletic-eligibility requirements are different from those of Divisions I or II. Instead, Division III requirements are determined by institutional, conference, and other NCAA regulations.

There are no partial qualifiers or nonqualifiers in Division III. Division III student-athletes must be full-time students who meet the requirements of their respective schools and the conferences within which those schools play. This means you have to check with the school you plan to attend to know exactly what its academic requirements are. If you meet the academic requirements, you're eligible to play.

NAIA and NJCAA Requirements

Like NCAA Divisions II and III, NAIA and NJCAA colleges offer the student-athlete excellent opportunities to play sports at the college level and get a quality education. You may be playing without benefit of an athletic scholarship, but if you excel at the junior college level, you may be able to transfer to an NCAA Division I or II school *with* an athletic scholarship. (See Chapter 18 for more information about transferring.)

In order to be eligible to represent any member institution of the NAIA in any manner (scrimmages, intercollegiate competitions), an entering freshman must meet two of three entry-level requirements. An *entering freshman* is defined by the NAIA as "a student who upon becoming identified with an institution has not been previously identified with an institution of higher learning for two semesters or three quarters (or equivalent)." In other words, an incoming freshman is considered to be a student who has had no more than two semester or three quarters with another college.

The three entry-level requirements for the NAIA are as follows:

- ✔ **Achieve a minimum overall high school grade point average of 2.0 on a 4.0 scale.**

- ✔ **Graduate in the top half of your high school graduating class.**

- ✔ **Achieve a minimum of 860 on the SAT or 18 on the ACT.** You must take the SAT/ACT test on a national testing day. Be sure that the testing place has been approved as a national testing site. Some schools may offer a testing site for a practice test. Make sure you don't confuse the two.

The NJCAA's requirements for entering freshman student-athletes are as follows:

- ✔ **You must have graduated from high school, received a high school equivalency diploma, or been certified as having**

passed a national test such as the General Education
Development (GED) test. The high school from which you've
graduated must be accredited or recognized by the
Department of Education within that state.

✓ **If you haven't graduated from high school, you can establish eligibility for athletic participation by completing one
term of college work, passing 12 credits with a 1.75 GPA or
higher.** This term must be taken *after* your high school class
has graduated.

✓ **If you haven't graduated from high school, but you've
already earned sufficient credit for high school graduation
status, you can establish eligibility for athletic participation
by completing one term of college work, passing 12 credits
with a 1.75 GPA or higher.** You can complete this term *before*
your high school class has graduated.

✓ **If you haven't graduated from high school, and you've established eligibility as a student-athlete by one of the two preceding methods (successfully completing one term of college
work before or after your high school class has graduated),
you may be added to the eligibility roster after completion
of the requirements and *after* the college term is over.**

If you're completing high school, and you're enrolled at the same
time in 12 or more credits at a junior college, you're eligible for athletic participation with the completion of the NJCAA High School
Waiver Form (Form 3-e). This form must be signed by your high
school principal and the college president. *Note:* This provision
applies only if your high school class has *not* graduated at the time
you enroll in college.

To find Form 3-e, go the NJCAA Web site at www.njcaa.org and
click Forms. Click Administration. Here, you'll be able to download
Form 3-e.

Reviewing Unusual Student Situations — and Making Sure You're Still Eligible

If you have a more unusual situations than the norm — maybe
you're an international student, you were home-schooled, or you
have a learning disability — there also are eligibility requirements
for you. And, like all other prospective student-athletes, you need
to be aware of what the most recent eligibility requirements are.

The most important thing to remember is that, regardless of your special circumstances, you still must fulfill the same minimum requirements that all other incoming freshmen have to meet.

International student-athletes

International student-athletes are expected to meet the same initial-eligibility standards as domestic students; however, there are different rules for nearly every country. For example, several countries require students to have a Leaving Certificate, which indicates they have completed certain core courses. The NCAA Initial-Eligibility Clearinghouse uses these Leaving Certificates to determine the eligibility status of international student-athletes.

So if you're an international student, you need to know the clearinghouse requirements for your specific country — in addition to needing to know all other requirements of the clearinghouse, requirements of the particular division or association in which you plan to compete, and the requirements of the specific college or university you plan to attend. That's a lot to keep track of — but you can do it with a little planning and organization (and with the help of this book!).

NCAA Initial-Eligibility Clearinghouse requirements

International students who want to enroll as incoming freshmen and compete in NCAA Division I or Division II athletics must — like all other incoming freshmen student-athletes, domestic or international — register with the clearinghouse.

There are several documents required to apply to the clearinghouse, and foreign students must submit all the following items:

- ✔ **NCAA Initial-Eligibility Clearinghouse Online Application for Foreign Student-Athletes:** Go to the NCAA clearinghouse Web site at www.ncaaclearinghouse.net and then click Registration Form for Foreign Students (Foreign Student Release Form).

- ✔ **A $30 payment by MasterCard/Visa:** The fee is not refundable if you decide not to attend an NCAA institution.

- ✔ **Original academic records (or certified [attested] copies of the original documents), and certified, literal-English translations of records not originally in English:** These must be mailed (not faxed) to the clearinghouse. That address is NCAA Initial-Eligibility Clearinghouse, 2255 North Dubuque Rd., P.O. Box 4044, Iowa City, IA 52243-4044 USA. The telephone number is 1-319-337-1492. (The clearinghouse office hours are Monday through Friday, 8 a.m. to 5 p.m. U.S. Central time.) Send any mail to the NCAA clearinghouse by regular surface or air mail.

International students must submit official records from all secondary or middle schools attended, as well as records from any universities, colleges, or professional schools attended. This includes any secondary or middle-school coursework completed in the United States. Academic records should show individual subjects studied and the grades you received. If your secondary or postsecondary records don't clearly indicate the subject studied or their content, you have to submit syllabi of the courses or descriptions of the curriculum along with the records.

✔ **Score(s) from either the ACT or SAT standardized test:** See the "Minimum academic standards" section, later in this chapter, for more information on these tests as they apply to international students.

If your original academic record is difficult to replace, the registrar — or other recordkeeping school official — from the original issuing institution should make a photocopy of your record and certify that it is the true copy of the original. He can do this by placing the institution's official seal or stamp and his signature on the document after photocopying it. (Do *not* send difficult-to-replace original documents — the clearinghouse will not return them.) Records certified by lecturers, professors, tutors, or any other school officials who do not hold primary responsibility for maintaining the academic records will not be accepted.

If the academic record is not in English, a translation must be sent *in addition to,* not in place of, the original record. The translation should be a literal translation, not an interpretive one. Any transcripts, certificates, translations, or examination results that appear to have been altered or are irregular will be forwarded to the appropriate school authorities or examination board for verification.

If an NCAA Division I or Division II school requests your eligibility status, the clearinghouse will review your final transcript and proof of graduation to make a final certification decision according to the NCAA standards (and give that information to the school that has requested it).

Note: If you don't submit all the documents required or the $30 fee, or if no member institution requests your eligibility status, your incomplete file will be discarded after three years, requiring you to pay a new fee if certification is requested after that time.

You can find additional information about some of the required items in the box labeled Important Information on the Student Release Form (Foreign).

Minimum academic standards

If you've never previously enrolled as a full-time student in a university, you must meet minimum academic standards in order to be eligible for practice, competition, and athletic financial aid your first year. The minimum required standards will vary depending on your country. The standards are outlined in the NCAA's *Guide to International Academic Standards for Athletics Eligibility* (which you can find at www.ncaa.org).

You'll need a minimum score on the SAT or the ACT in order to be eligible to play in the NCAA. International students *must* take the SAT or the ACT. Other tests, such as the TOEFL or TWSE, are not acceptable. If you haven't taken the ACT or SAT examination, contact your secondary school for information about taking one of these standardized tests. Enter the code 9999 on the registration form or answer document to have your scores sent directly to the NCAA clearinghouse.

If your secondary school does not have information about these examinations, you can contact the ACT or SAT directly:

- ✔ **ACT:** Outside the United States: Testing 61, ACT Universal Testing, P.O. Box 4028, Iowa City, IA 52243-4028 USA; Web: www.act.org; phone: 1-319-337-1448; fax: 1-319-337-1285. (The office hours are Monday through Friday, 8:30 a.m. to 4:30 p.m. U.S. Central time.)

- ✔ **SAT:** SAT Information, College Board — SAT Program, P.O. Box 6200, Princeton, NJ 08541-6200 USA; Web: www.college board.com; phone: 1-609-771-7600; fax: 1-609-771-1426. (The office hours are Monday through Friday, 8:30 a.m. to 9:30 p.m. U.S. Eastern time.)

If you're currently enrolled (or have previously been enrolled) as a full-time student at a university in a foreign country, you'll be considered a transfer student upon enrolling at an NCAA university. See Chapter 18 for more information on your eligibility as a transfer student.

Playing for NCAA Division III, NAIA, or NJCAA

All the terms for eligibility we cover in the preceding sections for international students are the eligibility requirements for NCAA Division I and Division II institutions. But if you plan to attend and compete for an NCAA Division III school or an NAIA or NJCAA school, you'll need to check with that particular institution to know what is required of you.

To see which schools are NCAA Division III institutions, go to www.ncaa.org/conference. To find out which schools are either NAIA or NJCAA member institutions, respectively, go to www.naia.org or www.njcaa.org.

Home-schooled athletes

If you've attended a home school or a nontraditional school for all or part of your high school career, and you plan to enroll in an NCAA Division I or Division II institution, you must register with the clearinghouse. In order for the clearinghouse to be able to evaluate your certification status for purposes of NCAA athletic initial eligibility, you have to submit specific documents to the clearinghouse. We let you know which ones in the following section.

If you plan to attend a school that is NCAA Division III or a member of the NAIA or NJCAA, see "Playing for NCAA Division III, NAIA, or NJCC," earlier in this chapter (the section is written for international students, but it applies to home-schooled athletes as well).

Register with the clearinghouse at www.ncaaclearinghouse.net. Click Prospective Student-Athletes, click Domestic Student Release Form, and follow the prompts.

Register with the clearinghouse after completion of your junior year of high school. The preliminary certification (see "Discovering the NCAA Initial-Eligibility Clearinghouse," earlier in this chapter, for more on this) is important because it lets you know if you're on track for graduation and in full compliance with academic requirements. The final certification from the clearinghouse will determine whether you'll be eligible for practice, competition, and institutional financial aid at an NCAA Division I or Division II institution during your freshman year.

After registering, you have to send the following information to the clearinghouse:

✔ **Standardized test score(s):** These must be sent directly from the testing agency.

The clearinghouse won't accept test scores received on home-school transcripts. Also, a Student Score Report or scores taken directly from a Student Score Report cannot be accepted by the clearinghouse for initial-eligibility purposes. Generally, three reports are sent out: One goes to the high school or home-school headquarters, one goes to the counselors, and one goes directly to the student's home. The clearinghouse will not accept any documentation that was in the student's possession. So, what does this mean for the home-schooled student/

athlete? Your score report must be sent to the clearinghouse directly from a counselor or established institute of education.

✔ **Home-school transcript:** The transcript must include course titles, course grades, units of credit for courses, the grading scale (if other than A–F letter grades), and the signature of the home-school administrator (the parent or other person who organized, taught, and evaluated your home-school coursework).

✔ **Transcripts from any other high school, college, or nontraditional program you've attended:** These transcripts must be mailed directly from the issuing institution.

✔ **Proof of high school graduation, including your specific graduation date.**

✔ **Evidence that home schooling was conducted in accordance with state laws:** This means a written statement from the home-school administrator verifying compliance with state home-school legislation. Attach any supporting documentation you may have received in working with public schools, churches, or national organizations in which you were honored school credits for your work.

✔ **List of texts used throughout home schooling:** Be sure to list the text titles, the publishers of those texts, and in which courses the texts were used.

If your home-school coursework was taken through an established nontraditional program (for example, a correspondence course, an Internet course, or a tutoring service) that evaluated your coursework and issued transcripts, have that program provide a copy of your transcript and provide contact information so that the clearinghouse can obtain further information, if necessary.

The clearinghouse will evaluate home-school coursework only after all required documents have been received. After this information is received, the clearinghouse may need to request additional information or clarification before completing your certification. Send all questions regarding this matter to the NCAA Clearinghouse, Attention: Home School Evaluation, NCAA Clearinghouse, 301 ACT Dr., Box 4043, Iowa City, IA 52243-4043.

The learning-disabled student athlete

Although the NCAA academic requirements for Division I and Division II athletics are the same for *all* students, including students with learning disabilities, as a student with a diagnosed disability,

Overcoming recruiters' worries

You may find that some coaches who are recruiting you are afraid that, because you're home-schooled, you won't be approved as a qualifier by the clearinghouse. To assure these doubters that you're taking all the right courses, you'll want to work with your parents or home-school instructor to ensure that you are, indeed, taking the required number of core courses in the appropriate subject matters.

You may want to consider providing coaches copies of your home-school transcript and ACT/SAT test score. Stay in touch with the coaches for whom you hope to play, and make sure you provide them with all the academic material possible to put their minds at ease.

you are entitled to some accommodations to enable you to meet these requirements.

One exception the NCAA makes for learning-disabled students is that a student with a disability who is a Division I nonqualifier out of high school may earn a fourth season of competition upon qualifying (whereas nondisabled students may earn only three seasons of competition, except if they graduate before their fifth year of college).

Many collegiate institutions provide academic accommodations for students with disabilities. However, you need to approach the college to determine if such accommodations are available. Do not rely on the athletic department of the college to provide this information. And don't send documentation of your disability to the clearinghouse (see the following section).

Documenting your learning disability

The *only* time disability documentation needs to be sent to the NCAA is when you, as a prospective student-athlete with a disability, would like to use core courses taken *after* high school graduation and you plan to attend a Division I college.

Be sure to send this information about your disability to NCAA Disability Services, *not* to the clearinghouse. If you submit them to the NCAA clearinghouse, other NCAA schools will be able to access your disability records — and those are records you may want to keep private.

To document your disability, send the following information to NCAA Disability Services, P.O. Box 6222, Indianapolis, IN 46206-6222:

> ✔ **A signed copy of the most recent professional evaluation report diagnosing your disability, including diagnostic test**

results: These reports and results must have been completed with the last three years.

✔ **A copy of your most recent Individual Education Plan (IEP); Section 504 Plan; or, for private high schools, a statement on the high school's letterhead describing the accommodations, if any, you received because of your disability.**

Core courses

If you're a high school student with a disability, and you've received help (for example, taken special classes or received extra time) because of that disability, you're eligible for the following:

✔ You can use courses for students with disabilities that are designated on the high school's list of NCAA-Approved Core Courses.

✔ You can use approved core courses taken before you enroll in college, including courses taken in the summer after your eighth semester of high school or after your high school graduation. *Remember:* For Division I, you must document your disability with the NCAA Disability Services to receive this accommodation.

Nonstandard tests

If you have a disability, you also may take a nonstandard test to satisfy SAT and/or ACT test-score requirements (or, more specifically, use SAT and/or ACT scores achieved during nonstandard administrations). Follow these guidelines:

✔ **Register for nonstandard testing as described by the ACT or SAT, submitting a properly documented and confirmed diagnosis.** This means that, after you've been tested by a physician and documented as learning disabled, testing exceptions may be made for you for the ACT or SAT. For example, the test may be read to you, or you may be offered an extended time frame to take the tests. But you must have proper documentation to support your special needs.

✔ **Follow procedures governed by the ACT or SAT.** The test may not be administered by a member of your high school athletic department or any NCAA school's athletic department.

✔ **If you take a nonstandard ACT or SAT, you may take the test on a date other than a national testing date, but you still must achieve the required test score for your GPA.** (Visit the ACT and SAT Web sites — www.act.org and www.collegeboard. com — to find out what their national testing dates are.)

✔ **Your high school counselor may help you register to take the nonstandard test.**

The GED

The General Education Development (GED) test may, under certain conditions, satisfy the graduation requirement, but it will not satisfy core-course GPA or test-score requirements. Contact the NCAA for information about GED submission. You can reach them at www.ncaa.org or write to the National Collegiate Athletic Association, 700 W. Washington St., P.O. Box 6222, Indianapolis, IN 46206-6222; phone: 317-917-6222; fax: 317-917-6888.

If you aren't certified

What if you've done everything as instructed, and you receive a final Initial-Eligibility Certification Report from the clearinghouse indicating that you are *not* certified?

In this case, you should contact the college/university where you've been admitted and ask the school to file an initial-eligibility waiver with the NCAA on your behalf. In considering a waiver of the initial-eligibility standards, the following may be factors:

✔ The extent to which your failure to meet the initial-eligibility standards is attributable to a disability

✔ Whether noncore courses you've taken were specified in your IEP, satisfied graduation requirements, and/or prepared you to successfully complete a planned course of study at a particular collegiate institution

✔ Your overall academic record, including performance on standardized tests

✔ Assessments of high school personnel attesting to the likelihood of your academic success in college while participating in athletics

✔ Accommodations for students with disabilities available to and used by you during high school

✔ Other factors useful in assessing your preparedness to succeed in college.

Remember: You cannot count on anything — a disability, a superb athletic résumé and reputation, friends in high places — other than yourself to get you into the college of your choice. Just meeting the NCAA academic rules does not guarantee your admission into a college; you must still apply for admission. The important thing to remember is that no matter how terrific an athlete you are, no matter how superior a student you are, no college or university will accept you if you don't apply. In short, you still must follow all the rules that every other would-be college student (athlete or not) must follow.

Remember: To be safe, don't pick one or two schools and assume you'll get in. Have backup schools. In life, you should always have a backup plan. And as the football-loving, late president Theodore Roosevelt said, "In life, as in a football game, the principle to follow is 'Hit the line hard.'" In other words, give everything you do — especially anything having to do with your academics and athletics — a 110 percent effort all the time.

Part II
Getting Recruited

In this part . . .

You'll discover what colleges are looking for when they begin their own recruiting process. Each school wants and needs student-athletes who will complement its program. You'll find out how to become the athlete recruiters talk about, how to handle the press, and how to talk to coaches.

Great ideas are just that until you put them into motion. In this part, you'll formulate a plan to promote yourself, talk to recruiters, and get your foot in the door. Because not every student-athlete has a recruiter knocking on his door, we help you figure out how to promote yourself and do a little door-knocking of your own.

Chapter 5

Knowing What Colleges Are Looking For

In This Chapter

▶ Knowing who the blue-chippers are

▶ Looking at who gets recruited and who gets scholarships

▶ Doing everything you can to be offered a scholarship

▶ Using your academics to pull in some money

*F*ootball still rules as the king of college athletics, with 43 percent of all Division I men's athletic scholarships in the NCAA (for 14 sports) going to football players. (Thirty-four percent of all men's athletic scholarships for 31 sports in Divisions I *and* II of the NCAA go to football players.) But even though football and basketball are the highest-profile sports, attracting far more television and media coverage than any other college sports, prospective football and basketball student-athletes are no longer the only ones to be actively recruited and get full rides. Today, schools recruit the best soccer players and volleyball players, the best hockey and lacrosse players, the best tennis and softball players — and that diversity of sports opportunities means greatly heightened competition for already-limited scholarship funds.

So what does this mean for you? If you're one of the top recruits in your sport, you may not have to worry about getting accepted to college. But if you're among the vast majority of prospective student-athletes who are *not* offered full rides, you'll probably have to work a bit harder to gain the attention of the college coaches. And either way, you still have to meet the academic requirements for the division and the school you plan to attend before you can be accepted and compete.

In this chapter, we give you helpful advice about how to get recruited, as well as how to maintain your eligibility status after you've been accepted to college, whether you're one of the elite or one of the slightly-less-than-elite.

Blue-Chippers Come in All Types and Sizes

The chance to compete in intercollegiate athletics and to receive scholarship money to do it is a once-in-a-lifetime opportunity for a relatively few lucky and talented student-athletes. Playing at the NCAA Division I level with scholarship money is an even rarer opportunity. In fact, less than 1 percent of all high school athletes receive any form of scholarship at the NCAA Division I level.

Blue-chip athletes are those lucky, talented, and rare student-athletes who not only get recruited to play NCAA Division I sports, but also receive full-ride scholarship. Although they're lucky and talented enough to play Division I sports, they still face tough odds when it comes to playing their respective sports professionally. For example, of the nearly 1 million high school football players, only about 250 make it to the NFL (6,000-to-1 odds, in case you're counting). And of about 550,000 high school basketball players, only about 50 make it to the NBA (10,000-to-1 odds).

But we're still only talking about football and basketball players. Though many people think of the typical blue-chip athlete as that 300-pound lineman or 6'11" basketball center, the reality is that blue-chip athletes now come in many types and sizes — from the thick, muscular football player to the long, lean swimmer to the compact, graceful gymnast. This is because as athletic programs have grown, so has the variety of sports (and athletes) sought out by Division I athletics departments: soccer, volleyball, tennis, golf, softball, fencing. . . . Combine this diversifying change with the soaring costs of colleges/universities, shake or stir, and you have the recipe for intense competition for very limited scholarship funds.

And this intense competition makes for stricter eligibility requirements for NCAA Division I and II athletics; it makes not only being noticed by college coaches but also, more important, being invited to join these teams even more difficult. But don't despair. You can do certain things to improve your chances, the most important of which is to focus on your grades and keep them up.

In order to be a college athlete, you must first be a college *student*. You must obtain and maintain the academic requirements for the college of your choice, or else the coaches will never look at you.

Being the parent of a blue-chipper

As the parent of blue-chipper, what can you do to help your talented student-athlete get into an NCAA Division I school? Take a look at the following list:

✔ **Make sure that this dream of playing in the NCAA's Division I is your son's or daughter's dream and not yours.** This is the most important item in this list — you can't relive your glory days through your child, and you certainly shouldn't try. Don't push your kid so hard to make a Division I team that you make his life miserable trying to fulfill everyone else's fantasies. Your pushing and meddling could adversely affect not only your child's mental health, but also his entire life.

✔ **Be honest about your child's true abilities.** You may have to get an outside, objective source — such as a professional scout or college coach — to evaluate your child's talent to make sure that she is, indeed, a blue-chipper. Overstating your child's abilities (see "The ones who recruit themselves," later in this chapter) can bring very negative consequences.

✔ **Assuming that your child really is a blue-chipper, do your homework.** Know what is needed for top athletes to be recruited and be well educated in the process. And don't take this job lightly, expecting someone else — like a high school coach or guidance counselor — to do it for you. High school coaches are paid to be full-time teachers or administrators and receive a small stipend for their added coaching responsibilities. You're the parent. Who will care more about and be able to take more time for this process than you?

✔ **Investigate every camp, recruiter, school, coach, and program.** You don't want to waste thousands of dollars sending your child to a showcase, for example, if the recruiters and coaches won't be there. More important, finding the school that fits your child's academic and athletic needs is up to you. (Be sure to read Chapters 4, 6, 7, 9, and 13.) Don't just *act* knowledgeable about the recruiting process; *become* knowledgeable about it — very knowledgeable.

A *showcase* is a kind of tournament that does not have a winner and is more common in team sports like soccer, volleyball, and softball. The sole purpose of these showcases is for college coaches to evaluate prospects in a competition setting. While the teams try to win, each team usually plays the same number of games regardless of wins or losses. Sometimes showcases also include drills where athletes can display their talents individually to the coaches who are in attendance.

✔ **Focus on academics.** In choosing a college, education should be the first consideration, not the reverse. And don't lose track of the importance of a college education and a college degree. Your child will be an athlete for only a comparatively short time, and anything can happen: injury, a change in plans, or a change in goals. But before that, your child has three basic responsibilities before he can receive a scholarship: (1) to pass designated core courses with a certain grade point average, (2) to achieve a certain score on a standardized test, and (3) to report both results to the NCAA clearinghouse. Stay on top of all three of these, and make sure they happen; otherwise, that Division I dream will not happen.

Analyzing the Three Kinds of Students

A very small percentage of student-athletes are actively recruited by colleges, some as early as the eighth grade. The vast majority of student-athletes need to recruit themselves. But both groups of athletes need to consider carefully the school they ultimately choose: the academic climate, the athletic climate, the social climate. The college you attend must be a good fit, or you won't benefit from your education as you should. And both groups need to be careful not to expect all the work of recruiting or being recruited to be done for them. Many a student-athlete finds himself out of luck and out of school because he took for granted that the work (getting the grades or test scores, or registering with the clearinghouse and responding to recruiting letters) would be done by someone else. Don't make those mistakes.

The ones who get recruited

The recruitment process is generally much less stressful for blue-chip athletes. They don't have to go out looking for college programs; the programs come looking for them. They don't have any of the stresses of finding appropriate schools and sending out mass mailings of letters introducing themselves, sending highlight films — it's all taken care of for them.

The problem is that these star athletes sometimes take the process for granted, getting used to having everything done for them. They may choose a school based solely on athletics (TV exposure, the promise of being able to go pro after college or before college is over) and lose sight of the main reason for choosing a school: *academics*. Often, these students don't have control of the recruiting process; the recruiting process has control of them. They simply listen to coaches, family, and/or friends who tell them how good they are in their sport, and they forget to ask questions about things other than athletics.

If you're one of the lucky few being actively recruited by college athletic programs, follow these tips to ensure that you get the most out of your experience:

> ✔ **Because you obviously won't be the only player on the team on scholarship, ask the coaches which players will be returning and whether you'll have a chance to compete for a starting position.**

✓ **Research the number of former players who have gone on to professional playing careers from the schools you're considering.**

✓ **Make sure you choose the right program for you and not simply the top-ranked or most recognized team.** For example, ask yourself whether the way the team plays is suited to *your* style of play.

✓ **Take your sport out of the equation, and ask yourself if you would be happy at the school.**

The ones who recruit themselves

Students who fall into this category generally have a much more challenging time picking a school, but more often than not, they have a more rewarding experience *in* school. This is because they appreciate the opportunity more — especially if they're rewarded with an athletic scholarship. (Remember how few athletic scholarships are actually awarded; in fact; more money is available through nonathletic and academic scholarships than athletic scholarships.) When a student recruits a school on her own, that student generally researches more than the athletics program and truly focuses on what it will be like to be a *student*-athlete. These student-athletes usually are in control of the recruiting process and do not allow themselves to be influenced by the process itself.

If this sounds like a good description of your situation, here are some thoughts to consider:

✓ **Do as much research as you can.** Take advantage of the Internet.

✓ **Consider schools that match your skills, preferences, and goals.** Everyone wants to play at the highest level possible, but be realistic about your skill level, and focus on colleges that have the same goals and values you have.

✓ **Initiate contact with the coach.** Send a brief letter introducing yourself and letting the coach know the type of student and player you are.

✓ **Just as we advise the blue-chip athlete, take your sport out of the equation, and ask yourself if you would be happy at the school.**

The ones who don't fit either category

Students who don't fit into either category are usually the ones who don't get recruited but think they should be, so they don't recruit themselves. They sometimes become very bitter toward student-athletes who *do* get recruited, and they generally believe they're better than they truly are. They've probably been told by well-meaning parents and/or coaches that they're the best and that they're as good as or better than those students being courted by Division I schools. They begin to believe this myopic hype and think they shouldn't have to pursue any schools — that the schools should be pursuing *them*.

We know too many stories of students who don't get recruited by Division I schools and who don't recruit themselves to these schools because they don't think they need or ought to. In the meantime, a Division II or III school shows some interest, but the student feels he deserves a higher level of athletic competition (forgetting entirely about the quality of education), so he ignores these offers or signs of interest. By the time scholarships should be being offered and signed, the Division II or III schools have moved on because of lack of interest or response from the student — and still, no Division I schools are showing interest. Guess where that leaves the overconfident, foolish student? High and dry.

If you're thinking, "Oh, this doesn't apply to me," here's a tip to keep in mind around scholarship/recruiting time: In Division I football, 98 percent of all scholarship offers are complete by Christmas, even though the signing date for scholarship offers is in early February. Yet, every year, hundreds of high school seniors are still waiting for scholarship offers in January and into February. Although this example is specific to football, the situation occurs in almost every college sport. Don't let your chance to get a scholarship at a lower-level Division I or II school get away by sitting around waiting for the "big boys" to come knocking on your door.

Keeping Score: Academics Do Count

During your first couple of years in high school, going to college seems so far away that it's easy not to worry about your grades. In addition, high school is a big step and can be a big adjustment for you, so you may slip a bit academically. Or you may think that you're a good-enough athlete that you'll get a scholarship and be admitted to a college regardless of your grades.

You can be the best player on your team and win all sorts of honors and awards, but if you won't be eligible to play, your chances of earning a scholarship usually lie somewhere between slim and none. There is a reason college athletes are called *student*-athletes.

By the time you begin your junior year, ideally you've started seriously thinking about college — especially if you want to play a sport in college. Many people believe the junior year is the year that makes or breaks a lot of prospects, and this section can help you make it a breakout year for you.

If you're a senior, and you're confident that you'll be offered a scholarship or if you've already been offered one, your senior year of high school still counts. The clearinghouse and colleges (including the one that may have already offered you a scholarship) look at what you're enrolled in your senior year and also get your final transcript after graduation to determine how well you did in all those classes. So forget about blowing off your senior year — unless you're willing to risk blowing off your athletic scholarship.

More and more frequently, recruited prospects are making verbal commitments during their junior year. If this is the case for you, staying on track both academically and athletically is even more important. If you're still undecided or not getting noticed as much as you'd like during your junior year, this year is equally important for you as well. If you're just about to start your junior year (or you're even younger and you're planning ahead), you need a timeline for that year.

You can't start paying attention to your grades or attending summer camps for your sport too early. And you should take the PSAT for the first time (without studying for it) during your sophomore year, to get an idea of where you stand and to get practice taking the test.

As a junior, you need to do several things:

- ✔ **Keep up your schoolwork.** We can't stress the importance of this enough.
- ✔ **Take the PSAT again in October.** Study for the test this time.
- ✔ **Register with the clearinghouse.** See Chapter 4 for help with this.
- ✔ **Register for the ACT and SAT.** Most students take these tests at least twice in an attempt to get the highest score possible.

(You'll need to decide whether the fall, spring, or summer test dates are best for you, depending on the sport you play and possible conflicts with your sports schedule.)

- ✔ **Make informal visits to college campuses throughout the year.** See Chapter 10 for more on college visits.

- ✔ **Send out your first contact letters at the beginning of the year.** Include copies of your fall and spring schedules, when available. Ask your high school coach to write letters of recommendation to a few preferred colleges. (Written contact by college coaches is allowed beginning in September of your junior year in all Division I sports other than men's basketball; in men's basketball, written contact by college coaches is allowed at the conclusion of the sophomore year.)

- ✔ **Travel with your team to recruiting events throughout the year.** Write college coaches, and make arrangements for them to evaluate your play. *Remember:* Now is the time to showcase yourself!

- ✔ **Prepare a highlight videotape of yourself to be sent out when requested.** Do *not* send out unsolicited tapes.

- ✔ **If a college coach sends you a player profile form/questionnaire to complete, return it immediately, even if you can't answer all the questions.** Send updates as you get the additional information.

- ✔ **Continue playing your sport as much as possible and trying to get as much exposure as possible.** If you're playing club sports, you need to be selfish and play for a team with a lot of exposure.

- ✔ **Prepare for phone calls from coaches.** During March of your junior year, one phone call from college coaches is permitted in all sports other than football and basketball. All subsequent calls may be made after July 1 (after your junior year) and are limited to once per week.

  If you're a football prospect, a coach may call you once during May of your junior year but may not call you again until September 1 at the beginning of your senior year. At that time, coaches are permitted to call you once a week except during a contact period when they can call you as often as they like.

  If men's basketball is in your future, you may expect one call a month from coaches starting June 15 after your sophomore year. From August 1 after your junior year until the beginning of your senior year, coaches can call you twice, but when your senior year starts, that goes to once a week.

  Women's basketball is slightly different. Coaches get to call you once a month during April and May of your junior year and then once more from June 1 through June 20 of that year. From June 21 through June 30, one call is permitted; then three total calls can be made in July. When August 1 hits, the calls are limited to once a week!

In all Division II sports, coaches may begin calling you once a week on June 15 after your junior year. Division II football coaches have the same leeway as Division I coaches during a contact period when they can call as often as they like.

There are no restrictions or limitations when it comes to *Division III* coaches calling you, so don't be surprised if they call you as early as your freshman or sophomore year.

A *contact period* is exactly what it sounds like: It's the time when college coaches are allowed to meet with you and/or your parents, in person and off campus.

✔ **Remember to maintain your academic performance (keep those grades up!), and keep up your level of athletic performance.** You may be attracting the attention of colleges now.

✔ **The summer between your junior and senior years, focus on attending "select," "advanced," "elite," or "showcase" camps.** In this environment, you'll be able to gauge your play against the best players at the camps. The college coaches will be able to do the same. (The summer between your junior and senior years is very important.)

Analyzing the Athlete off the Field: Looking at the Whole Athlete

If you aren't a blue-chip athlete, you still have the chance to participate in an intercollegiate sport. You can market your best qualities in ways that will gain the attention of a coach at any level.

Beyond raw or polished athletic talent, beyond media coverage and cocky attitudes, colleges and universities are now preferring to recruit the complete student-athlete — in other words, the whole package. Schools are looking for a diverse student body, so your gender, ethnic origin, geographic origin, personal character, and academic performance are among the criteria that colleges and universities consider. Although more and more schools at all levels are doing this, Division III schools (nonscholarship schools) have been using these criteria for years.

Your athletic ability is not all that the schools will look at. Your grades matter; your extracurricular activities matter. If you're active in your church, synagogue, or mosque; if you're politically or environmentally active; if you hand out food to the homeless at Thanksgiving — all of these activities matter to colleges and universities. They all say something about you, and what they say may be just what a particular college wants to hear.

So, besides playing your heart out and keeping your grades up, stay busy being an important individual in this very large, busy world. In other words, *make a difference.*

Chapter 6

The Game Begins: Getting Noticed

● ●

In This Chapter

▶ Understanding club ball and sport camps

▶ Learning from your coaches

▶ Thinking of your parents as teammates

▶ Working with the media

▶ Building your portfolio

● ●

*I*f you're reading this book, you must be committed to your sport — you understand the commitment involved to get to the next level. Most likely, you've passed the preteen (adolescent) stage where the majority of your peers began to walk away from sports. For whatever reason — hormones, fashion, peer pressure, or insecurities — the desire to be an athlete becomes less and less appealing for some, but it only grows in you. You're willing to give the time, energy, blood, sweat, and tears needed to make it in your sport. For you, understanding the evolution of the college/elite athlete is very important. These athletes aren't born; they're trained — and that training begins at the recreational and club-ball level.

In this chapter, we show you how to begin. Most people are under the impression that the game of recruiting begins when you pick up your first ball or run your first race. Not so. The game of recruiting — or getting noticed — has its own rules and begins only when you start. Knowing how to use your current coaches, family, local media, and teammates is just the beginning. As you build your own portfolio, you'll better understand how to promote yourself while doing something you love.

What's that old sports saying: "There is no *I* in team"? But as you enter the recruiting game, you'll (temporarily) find that there *is* an *I*. And you have to know how to promote yourself effectively.

Discovering the New Kid on the Block

The first of many questions you must ask yourself as you step into this arena is "Why am I playing a sport?" You'll find soon enough that playing on the field or court has been the easy part. As you step into the far more competitive world of select or club ball, college recruiting, and playing in the big leagues, you have to be sure of what you really want.

In the movie *Grease,* Danny (John Travolta) turns his back on his leather-wearing, drag-racing ways to earn a letter in sports — all because he wants to impress Sandy (Olivia Newton-John). The theme is common in Hollywood and real life. Sports are cool! And kids who play sports are cool, right?

The social status attached to being an athlete cannot be denied, and parents are all too aware of this. For this reason, parents, guardians, friends, and even coaches often push kids to the limit in the name of scoring the winning goal or making the final shot. They push and push until, quite suddenly, a star is born. After all the hours on the field or court, all the time running drills and working the hand-eye coordination, something clicks.

For all the pushing that parents and coaches do, however, it is *you,* the athlete, who makes the final call. You have to feel the desire in your gut. You have to be able to say, "I really want this" — and *mean* it.

Statistically, the majority of athletes drop out of competitive sports by their early teens. The time commitment, money, energy, and/or agility is more than they can handle. Others understand that this is just the beginning. You may be one of these others.

What happens after your decide to take sports to the next level has as much to do with athletic ability as it does with the kind of support you receive from your coaches and parents.

Playing club ball

Check the by-laws of any ball club, traveling club, or select club, and you'll find the same mission statement: to promote the *advanced* players. In the late 1970s, the idea of creating teams — select teams with more advanced players — gained popularity as parents and coaches attempted to provide more challenging matches among better, advanced athletes. Whether or not you like the premise, these teams played against the better teams from the communities, cities, and even states for title matches. Thus, the term *traveling team* was born.

Select or traveling teams do offer more challenging games to young athletes. But another driving force behind the club movement is prestige. Both kids and parents feel a great deal of pride in being associated with a "select" group of athletes.

The process typically works like this: You're invited by a coach who has seen you play, or you may try out for a team that you've heard about from other parents or through an ad. If you make the cut, you're asked to sign a one-year contract. This is a binding contract in which your family is obligated to pay a flat-out fee or make monthly payments to the club — fees that can cost hundreds or thousands of dollars. The contract may also forbid you to play with any other teams during the off season. When you've signed that contract, you must adhere to the club's practice and to game times and places.

No scientific data proves that club ball advances young athletes to the elite status any faster or better than recreational ball.

Scientific data aside, there is a very positive and undisputable reality about playing select ball: You get noticed. Because college recruiters' funds and time are limited, select tournaments allow recruiters to see a wide variety of talent from all over the region in one place. These games are a recruiter's paradise. And if you're playing select tournaments, you'll increase your chances of being seen.

Another positive of playing select or club ball is the experience. Although recreational sport is wonderful, athletes who play select often have a higher level of commitment. Because these athletes have paid a higher price (literally), and are willing to travel and train more intensely than recreational athletes, the competition will be more fierce.

If you decide to play with a select team, you're making a commitment beyond the tryout and practice times. Some select teams travel across state lines or to faraway cities. Tournaments may turn into three-day events, which means greater food and lodging bills.

Be sure to take a look at the investments required before signing on, including the following:

 ✔ Uniform and equipment

 ✔ Lodging and food

 ✔ Transportation

   ✔ Separate tournament fees

   ✔ Tournament T-shirts and souvenirs

Be sure to talk to other parents and athletes to determine costs you may not have thought of.

Also consider the travel schedule to determine the hours or days involved in individual games and weekend tournaments.

Before you try out for a club team, ask the club coach the following questions to determine whether playing club ball is right for you:

   ✔ What will be the time requirement for you and your family?

   ✔ Does the coach give equal playtime to all the players?

   ✔ What is the team/club policy for sportsmanship? Are parents and coaches required to sign a code of conduct as well as the players?

   ✔ What if you miss a practice or game?

   ✔ Is there an academic standard?

   ✔ Do you have to sign an agreement? If so, what are the terms?

   ✔ What kind of experience does the coach have?

   ✔ Can the coach provide references from previous and current players and parents?

Then ask *yourself* and your family the following questions:

   ✔ What will my siblings or parents have to sacrifice so that I can play?

   ✔ What will I have to give up so that I can play with the club?

   ✔ How will playing club ball affect my schoolwork?

   ✔ How will playing club ball affect my social life?

   ✔ How much time will I be on the road?

Be sure also to talk to your family before you join a club sport. Ask them whether they're all ready for the time commitment that will be involved.

Choosing sports camps

Sports camps are an excellent place for you to showcase your talent for coaches and recruiters, as well as to learn valuable skills from coaches from around the nation. They're also full-fledged businesses that offer one- and two-week sleepover camps with intense training programs in a variety of sports, such as tennis, soccer, basketball, and swimming.

The camps are generally held on college campuses and are run by college coaches — an excellent way for you to be seen by that college's coaches and recruiters, as well as to tour the campus, meet and interact with the coaching staff, and see the athletic facilities. In recent years, shoe and other sports-apparel companies, such as Nike and Reebok, have begun offering select sports camps of their own.

At a sports camp, you also have an opportunity to learn from more-skilled coaches than your high school or club coach. This is not meant to knock your high school or club coach, but he or she may not have had the chance to learn the coaching skills to help you get to the next level. The coaches you'll work with at a sports camp likely will.

At camp, you'll have the chance to test your skills and talents against those of other potential college players. If you're able to compete well in a good camp, chances are you can play at the next level.

Attending a sports camp adds to your athletic résumé. A coach who may be on the fence about recruiting you may be more willing to take a chance if you've attended multiple camps. Going to sports camps shows the coach you're serious about your sport and trying to improve your game.

Sports camps are a good way for you to continue playing in the off season. Because most camps are held in the summer, they can give you an opportunity to work on your skills at a time when you may not otherwise be able to. Most high school associations have rules against organized practice and/or competition during the summer, so camps may be the only way for you to play in a competitive setting during the summer.

On the downside, camps can be very stressful, with undue pressure from expectant, demanding coaches, parents, or fellow teammates. They can also be very expensive and time consuming.

The most popular reason for attending a sports camp is recruiting. Attending a camp may get your foot in the door at a college that otherwise might not know who you are. This can especially be the case for a small Division I school or one in Division II or III, where the recruiting budgets are scarce. Specialty camps, or *position camps* (for example, a quarterback camp in football), can be a great way for you to showcase your talents because those camps are generally used only for recruiting purposes by coaches.

Working with the coach

Deion Branch of the New England Patriots called all his coaches hours before he was named MVP of Super Bowl XXXIX. He called all the Little League, high school, recreational, and college coaches he ever had to thank them for the time and dedication they gave him while he was growing up. Without them, he said, his dream of playing in the "greatest show on earth" would not have been possible. Branch's coaches served him as guidance counselors, educators, personal trainers, and motivators. The message from Deion Branch is that, whether you're working with a recreational coach, a club or select coach, or a sports-camp coach, view it as a learning experience.

Like every athlete, coaches have their strengths and weaknesses. You don't have to like your coach, but you must respect the position of the coach on your team.

Learning from your coach

Coaches wear many hats. Not only must they strategize games, calls plays, and organize games and/or staff, but they're also responsible for teaching you how to deal with pressure before and during games or matches. They instill a strong work ethic and must figure out what motivates you.

While you play at the club or select level, your coach asks far more of you than the typical recreational coach may. But remember that you may also expect more from your coach. You're paying for a service — make sure you get your (or your parents') money's worth.

In club sports, the coach often works directly with or has personal contact with many college recruiters. Not only can successful select coaches get recruiters to come watch a game or practice, but they also can also tell you what recruiters are looking for. From the way you warm up to the way you behave on the sidelines, recruiters know what they want, and your select coach can help guide you in the right direction.

As you begin to think about what college you would like to attend or dream about your collegiate future, talk to your coach. If you're a freshman in high school, your coach may give more instructional advice on athletic strategy. But if you're a junior, ask your coach about his or her own experience with college recruiters. What should you ask when speaking with a recruiter? How do you get recruiters to notice you? What are your strongest and weakest points on — and off — the field?

Your coach is dealing with a variety of personalities on the team: the extroverts, the introverts, the show-offs, the wallflowers, the easily discouraged, and the overly confident. Don't demand his or her full attention. Choose your time carefully. Ask to set up a time to speak one on one with your coach — and listen to what he or she has to say.

By learning to accept criticism, and following and carrying through instructions, you'll become the kind of athlete coaches enjoy most.

Here are some things you *don't* want to do with your coach:

✔ Nag or complain about playtime

✔ Pout when the game doesn't go the way you want

✔ Gloat over a successful shot or awesome throw

✔ Call positions you think you should play

✔ Make excuses when you're corrected

Is this the coach for me?

Despite your best efforts, there are times when you and your coach simply don't mesh. It may be a matter of miscommunication or differing personality types.

Ask yourself the following questions to determine whether this coach is the right one for you:

✔ What is his or her philosophy on winning? Is it "Win at all costs"?

✔ What is my philosophy on winning? Does it mesh with the coach's philosophy?

✔ Is my coach a role model?

✔ Does my team respect this coach?

✔ What do my coach's peers think of him or her?

✔ Is safety important to my coach?

✔ Is he or she trained to deal with injuries?

✔ Why does he or she coach?

If you aren't satisfied with the answers you receive, talk to other athletes and parents. A coach and athlete may knock heads from time to time but be able to work through their differences. But if the coach and coaching staff have a completely different sports philosophy from yours, it may be time to step away and find a new school or coach.

You cannot and will not develop as an athlete if you're miserable where you are.

Before signing with a select team, consider the coach and his or her reputation. All too often, both parents and student-athletes are so excited to have made the team, they forget that there was actually a "second tryout." What's the second tryout? As you go out for a club or select team, you aren't the only one trying out. Your coach and the club must also impress you. You shouldn't care about a club because your best friend is playing in it — you have to consider your select team as you will a college. It's not about team colors or friends. This is about top-level competition, and you need to consider the experience and reputation of your coach. Just as you hope to get a scholarship to college so that you may earn a higher education, you're getting an education (of another sort) from your select coach.

Don't be embarrassed or shy about investigating the club or select coach. Check references. Talk to other parents and players. Ask the coach for his coaching résumé.

Working with Your Parents

Just as you have a very specific role you need to play as an athlete, your parents have very specific roles they need to play in your sport. In this section, we provide some guidelines for parents.

Parents should

- ✔ Teach their kids sportsmanship.
- ✔ Teach their kids integrity.
- ✔ Offer financial support.
- ✔ Offer emotional support. Be a good cheerleader!
- ✔ Work with the coach or team. Parents can contribute to the team by doing anything from making phone calls to driving other players when they don't have a ride to a scheduled practice or game.
- ✔ Find out more about the coach and/or league. Check their safety guidelines and zero-tolerance policy.

Parents should *not:*

- ✔ Expect more playtime for their kid
- ✔ Demand more coaching time for their kid

The stage mom: How aggressive parents can cause a foul

We've all seen the headlines in recent years. A father knocks down his son's football teammate after a disagreement between the boys. A mother heckles an injured soccer player during a match between 8-year-old girls until an enraged father punches her in the face, clearing both sidelines; police have to be called to separate the parents. A father beats his son's hockey coach with hockey sticks when he disagrees with a coaching decision. A tee-ball game erupts into a full-blown brawl over an umpire's call. A father attacks a fellow parent during a game. The list goes on and on. And while everyone was deeply saddened, no one was particularly surprised when a father in Massachusetts beat another man to death over a disagreement during a boys' recreational-hockey practice. Many sports fans have asked over and over, "Why is this happening?" The easy answer is entitlement and rage.

Parents devote an enormous amount of time and energy to their children's hopes and athletic dreams. More important, far too many parents connect their own personal hopes and dreams to the athletic abilities of their children. They live vicariously through their children and expect greatness. In time, parents begin to feel a powerful sense of entitlement: We deserve this! You deserve better! You should be playing more! You're one of the best players on the team — why doesn't your coach use you more often?

With this kind of thinking comes the idea that parents should have more input with the team, with how the games are run and how the coach thinks. But the reality is that only a select group of kids will wear the celebrated high school varsity jersey. Fewer will ever be offered an athletic scholarship, and even fewer will eventually make the pros. These are hard facts for parents to accept.

In *Coaching Kids For Dummies,* Rick Wolff discusses how to deal with difficult parents, placing them in categories from the "know-it-all" and "loud-mouth" to the "comparer" and "flatterer." Wolff identifies what college coaches and recruiters have known for some time: There are certain parents who need to be avoided or appropriately dealt with. Although coaches have learned to walk the fine line between encouraging parents to participate and risking parents' running the game, this is not a problem you want to have if you're being considered by a school. From recreational ball to high school or select sports, a parent can be a deal-breaker, and coaches have been known to pass on a star athlete because of his or her parents' behavior.

After two years of recreational soccer, a very gifted center forward left her team to play club ball. The athlete had been a strong force for the team, and her absence was felt quickly. The following season, the team lost the majority of its games, and parents worried that the girls would be downhearted. After the fourth straight loss, the coach met with the parents and players to talk about their future.

(continued)

(continued)

He began the discussion by saying, "Now, I know we all miss Monica." To his surprise, not only did the parents disagree, but so did the players. The girls unanimously agreed that while they liked the girl, they hadn't missed her because her parents caused so much stress and distraction to the team. The girls said that, although they were losing, they were enjoying the sport more than ever. One season later, the coach attended a tournament and stopped to watch his old player, Monica. Nothing had changed, he noted, as he watched the girl's parents scream and berate Monica, her teammates, and the officials. After the game, he spoke to the club coach to see how Monica was doing. "Nothing is worth this. I don't care how good she is — she won't be playing with us next season."

✔ Make plays or offer their own ideas for a lineup

✔ Talk to the officials

✔ Talk negatively to the parents of the opposing team

✔ Compare their kid to their kid's teammates

 A scholarship is truly a gift that is often overlooked or unappreciated. Often, parents overestimate their kids' abilities and expect a slew of scholarship offers. Full scholarships are rare (except in football, basketball, and certain women's sports at the upper Division I level), so parents should be careful when attempting to persuade a student to turn down a partial scholarship in hopes of being offered a larger one later.

Maximizing Your Exposure

Like the behavior of your parents and coaches, how you conduct yourself is critical in the game of college recruiting. You have to think of yourself in business terms.

Not many years ago, a young man began his own taxi service to help pay for college. We like the idea of supporting an enthusiastic, up-and-coming businessman, but there was a problem. The bumper sticker on the back of his cab read:

THERE'S A PARTY IN MY PANTS
AND EVERYONE IS COMING!

You have to wonder: What kind of image was this guy trying to sell?

You are your brand name. Beyond your athletic abilities, you want to find a strategy that makes you different and memorable (but you don't want to be remembered for having a party in your pants). Hard work alone won't get potential colleges to take notice. You have to promote yourself, and in this section, we show you how.

Thinking outside the box or beyond the game

Getting a college scholarship is about much more than how fast you can run or how high you can leap. It's also about commitment, strategy, phone calls, interviews, and follow-ups. In short, you need to create your own business plan. You need to ask yourself a series of questions about your future goals, just as a businessperson might do.

Sit down with your parents, guardians, or coach, and honestly answer these questions:

- ✔ What would you most like to do with your life?
- ✔ Where are you now?
- ✔ How can you achieve your goals?
- ✔ What is your time frame?
- ✔ What kind of networking system do you have?

The one that got away

While working at the NCAA, co-author Pat Britz fielded many phone calls from angry parents about lost scholarship deals. In one instance, a parent called, angry because a school that offered a verbal commitment later declined a scholarship. The parent was upset because she (and her son) had previously withdrawn a verbal commitment to a smaller school when the other school came a-knockin'. Suddenly, they were without any offer at all. The parent turned to the NCAA for assistance, but there was none to be given — the parent let the big one get away in her quest to get something even bigger!

You can easily believe the initial hype when colleges show interest: "They want me! I'm the best!" But the reality is this: Colleges are simply looking around to see what and who is out there. The early stages of recruitment are quite similar to trying out for a club or select team. This is the tryout phase. Don't rule anyone out; don't overestimate your abilities or appeal; and never disregard another player.

✔ How can you gain access to the information you need?

✔ What are the costs?

✔ What are the risks?

✔ What is the payoff?

✔ Who may be interested in you as a student-athlete?

By answering these questions, you'll have taken the first steps to promoting yourself in a timely, organized fashion. You'll know who is willing to help, what schools to focus on, what deadlines you need to meet, and what you really want.

If you're like most student-athletes, the one question that you'd rather not have to answer is "What are the risks?" There are several:

✔ You could fail.

✔ You may not be offered a scholarship after all.

✔ You'll have to talk to people about yourself.

✔ You'll have to take the initiative, calling up strangers to discuss your athletic feats.

✔ You may feel very intimidated or embarrassed.

Picking up the phone: Don't be afraid to do PR

You've put in hours and hours on your jump shot, slap shot, corner kick, swing, or long jump. You understand the importance of "practice makes perfect." *Networking* (talking to and getting to know people who can help you reach your goals) is no different — you'll get better the more you practice.

Networking is an extremely important aspect of the college recruiting process. Too many student-athletes overlook the importance of networking, probably because it requires overcoming fear — fear of exposure, rejection, or obligation.

In this section, we show you how to make your network work for you.

Networking the sports community

A big mistake student-athletes make is not sharing information. Their thinking is "I don't want anyone else to know what I'm doing. They might get ahead of me." But when you share information with other athletes, teammates, and parents, you actually create more opportunities for yourself.

The sporting world is a small community built around a shared interest. While writing this book, we met numerous coaches, trainers, counselors, athletic directors, parents, and athletes who wanted to share their interest and knowledge. Sports folks like to talk about athletics and athletes.

This behavior works two ways:

✔ If you misbehave, coaches and others will talk about you. Coaches have a great memory when it comes to recruiting time.

✔ If you share and ask for information, sports people will talk to you, sharing their expertise and supporting young athletes' efforts.

Expecting paybacks: Don't!

Part of sharing in a network requires

✔ Faith in the importance of being generous

✔ Knowledge that what you have is worth sharing

Don't calculate your actions for rewards — don't always think "If I do X, then Y will happen." Exchange information because it is the right thing to do. You'll earn a reputation as a student-athlete who is open, honest, and fair. When you do this, your networking relationships will grow. Your cooperative and helpful attitude will bring you more paybacks than you could ever get by scheming or holding out.

Playing phone tag

Part of networking means that you have things that others want, and they have things that you want. A recruiter is interested in having you play for his or her school. You want a scholarship, and you hope to wear the colors of your choice.

But this relationship doesn't always mean that both parties have to be active in the relationship at the same time. For example, you call a recruiter who is talking to several athletes at the same time. At this point, the recruiter is digesting information and trying to decide who the better student-athlete would be to represent the college. You want the recruiter's full attention, but you have to wait for a decision or further conversation when the recruiter has more time.

Stalking or bombarding the recruiter with phone calls won't work to your advantage. All you can do is thank the recruiter for his time and carry on. Tag. Now he's it.

One day, one week, or one month later — no matter how long it's been, the recruiter may call back. Now you have something the recruiter wants. You've been noticed, and the game moves on.

Making cold calls

The cold-call relationship can be with a complete stranger or someone you knew before but only now recognize as someone with potential for future contacts. Your cold-call contact can be a recruiter, journalist, coach, teammate, or parent. What you hope to do is turn the cold call into a more personal contact — someone with whom you share information and through whom you can expand your network.

Get out the Rolodex cards, and start making notations of names, addresses, phone numbers, and e-mail addresses. Make notes to yourself about people, their titles, and personal information you may have gathered (special interests, names of family members, special events), and note the best times to contact each person.

Developing relationships with coaches, trainers, and local media is a great way to expand your contacts, gain valuable inside information, and get your name out in front!

Creating your own portfolio

Most student-athletes give recruiters their college applications, résumés, and highlight tapes when meeting recruiters. Then they cross their fingers and hope they've given the recruiters enough information.

But *you're* not most student-athletes. You're going to create an impressive portfolio that leaves no doubt in the mind of any coach or recruiter that you're the best choice to wear his or her school colors.

Buy a leather-bound portfolio (you can get one in any office retail store, starting from $30) to hold all your vital information. Here's what you want to put inside the portfolio:

> ✔ **Awards:** Place all certificates of achievement you've earned in the front of the portfolio so that they're the first things people see. Make copies of these certificates, and keep them in a separate file.

- ✔ **Articles:** Whether it's a mention in the local paper naming you along with your teammates or an entire article dedicated to your athletic achievements, fill the portfolio with these accolades. Be sure to put the best headlines in front. Again, make copies for your records.

- ✔ **Statistics:** You may be sure that the coaches or recruiters already have this information, but include your stats with the portfolio package. They're something to be proud of, and you want to show what you've done.

- ✔ **Sports-camp/club-ball certifications:** Include this information as another way to show your commitment, time, and dedication to a sport you love. You're not a prima donna — you're the real deal!

- ✔ **Academic achievements:** This includes your grades and a list of extracurricular activities that will set you apart from your competition. Did you win an art contest? Compete in a science fair? Join the chess club? Colleges like to see a well-rounded student who can bring more than just great hand–eye coordination to the school.

- ✔ **Letters of recommendation:** Ask your coach, trainers, team managers, school counselors, and teachers to write letters of recommendation. These letters should mention your work ethic as an athlete *and* as a student. Again, recruiters like to know that they're dealing with a team player — someone who can follow directions, take criticism, lift team morale, and be counted on as a leader. This list of letter-writers can also include parents of fellow teammates, your spiritual leader, and tutors.

- ✔ **Virtual records:** Include any copies of highlight films, pictures, or videos that showcase your best work (see the "Putting together highlight films" section, later in this chapter).

 If possible, make copies of articles and letters so that you can leave material with whomever you meet. *Remember:* You're your own brand name. Nike has the swoosh, Starbucks has the green-headed lady with flowing hair, and *For Dummies* has the black-and-yellow cover. These images are universally recognized! But you can create your own image. Reinforce your image by leaving some copies of your information in the hands of everyone you can.

Corresponding with coaches

Even if you're ready to take it to the next level, you can't assume coaches will know this or will be able to find you. Don't wait for coaches to find you. NCAA rules or financial restrictions may hold them back, so you can make the first move if necessary.

Presenting the letter and questionnaire

As a general rule, because coaches are not permitted to contact you in writing until September 1 of your junior year in high school, you may *have* to take the first step by sending a letter, e-mailing, or completing a questionnaire (which you can find on the school's athletics Web site). The main purpose of such correspondence is to give the coach enough information so she knows you're talented enough and have the grades to be eligible for and be admitted to the school.

You may find questionnaires on most college athletics Web sites. These are generally sport-specific and can be found in the menu for the particular sport in which you're interested, but some are generic and can be found on the recruiting page of the Web site. Completing this questionnaire almost always guarantees a response; if you complete a questionnaire, you may not need to send an initial introduction letter, because most of the information you would put in the letter will be asked on the questionnaire.

If you're completing the questionnaire prior to September 1 of your junior year, don't be surprised if you receive a generic letter from the coach thanking you for your interest and letting you know he'll be in touch as soon as he's allowed to do so. Eventually, you'll probably get a response stating the coach's interest level and what your chances of making the team actually are. Either way, sending a quick thank-you note or e-mail to the coach can go a long way.

If you're interested in a big Division I school, don't be surprised if it's not as easy to find contact information (phone number, e-mail) for coaches. Most of these schools have a list of individuals they want to recruit, and they try to limit the contact they get from prospects who probably aren't gifted enough to play there. If you have trouble finding the coach's contact info, a simple phone call to the main athletics department phone number will do the trick. Ask the operator for the best way to get in contact with the coach. The operator may also be able to tell you where the information is online, in case you just overlooked it.

If you can't find a questionnaire on the school's Web site, you should write a letter of interest to the coach. Your letter should be concise and to the point. You want to provide the coach with the vital information about you. The letter should include

- ✔ The position you play and a brief description of your success and athletic qualifications

- ✔ Your academic credentials and the field of study in which you're interested (don't worry — you can change your mind)

✔ Your highlight tape or DVD (see the "Putting together highlight films" section, later in this chapter)

✔ The fact that you're familiar with the program and its recent successes or troubles

✔ A request for the coach to respond

You may be amazed at how much time and energy you can save a coach with such a simple letter. The coach should now be able to make a good estimate of your ability to be part of his program without ever leaving the office. Coaches like this.

Be sure to proofread your letter. Nothing can turn off a coach more than having a letter sent to her with the name of another school, the name of another coach, or misspelled words on it.

Don't be discouraged if you don't hear back from the coach. The coach has probably received hundreds of letters just like yours and may not have the time to respond to each one or may already be recruiting people for your position that she's seen play in person. In fact, many coaches are known to wait for a follow-up phone call from the prospect to see how interested you really are. Just because you send a letter doesn't put you at the top of the coach's list. Chances are you're still an anonymous player at this point, so the coach will need a more convincing reason to recruit you over the other players she may already be tracking.

Don't assume that the coach received the letter. Letters can get lost or mishandled, or can simply fall behind a desk. Checking up on the status of the letter can be enough of a reason to place a follow-up phone call.

Putting together highlight films

When they're able, coaches and their staff will review as many highlight films as possible to create the best team they can. Remember the key word: *highlight*. You must choose a winning run, shot, or throw that best illustrates your abilities as an athlete.

Keep it brief. Think ESPN's "Play of the Week" segments. Coaches don't have time to watch an entire game or event. They'll lose interest and move on to another prospect.

Appreciating the Role of the Media

Baseball's volatile Barry Bonds has had an ongoing feud with the media. Few sports fans have missed his continued complaints that the media have unfairly ridiculed and berated him for his behavior with fellow teammates and fans. After his testimony about steroids was leaked to the press, he lashed out once more, calling reporters liars.

Whatever you think of Bonds or how he's been treated by the press, we assure you that he once used every press clipping, every write-up, every interview to wow recruiters and coaches at both the collegiate and professional levels. The point is, you need the press. Use it wisely.

Maximizing your 15 minutes of fame

The press has certainly earned a bad reputation over the years, particularly when reporters crowd the locker room after a bad play, asking athletes to relive the moment. This experience is a frustrating one, and nobody wants to have his slip-up highlighted. But take a lesson from Bonds: Don't overreact. Don't whine. Don't complain. Respectfully answer the questions, remembering that the reporters are simply retelling a story the fans want to know. Take it in stride, and know that better days are coming.

And if you are the MVP, grab hold of the spotlight. Don't avoid or dodge reporters out of embarrassment. You don't have to jump up and down in front of cameras. Simply smile, answer the questions, and enjoy the moment.

You've got 15 minutes — ready, set, go! How do you want to use that time? Whether it's a local match or a state championship, this is your time to meet the press and talk to individual reporters, providing as much information as possible.

Your parents can be extremely helpful, making sure the reporter gets the proper spelling of your name, your jersey number, other stats, and any personal information that might make a great storyline.

Be sure to mention fellow teammates who assisted in a specific play, and compliment the entire team effort and the coaching staff.

Getting what you want printed

Every day, reporters around the world receive phone calls from well-meaning parents and athletes. They want a story in the newspaper about the budding athlete. But frequently, when asked for their *pitch* (story idea), they've got nothing. "Well, he's really, really good at hockey."

"Really, really good" doesn't sell copies. "ATHLETE OVERCOMES LEARNING DISABILITY TO PLAY STARTING POSITION," "LOCAL ATHLETE DEDICATED TO COMMUNITY SERVICE," "HOMELESS STUDENT HITS WINNING RUN IN BASEBALL AND EDUCATION" — those are headlines that sell copies.

Whether you'll graduate early, you help senior citizens in your spare time, you fix computers for extra dollars, you're an avid chess player, or you secretly enjoy knitting, you must have a story that will make you more personable and add to the sports angle.

Reporters have deadlines and must move quickly. If you don't return phone calls or offer enough information, they'll move on to the next story. An, ultimately, the story is in the hands of an editor. The reporter doesn't always get to write about what she wants, so your story has to be compelling enough to interest the editor who has not met you — or maybe even heard of you.

Working Mom and Dad as Your Public Relations Firm

A good public relations director will work to keep his client in the spotlight, in the game, and attending all the main events. The PR parent needs to have that same agenda.

Choosing what's on the agenda

Parents can help by making and keeping an agenda. If your parents know the calendar of events for college applicants, athletic scholarships, and recruiter guidelines, you'll be ahead of the game.

Parents can create their own press kit, which should include

✔ College/scholarship application deadlines and notification dates.

✔ Testing dates and times.

✔ A filing system of addresses for colleges and coaches.

✔ A personal information package that includes your Social Security number, academic records, medical history, and athletic statistics. (It's helpful if your parents can answer questions such as what sports camps you've attended or what awards you've earned.)

✔ Copies of your test scores.

Keep all these important papers together.

Although having a calendar of events to mark your personal calendar with is nice, you don't have to wait for schools to publish anything. You or your PR parent can also check out scholarship Web sites, such as www.fastweb.com, for a free Internet scholarship that will match you with a scholarship that best suits your academic, athletic, and financial needs.

Beware of scholarship search services that make guarantees or require fees. Numerous legitimate services offer free advice and information about the latest and greatest scholarships. Use the services designed to help young athletes, rather than those focused on making a profit.

How to help, not hinder

You'll always find pushy parents on the playing field. Just as these parents can be annoying to coaches, the pushy PR parent can be equally troublesome. Parents can easily convince themselves that their kid is being overlooked, ignored, or underestimated. They tend to adopt the philosophy "Well, if they won't listen, we'll *make* them listen!" The squeaky wheel gets the grease, right? But sometimes, a squeaky wheel is just really annoying.

Relentless phone calls and letters to reporters, recruiters, and coaches will not endear you to anyone.

The opposite problem is the parents who simply wait too long to act on behalf of their kids. Afraid of being too intrusive, these parents simply let deadlines come and go. Although you don't want loud, aggressive parents, you *do* need strong team players. Talk to your parents, plan with them, and work with them to build an effective PR effort.

Working as a team

Okay, so your parents or guardians are on board, and Team Scholarship is ready to rock! Recruiters have taken notice; coaches are talking; you're having the best season of your life; the local media has written some nice pieces about you; and you're ready to take it to the next level. But is your team ready?

Ask your parents:

- ✔ Do they really believe you can get a scholarship?
- ✔ Do they have time as a family to create Team Scholarship?
- ✔ Is this appropriate for the family?
- ✔ Are they ready to create a PR packet, contact coaches, and deal with the media?
- ✔ Are they willing to help you research schools and Web sites?
- ✔ Are they willing or able to travel?

If the answers are yes, and Team Scholarship is ready to go, create your PR checklist. Network and share information. Research the schools you're interested in, looking at each school's records, location, and academic standards. Take a serious look at your parents' behavior during games and with other parents. Be media savvy, and use the Web to find out more about scholarship services and marketing ideas.

Here's a PR checklist you can use as a good starting point:

- ✔ **Set your goal.** What is your final objective? (If you don't set a goal, how will you achieve it?)
- ✔ **Understand the market.** How can you best sell yourself and your name?
- ✔ **Research.** Find out how other athletes — perhaps your teammates — have successfully marketed themselves with the local press and recruiters.
- ✔ **Identify your resources.** What resources can you use to learn more about the marketing and recruiting process? With whom can you network?
- ✔ **Make lists.** Write down and continuously check out various books, Web sites, and services. Don't just look once and walk away.
- ✔ **Create a Rolodex of all your contacts.** Network, network, network.
- ✔ **Play the PR agent.** Hone your people skills, and learn to sell your story, successes, and potential.
- ✔ **Restate your agenda.** Continuously remind Team Scholarship why you're doing this and what the goal is.

It's never too early to begin researching schools and coaches. The more people you talk to and the more questions you ask, the more easily you'll be able to pinpoint what it is you want from a college and where you hope to go.

But don't panic if you don't know yet. Many young athletes worry because they don't yet have a precise top-ten list of the schools they want to attend. You may get offered an athletic scholarship to a college you never even thought about. By discussing your options with your parents and working the media angle, however, you'll open as many doors as possible.

Chapter 7

The Full-Court Press: Calls, Letters, and E-Mails from Coaches

*H*ave you ever bought a car? Or at least been around to watch a parent or sibling buy one? On the surface, the process appears to be pretty straightforward, and it's very similar to choosing a college: You pick the model or make you like (a type of college), visit a few dealerships (campuses), and talk to salespeople (recruiters and staff) to get a feel for what you want and need. When you know what you want, you ask for a test drive (the official campus visit), kick the tires (try the cafeteria food), and then begin the negotiation process.

But if you're sharp, you know there is much more than that to buying a car. For instance, some dealerships are overstocked and need to sell, whereas others may not negotiate on the sticker price. Dealerships often have end-of-the-month or end-of-the-quarter sales quotas that may allow you more room for haggling. You need to shop and compare, know the blue-book value on a car, and consider gas mileage and the practicality of a car before buying in.

So soon, so fast

By the age of 12, world-champion rock climber and pole vaulter Tori Allen had her academic and athletic career planned. "By my sophomore year," says Allen, "I knew what I needed to do, where I needed to go. I know I'm competing against other athletes who have their athletic careers planned out, so I have to be just as organized, if not more. If I'm going to be the best, I have to plan everything in the best way possible."

Just as Olympic athletes prepare and train four years in advance of the chance to try out for a position on a national team, so must the high school athlete who has collegiate aspirations. The games start now, not next year. Sports camps around the nation are reaching out to, training, and profiling students as young as 10 and 12 years old. And while the debate rages on among educators, parents, coaches, and boosters on the ethics of these practices, the competition is heating up.

Colleges are already reviewing new talent, identifying those prospects who fit their needs and weeding out those who don't. Remarkably, a high school athlete can be cut from a college recruiter's prospect list without even knowing it. In Chapter 6, we fill you in on ways to market yourself effectively and keep your name out in front, which are critical to staying in the game.

Choosing a college is no different. Each year you're in high school is about more than the curriculum that your teachers want you to learn. As you play sports as a sophomore, junior, and senior, you and everyone involved in your athletic career must follow certain guidelines. In this chapter, we fill you in.

Vying for the Sophomore

You become something of a prospect at the beginning of your *freshman* year. The wheels are in motion. But you're only likely to become a *real* prospect in the recruiting game as a *sophomore*.

What does this mean? If recruiters haven't identified you as a prospective college athlete by your sophomore (or early junior) year, there is a good chance that you may never be looked at closely without aggressive marketing by your family.

You're not alone if this comes as a huge surprise to you and your parents. All too often, we hear about parents and athletes who are considering the scholarships and recruiting game only at the end of the junior year. In most cases, if you wait 'til you're a junior, you're behind the game. Although you may only be finding your academic groove as a sophomore, this is a pivotal year for you as college-athlete-to-be.

Letters of promise: What they really mean

Receiving a letter in the mail that makes promises of academic and/or athletic advancement can be very exciting and confusing. But does acknowledging such a letter mean that you're committed to a particular school? Should you respond immediately to the first school that writes? More important, is it a letter or a questionnaire?

When you're a sophomore, the first two questions can be answered with a simple "No." Colleges are not allowed to contact you by mail before September 1 of your junior year except in the sport of Division I men's basketball (in which you can start to receive mail from colleges after June 15 of your sophomore year). Before that date, you shouldn't even have to deal with any letters of promise.

What you may receive as a sophomore is a questionnaire. This is the college's way of expressing interest in you — nothing more. The college is checking you out, and you're checking out the college. By filling out the questionnaire and promptly sending it back, you're letting the coaching staff know that you're interested in their program. After you return the questionnaire, the coaching staff will likely begin to follow your high school athletic achievements.

Although you don't have to fill out a questionnaire, we highly recommend that you do. You're in a pool with hundreds, perhaps thousands, of equally talented athletes. But for argument's sake, let's say that in the entire nation, there are only two other athletes equal to your own abilities. The other two athletes fill out their questionnaires and send them back in. Their response was courteous, prompt, and enthusiastic. But the college recruiter hasn't heard from you. Come decision time, who do you think will be dropped first?

One of the most violated rules in the NCAA just may be the letter sent by an overzealous recruiter to a prospect before his or her junior year of high school. Be warned: You could be subject to penalties under NCAA guidelines, and you definitely don't want to mess with the God of Collegiate Sports!

Even by receiving mail from recruiters before your eligibility status, you can unwittingly be violating NCAA guidelines. If you receive any mail or phone calls before your junior year, be sure to forward all communication to your coach, letting him or her explain your current status to the recruiter. By working closely with your coach, you'll also be able to clarify the difference between letters of recruitment and questionnaires (forms of standard questions about you and your sports involvement).

Table 7-1 provides the NCAA rules about who can contact you in your sophomore year. In the table, you'll notice a few terms you need to be familiar with:

- ✔ **Off-campus contact:** This is contact such as letters, phone calls, or in-home visits.

- ✔ **Official visit:** An NCAA-approved visit on campus that allows you to meet with the coaching staff and discuss your future with a specific college.

- ✔ **Unofficial visit:** A visit you make to any college on your own dime and time.

Enjoy the ride: Keep on pedaling

Something important happens to the high school sophomore who has two or more letters of interest or questionnaires from college recruiters. Although high school coaches and guidance counselors assure you that you need to stay focused on academics and continue to play strong and with confidence, you and your family often hear something else: "It's in the bag." "It's only a matter of time before we make you a firm offer." "Sit back and enjoy the ride."

High school is not the time to become a prima donna. Coaches have very little time or interest for that kind of attitude — even less for the high school student who has yet to prove his worth on the field. The enjoy-the-ride theory often lands an otherwise-strong high school athlete in the weeded-out pile.

Your sophomore and junior years are critical legs of the path to a college athletic experience for the high school athlete. Don't sit by as the chance for the real ride of a lifetime passes you by.

We've often heard that a high school coach is able to seal the deal with a specific college. In truth, most high school coaches are full-time teachers in charge of an entire team of 20 to 50 athletes. They, too, are overwhelmed — so relying upon your coach to manage your deal of a lifetime isn't smart. Your coach can write letters of recommendations and, in some cases, make a well-placed phone call to an old friend, but getting the wheels rolling is up to you.

Table 7-1   Sophomore-Year Recruiting Rules for Division I

Recruiting Method	Men's Basketball	Women's Basketball	Football	Other Sports
Recruiting material	You may start to receive on or after June 15.	You may receive brochures for camps as well as questionnaires.	You may receive brochures for camps as well questionnaires.	You may receive brochures for camps as well as questionnaires.
Telephone calls	*College coaches are allowed to:* Accept collect and toll-free calls from you at the end of your sophomore year. Call you one time per month after June 15 after your sophomore year.	*College coaches are allowed to:* Accept calls from you made at your own expense. ***Note:*** College coaches are not allowed to call you.	*College coaches are allowed to:* Accept calls from you made at your own expense. ***Note:*** College coaches are not allowed to call you.	*College coaches are allowed to:* Accept calls from you made at your own expense. ***Note:*** College coaches are not allowed to call you. ***Note:*** If you are an international prospect in the sport of ice hockey, college coaches are allowed to call you one time in July after your sophomore year.
Off-campus contact	None allowed.	None allowed.	None allowed.	None allowed.
Official visit	None allowed.	None allowed.	None allowed.	None allowed.
Unofficial visit	Allowed.	Allowed.	Allowed.	Allowed.

Tracking the Junior and Senior Rush

As a junior or senior, you understand the athletic level at which you're performing and just how many colleges are starting to take notice. The level of your athletic and academic achievement will be measured against Division I, II, and III standards. Although Division I is considered the most competitive in sports and scholarships availability, all kinds of exceptions or surprise bonuses can be found in the other divisions. (See Chapter 3 for more on the divisions.)

In the following sections, we help you navigate this exciting time.

The phone is ringing off the hook

Division I colleges are not allowed to send you formal correspondence (that is, a *letter of promise*) until September 1 of your junior year (except in the sport of men's basketball, in which colleges may contact you after June 15 of your sophomore year). Prior to that date, the only documents that colleges can send are questionnaires and NCAA educational materials, such as *Guide for the College-Bound Student-Athlete*.

After September 1 of your junior year, you may expect an all-out mail war. Letters, postcards, and media guides are mailed. More commonly, e-mails — based on your response to the questionnaire the schools may have sent you while you were a sophomore — are sent as a way to establish contact. We've heard stories of standout athletes receiving a letter a day from various schools expressing their interest. This practice is time consuming (and costly) to the school, and it can be overwhelming, as well as flattering, for the athlete.

Like letters, the general rule is that coaches (or athletic department staff members) are not permitted to call you until July 1 after your junior year, and such calls are limited to one per week. A few exceptions to the July 1 rule exist:

✔ **Football** prospects may be called one time in May during their junior year, but not again until September 1 of their senior year.

✔ **Women's basketball** prospects may be called one time in April and again one time in May of their junior year. They may be called one time between June 1 and June 20, and one time between June 21 and June 30. Three calls may be made during July, with no more than one call per week, and from August forward, calls are limited to once a week.

✔ **Men's basketball** prospects can be called once a month on or after June 15 of their sophomore year through July 31 after their junior year. Beginning August 1 after the junior year, two calls per week are permitted.

In all other Division I sports, one call is permitted in March of your junior year. For more sports-specific information, contact the NCAA and NAIA.

Table 7-2 spells out the rules for Division I junior-year recruiting; Table 7-3 gives the scoop for Division I senior-year recruiting; and Table 7-4 has the lowdown on Division II and Division III rules.

Table 7-2   Junior-Year Recruiting Rules for Division I

Recruiting Method	Men's Basketball	Women's Basketball	Football	Other Sports
Recruiting materials	Allowed.	You may begin receiving after September 1 of your junior year.	You may begin receiving after September 1 of your junior year.	You may begin receiving after September 1 of your junior year.
Telephone calls	*College coaches are allowed to:* Call you one time per month through July before your junior year. Call you two times per week beginning August 1 before your junior year. Accept collect and toll-free calls from you.	*College coaches are allowed to:* Call you one time during each of the months of April and May. Call you one time between June 1 and June 20 after your junior year. Call you one time between June 21 and June 30 after your junior year. Call you three times in July after your junior year, with no more than one call per week.	*College coaches are allowed to:* Call you one time during May of your junior year. Accept collect and toll-free calls from you.	*College coaches are allowed to:* Call you one time during March of your junior year. Call you one time per week starting July 1 after your junior year. Accept collect and toll-free calls from you.

Recruiting Method	Men's Basketball	Women's Basketball	Football	Other Sports
		Call you one time per week beginning August 1. Accept collect and toll-free calls from you.		
Off-campus contact	None allowed.	None allowed.	None allowed.	Allowed once during April only on your high school campus. Allowed starting July 1 after your junior year. This applies to all sports other than football and basketball. A current proposal would eliminate this contact during the junior year; if enacted, it will be effective in July 2006. Proposals for gymnastics and women's ice hockey would push back the first contact opportunity to the first day of classes of your senior year.
Official visit	None allowed.	None allowed.	None allowed.	None allowed.
Unofficial visit	Allowed.	Allowed.	Allowed.	Allowed.

Table 7-3	Senior-Year Recruiting Rules for Division I			
Recruiting Method	*Men's Basketball*	*Women's Basketball*	*Football*	*Other Sports*
Recruiting materials	Allowed.	Allowed.	Allowed.	Allowed.
Telephone calls	College coaches are allowed to call you twice per week.	College coaches are allowed to call you once per week.	College coaches are allowed to call you once per week beginning September 1 of your senior year.	College coaches are allowed to call you once per week.
Off-campus contact	Allowed starting July 1 after your junior year.	Allowed starting July 1 after your junior year.	Allowed starting July 1 after your junior year.	Allowed.
Official visit	Allowed beginning first day of classes of your senior year.	Allowed beginning first day of classes of your senior year.	Allowed beginning first day of classes of your senior year.	Allowed beginning first day of classes of your senior year.
	You may make only one official visit per college and only up to a maximum of five official visits to any colleges.	You may make only one official visit per college and only up to a maximum of five official visits to any colleges.	You may make only one official visit per college and only up to a maximum of five official visits to any colleges.	You may make only one official visit per college and only up to a maximum of five official visits to any colleges.
Unofficial visit	Allowed.	Allowed.	Allowed.	Allowed.

Recruiting Method	Men's Basketball	Women's Basketball	Football	Other Sports
Evaluations and contacts	A coach can see you or talk to you off the college's campus as many as seven times during your senior year, with no more than three times being in-person contacts.	A coach can see you or talk to you off the college's campus as many as five times during your senior year, with no more than three times being in-person contacts.	A coach can see you or talk to you off the college's campus as many as six times during the allowed contact period (thepermissible time when a recruiter may contact you). The contact period begins the Sunday after the last Saturday in November and ends the Saturday immediately before the initial signing date for the National Letter of Intent (NLI). If a coach only evaluates you during this contact period, it still counts as one of the permissible six contacts. Each Division I-A head coach is allowed to make only one in-person contact with you. A coach is allowed to make one evaluation of you during September, October, *or* November	A coach can see you or talk to you off the college's campus as many as seven times during your senior year, with no more than three being in-person contacts.

Table 7-4 Recruiting Rules for Division II and Division III

Recruiting Method	Division II	Division III
Recruiting materials	College coaches may begin sending you printed recruiting materials September 1 of your junior year in high school.	College coaches may begin sending you printed materials any time.
Telephone calls	College coaches may call you once per week beginning June 15 between your junior and senior years.	There is no limit on the number of times college coaches may call you or when the calls can be made.
Off-campus contact	College coaches may contact you or your family off the college's campus beginning June 15 after your junior year. Coaches are limited to three in-person contacts off campus.	College coaches may have contact with you or your family off the college's campus after your junior year.
Unofficial visit	You may make an unlimited number of unofficial visits any time.	You may make an unlimited number of unofficial visits any time.
Official visit	You may make official visits beginning the first day of classes of your senior year. You may make only one official visit per college and only up to a maximum of five official visits to any college.	You may make official visits beginning on the first day of classes of your senior year. You may make only one official visit per college.

The NCAA is an ever-changing, ever-evolving organization — which means rules can change. Always be sure to talk to your coaches and check online at www.ncaa.org to verify dates.

Before those designated dates, you can call a coach at any time at your expense. In fact, calling a coach can sometimes be beneficial. For example, when high school senior Elizabeth Flores learned that a fellow track athlete was being recruited by a local NAIA college (Northwood University), she picked up the phone and called the coach. Although her running times were not as strong as she wished, Flores had learned that head coach Shawn Winget was trying to build a women's cross-country team, which gave Flores a logical reason for her to call. Flores used that small window of time to establish contact, earned a scholarship, and went on to be an NAIA All-American.

On the designated dates, you can use toll-free numbers established by the university or college in question. Most schools, and in particular the athletic departments, provide toll-free numbers for prospective athletes.

The NCAA has a tough time monitoring whether calls are made within the designated dates, so many athletes make toll-free calls during their freshman, sophomore, and junior years. Just because this is a common practice doesn't make it okay — breaking the rules is dangerous. According the very strict NCAA Eligibility Guidelines, you could lose your eligibility and possible scholarship status if you're caught communicating with a college when you're not allowed to do so.

You can check the most up-to-date recruiting calendar for your sport at www1.ncaa.org/membership/membership_svcs/ recruiting_calendars/index.html. Note the times when you may speak to recruiters. Until then, let your on-court or on-field actions do the talking.

What the recruiter really wants

Beyond points scored, college scouts are looking at academic achievement, after-school and community-service activities, and player-to-coach and teammate relationships in order to see the whole package. With a scholarship on the line, coaches need to know that you'll stay in school, stay out of trouble, and remain a viable member of the team.

Recruiters also want to be able to have intelligent conversations with you, to understand what you want from a college and what ideas you have for your future. We've spoken to many recruiters whose chief complaint about young athletes is the "I dunno" followed by a shrug.

College recruiters are trying to understand who you are. They want to know that you'll fit with their program. Giving them concrete answers is *always* better than shrugging.

Before you speak to a recruiter, know what you want and who you are:

✔ Know your current stats as an athlete (what your strengths are on the field and what you offer to a team).

✔ Know your grades and class standing.

✔ Be able to communicate what you want academically from a college.

✔ Be prepared to talk about your future and what you want or expect.

✔ Be prepared to tell a recruiter what you expect from a college and how the college in question may have what you want or need.

In-home visits

When a coach comes to your home, you can generally assume that he or she wants you to sign. The coach may bring a media guide and a most recent highlight film for you to watch — this is the coach's turn to try to impress you.

Athletes are no longer allowed to sign in front of a coach, which means you won't be signing during a home visit. Even so, the coach may still push you for a verbal commitment.

In the 1994 documentary *Hoop Dreams,* featuring basketball players William Gates and Arthur Agee, a college recruiter shows audiences just how intense recruiting can be. Cameras follow two high school boys in the Chicago area for five years as the boys try to realize their hoop dreams while struggling with school, their personal lives, and making the NBA. In one poignant scene, a recruiter tells William Gates that if he doesn't sign with the recruiter at that moment, he'll be dropped. The recruiter effectively tells Gates that he (the recruiter) has another athlete who is interested and will sign. Even though the recruiter has named Gates as his first choice, he'll drop him and pick up another player who wants it more. Gates ends up signing.

The purpose of the in-home visit — from *your* perspective — is to get to know the coach and get that personal one-on-one meeting in which you can ask direct questions about student-athlete responsibilities, what the coach expects from you, the athletic department's goals for its students, and more. This is your time to interview the coach.

A verbal commitment is just that — verbal. It is not a legally binding contract. Sadly, this reality has worked against many student-athletes who believed they had a binding contract with a college based on a verbal agreement, only to discover that there was no scholarship offer down the road.

Although the verbal agreement is not binding, many coaches still push for one. We recommend that you and your family make it clear from the beginning of the meeting that you'll need time to discuss any offer as a family — after the coach has gone. This very reasonable demand offers you and your family time to think, review your notes, and discuss your options without making any hasty decisions.

Understanding the Misunderstandings

You know the saying "Knowledge is power." When you understand the rules, you're empowered to move forward and make the right decisions for your future. Take the time to memorize the dates for recruiting (see the tables earlier in this chapter). Revisit the official NCAA and NAIA Web sites, and refresh your memory on rules and regulations. And know what your recruiter wants of you.

Understanding that there will always be misunderstandings is half the battle. As Grant Teaff, executive director of the American Football Coaches Association, once said, "One man's fact is another man's negative recruiting." Each person has his own perspective of the recruiting process, which is all the more reason to arm yourself with knowledge.

Negative recruiting

The athletic associations have strict rules about how and when coaches can recruit (refer to Tables 7-1 through 7-4), and those rules include a code of conduct that recruiters are expected to uphold. Yet, every year, there are stories of improper behavior. Money and pride are on the line. Jobs are at stake. And the thrill of landing the supreme athlete drives some recruiters to the edge, which can be a very gray area.

Recruiters have been known to discuss the downside of another college, citing its poor geographic location, weak academic ranking, party reputation, or lesser coaching staff in order to sway athletes. You may find yourself sitting across the table from a recruiter who delights in telling you all that is wrong with another college you may be considering. What do you do? Nothing. Don't smile. Don't laugh. Don't ask the recruiter to explain why he thinks the other college is bad or failing or otherwise inadequate. Simply do not respond.

After the recruiter has left, you may want to research some of the statements the recruiter made regarding that other college. But do not engage in any anticollege conversation with another recruiter.

The collegiate world is vast, but the recruiting circles are small. As inconceivable as it may seem, your name could easily be dragged into a he-said/she-said situation, in which one recruiter tells another recruiter that you weren't such a fan of the other recruiter's school. If that happens, you've just tarnished your reputation and limited your opportunities.

This negative wordplay is only one pitfall in the recruiting process. High school athletes and their families can be bullied into a commitment while sitting in the presence of a coach, believing that this is the best and only offer. This situation is particularly tricky when the athlete is alone and likely to be unwilling to fire back questions at this adult — the expert. All the more reason for you to be informed.

Simply put, when you're informed, your chances of making a sound decision without being bullied or intimidated are far greater.

Who to talk to

Every year, because of a misunderstanding, extraordinary athletes are not recruited. In most cases, the fault lies with the student-athlete, who simply didn't understand the recruiting system. Whether the athlete missed a deadline, didn't take a required academic course, or spoke to the wrong person, the bottom line is simple: He missed out.

Your most valuable weapon is research. In addition to what we share with you in this book, you may gather additional info from guidance counselors, high school coaches, fellow athletes, and recruiting agencies. Your counselor or former teammates may tell you about mistakes they've seen (or made themselves), steering you away from similar mistakes. If they've been in the recruiting business or have gone through the system, they can dispel rumors or misconceptions you've heard about recruiting — for example, no, it's not okay to take a phone call from a recruiter (even in secret) when you are a freshman; no, you shouldn't throw away questionnaires. Beyond that, the guidance counselor or former athlete can offer you tried-and-true tips, such as their own personal note-taking or color-coding system that will help you make final decisions.

Approach this process much like a businessperson would. Before beginning any business, you would review the market, see if there is a need for your product — in this case, you're the "product" — and talk to other business owners who are or were in a similar business. You'd want to know how they did, what problems they ran into, and what advice they're willing to offer. Being recruited is no different.

Ensuring the Best Results

You're standing in the locker room after the game of your life in your senior year when a college recruiter seeks you out, thrusts a card at you, and proclaims that you're the superstar he's been searching for. It could happen. But just because there is no face-to-face meeting in a locker room doesn't mean you won't get a scholarship.

You are your own best cheerleader and supporter. Through your own work and determination, you can make recruiters stand up and take notice.

Toeing the line

A father of a top-ranked national track athlete walked into his living room to hear his son talking on the phone. He listened for a moment as his son, just a freshman, appeared to answer questions about his grades, his latest track record, and his future. It was then that the father stepped forward. Who was his son speaking with?

An overzealous recruiter, eager to get his hands on one of the hottest young track athletes in the nation, had called the prospect. When the student-athlete just set another national record, the recruiter didn't stop to look at the athlete's age. Because his success had been so overwhelming, and because so many recruiters had expressed interest in his achievements, the student-athlete didn't think to say he was only a freshman.

When the freshman said, "Well, when I'm a junior . . ." the recruiter instantly stopped the call, saying, "Oh, I have to turn myself in for recruitment violation!"

As eager is everyone is to get you that college scholarship and have you compete at the collegiate level, toeing the line is up to you. You can and should speak with guidance counselors, teachers, high school coaches, and fellow athletes, but you need to understand the rules, time restrictions, number of visits and phone calls, and dates allowed for the contact you have with recruiters and coaches. Both you and the college recruiter can get into trouble if one or both of you break recruiting rules.

So what about the story of the overzealous recruiter who called a freshman? In this example, neither was aware of the mistake in the beginning. The recruiter hadn't properly read the material in front of him. If he had, he would have noted that the athlete was only a freshman. Likewise, the freshman was completely unfamiliar with NCAA guidelines on speaking with recruiters. In this case, the recruiter reported himself to the NCAA and received a warning. His mistake was unintentional. No harm, no foul. But this situation could easily have turned into a recruiting violation in which both athlete and recruiter were penalized.

This business has one clear motto: Survival of the fittest . . . or the most informed.

The role parents can play

Just as you're expected to know dates and restrictions when it comes to recruiting, you need your parents or legal guardians to be involved in the recruiting process. Your parents are in your corner — they're invested in your health, your education, your dreams, and your future. College and recruiting are big business. Coaches are most interested in how you can help the *team,* and they may overlook what's best for you. Your family is vested in what is best for *you.*

Talk to your parents about creating a filing system for your college questionnaires, letters, and cards. Together, you can review the history, academic records, graduation rates, geographic locations, coaching staffs, and general impressions you have of each college you're interested in.

As you begin to wade through all the letters and questionnaires, talking with your family about all this will certainly help you make more-sound decisions. But you may also want to delegate important roles to your parents or guardians. By having someone else in your corner, you can feel more at ease about all the new rules and about the strangers contacting you.

During the school year or at summer sports camps, you may be approached by an agent who is interested in representing you in commercial endorsements or who promises to get you into a big-name school. As tempting as the agent's offer may sound, leave this conversation for your parents. NCAA rules don't prohibit you from talking to such a person, but you could easily lose eligibility status if you enter into any kind of written or verbal commitment with an agent. (For more information about recruiting and agent services, see Chapter 8.)

Here's a list of other things your parents can help you with:

✔ Your parents can create index cards or a checklist with important phone numbers and names of various coaches. When the rules allow it, you can use this information to contact various coaches or colleges.

✔ Your parents can organize a travel plan for the unofficial and official visits you make.

✔ Your parents can create a checklist of all the questionnaires you've filled out and mailed back, including a ranking system of which schools are most important to you and why.

✔ Your parents may also search the Internet for information on colleges you're interested in but that have not yet contacted you. *Remember:* Just because they haven't sent you a letter of interest doesn't mean *you* can't contact *them*.

What Recruiters Wish You Understood

We've talked to parents, athletes, and coaches from all different sports and divisions, asking what some of the most common misunderstandings are between recruiters and athletes.

Recruiters wish that both parents and athletes were more informed about the recruiting process. They also wish that parents understood that just because an athlete receives a number of letters from schools, that doesn't mean the athlete is being recruited. As one recruiter put it, "Parents will say, 'My kid is being recruited by 18 different schools.' No, you've got letters of interest, but you're not being recruited." This distinction is an important one.

The act of being recruited can come only when you're eligible both academically and within the time frame for your sport (see Tables 7-1 through 7-4).

Letters of interest are simply feelers that colleges put out to see which students might be interested in their college programs. The letters of interest are simply the first play in a very long game.

Recruiters want athletes to take the process of recruiting into their own hands. When you know the system, when you know what's at stake, and when you understand the rules and regulations, you'll be far more appealing to recruiters. You'll also make fewer mistakes. Know what you're getting into, and there should be no surprises.

Chapter 8

What to Do If You Don't Get Noticed

- -

In This Chapter

▶ Knowing how you can play without a scholarship

▶ Understanding the benefits of being a walk-on athlete

▶ Talking about possible scholarships

▶ Researching and using recruiting services

- -

*N*ot every successful high school athlete simply transitions from local phenom to Division I greatness. Instead, you can find plenty of examples of high school athletes with talents unrecognized by recruiters who nonetheless persevered to make a college team and then gained scholarships. There are also high school athletes who seemed slated for greatness yet never really rose to the recruiter's expectations. Some had dreams of Division I glory but actually played Division III, while others specifically went for a Division III school after declining offers from Division I.

What makes these athletes successful is how they played when they got to college. In college, coaches don't care how the athlete got to the team; they just want to know what he or she will do with the opportunity. If it turns out that a talented athlete is willing to work hard, there will be a place on the roster. And that place could be yours.

Playing without an Athletic Scholarship

So, do you want to hear your chances of getting the full-ride scholarship? They're not good. According to the NCAA, high school boys' basketball has approximately 500,000 players; 157,000 are seniors. There are close to 4,500 available freshman positions open in college ball, leaving an opportunity for just 3 percent of high school senior basketball players to pick up an NCAA scholarship. If you're a swimmer, track-and-field athlete, tennis player, or gymnast (just to name a few possibilities), your chances of getting that all-gloried full ride are even *more* difficult.

None of this, of course, is meant to discourage you. Quite the opposite. We believe that when you know what you're up against, you'll work that much harder, fight that much longer, and research that much more to make your dreams come true.

The reality is this: Even the very best of players can be passed over or overlooked. If this happens to you, it doesn't mean you can't play without a scholarship. Perhaps the most important question you need to ask yourself is: How much do I want to play?

Surprisingly, some athletes have walked away from an opportunity to play because it wasn't under the bright lights of a Division I school. We would argue that they didn't really want to play the sport — they wanted to play at a Division I school.

There are two kinds of prospects: players and athletes. The lion-hearted athlete will play on with or without a scholarship. And he will be rewarded tenfold.

In the following sections, we let you know the realities of playing without a scholarship.

Understanding the benefits

NCAA Division III and the NJCAA Division III schools are excellent avenues to play sports at the college level while earning a college education. Beyond the educational experience (which we hope is a top priority for you), these divisions can provide you with great exposure to other coaches.

College coaches are always looking for an athlete who can fit well within their roster but also help the program succeed. One successful season with a Division III school may allow you to transfer (with or without a scholarship offer) to a larger school, if this is your goal. By using your natural talents and by showing grit, determination, enthusiasm, and a willingness to take one for the team, you may garner more attention from other coaches within a Division III school than you did at the high school level.

In addition, many student-athletes commit to a larger school, paying their own expenses and testing their own abilities for the sake of having the full student-athlete experience. Many of these dedicated athletes simply wanted to take their competition to the next level. They're fulfilling a dream while earning a degree. If you go this route, you'll have first choice of classes, preferred housing, the experience of traveling and training with the team, and more.

At the University of Washington, for example, a high percentage of the athletes are competing without a scholarship because of the school's high academic standing. In 1999, four of the state's strongest runners were walk-ons at UW, two of the athletes running a mile under 4:20. As many as 30 of the team's football players were also walk-ons. For these athletes, the benefits began to come as soon as they donned their first Huskies uniform. Hearing the cheers from the crowd, having the opportunity to travel, and continuing to play made all the other sacrifices well worth their time.

Taking that first step

Perhaps the first step in playing without a scholarship is accepting the idea that playing as a nonscholarship athlete is an honor and does have many benefits. Sports history is filled with Olympic, professional, and world-record-setting athletes who began their affluent careers as nonscholarship athletes.

There are even more stories of athletes who, for one reason or another, gave up a scholarship to play at a different college without a scholarship. Take, for example, Dylan Leal. The basketball standout was offered an athletic scholarship to a number of schools, such as Holy Cross and Lehigh College. But Leal wanted to stay close to his two brothers in Texas and, as a result, chose to play at Texas A&M without a scholarship. Coaches said his dedication and determination to play were so great that he played as a freshman, and in his senior year, his own teammates named him captain of the team. Because Leal lived, trained, ate, and played with the team, most of the team members were unaware of the fact that he hadn't been offered an athletic scholarship, dispelling the myth that the nonscholarship athlete is ostracized or made to feel like an outsider.

Deciding where

As the story of Dylan Leal illustrates, knowing where you want to be is important. Maybe you've decided you don't have to wait for the offer of an athletic scholarship, or you recognize you may not be offered one at all. Believe it or not, this could be good news: You now have the freedom to decide where you really want to go to school.

Whether you want to be close to family, remain in a small-town setting, or go big — attending large schools and taking in the big-campus lifestyle — you have a great number of schools to choose among. Wherever the geographic location, research the school to be sure it offers your sport and to find out how receptive the school is to nonscholarship and walk-on athletes.

Survivor: Getting noticed

The motto of the reality-based television show *Survivor* is "Outwit, Outlast, Outplay." Many recruiters have their own motto: "Outwork, Outmaneuver, Outrecruit." Many recruiters love the entire process of finding talent, tracking them down, and wooing them. They love the rush of beating deadlines and beating out other schools.

Other recruiters hate it. They dread the entire process, understanding all the while that it must be done for the good of the program. But for this reason, they're often less agreeable, less accessible, and less interested in taking on any more talent than they have to. So, when a walk-on hopeful comes along, these coaches groan audibly. It isn't personal, but you — the walk-on — are representative of more time, more paperwork, and just one more person to talk to.

You can save yourself a lot of time and heartache by researching a particular program and coach. Call ahead of time, letting the head coach know you're interested in walking on. If the coach is receptive and wants to learn more about you, you may earn an informal invitation to practice with the team. This walk-on status allows you and other nonscholarship athletes to participate in a two-day practice with the team prior to the new school year.

You can't just appear at a scheduled practice with the hope of playing. You have to tell the coaching staff who you are and what your intentions are before you ever set foot on their field, court, or track.

The NCAA rules state that only 105 players may be invited to preseason football practices prior to the start of classes. As many as 85 of those players are athletes with a scholarship, leaving just 20 positions available. The 20 remaining positions may include the nonscholarship athletes who are already on the roster, which makes for very few positions available for incoming freshman.

Understanding the expectations

When you believe you have the opportunity to show your stuff, you must understand that this opportunity — and indeed, it *is* an opportunity — is not free. As a walk-on, you pay your own way. The positions available may be greatly limited, and the competition will be fierce.

Walking on, walking tall

Even during the walk-on stage, your past can be a big part of the process. Your attitude and work ethic as a high school athlete, your grades, your relationship with coaches and teammates, and your performance in sports camps can give you a leg up on the competition.

Former soccer player Jonathan Funston had hopes of attending NCAA Division I institution Purdue University as a football kicker. He had been offered a scholarship at a smaller school but really wanted to play at Purdue. Purdue, however, had already signed a kicker, Jonathan Phillips. But when Phillips changed his mind, Funston's past came back to help him.

Phillips decided to go with his home state and kick for the Florida Gators, leaving an opening on the Purdue roster.

Funston had attended an elite kicking camp in Miami, Florida, ranking third among many kickers who had already signed with various schools. Because of his performance at this camp, his constant contact with the Purdue coaching staff, and the partial academic scholarship he had been offered by Purdue, Funston was a natural fit for the Purdue Boilermakers.

As a member of the team, scholarship or nonscholarship, you need to adhere to the rules and guidelines of the NCAA, NJCAA, or NAIA. Behave and perform as a college athlete.

Walking On

One of the most beloved sports movies of all time is *Rudy*, the story of the kid with heart who wanted to play at Notre Dame. Rudy Ruettiger wasn't particularly athletic and didn't have a great academic record or a big, strong, athletic build. In fact, he was half the size of the other players. But he had drive and determination. He was willing to — and did — work harder than anyone on the field. The story of Rudy is so popular because it is representative of the notion that if you want something badly enough and are willing to work for it, dreams can come true — no matter the odds.

Not every walk-on story is like the story of Rudy Ruettiger. In fact, some colleges make the walk-on experience downright easy. Take, for example, Stanford University, which actually ran an article in the college paper recruiting possible athletes for the school's rowing teams: "We are looking for individuals who enjoy being athletes and who want to commit to being part of a Division I team. . . . No prior rowing experience is required."

In the following sections, we let you know what you may expect as a walk-on. Some athletes have reported being more nervous trying out as a walk-on than having to stand up for an oral presentation in class. Don't worry — you don't have to go through that kind of stress. If you have your affairs in order, shoelaces tied, and game face on, the walk-on process should be a walk in the park — or your game-winning point.

In the following sections, we show you what you need to do in terms of paperwork and medical information, and how to move forward as a walk-on athlete.

Prep work

You've contacted the coaching staff, and now you're ready to practice with the team. Not so fast. Before you lace up, you need to take care of a few things:

- **Medical-history documentation:** The athletic department will provide a form for you to fill out.

- **Physical examination:** This is pretty straightforward; you just have to have a physical. You may want to ask in advance how to get your physical; some colleges require their own team doctor to give the physical, while other schools expect you to already have your physical in hand.

- **Complete blood work:** The lab report must be included with the physical paperwork, or you may not be allowed to work out with the team.

- **Electrocardiogram (EKG):** The EKG report must be included with the physical paperwork, or you may not be allowed to work out with the team.

- **Record of shots:** This should include a tetanus shot and a thorough record of all your childhood vaccinations.

- **Drug testing:** Be prepared to give a blood and/or urine sample.

- **Previous surgeries/injuries:** Any recent injury or surgery procedure that may interfere with the rigors of training with the team must be documented and attached with all physical paperwork.

- **Insurance:** All nonscholarship and walk-on athletes must have proof of insurance. You won't be allowed to participate on the field or court or in the gym without current medical insurance. Nonscholarship and noninvited walk-ons should expect to pay for all physical and medical exams (your insurance may cover this).

The tryout

Most schools have a slated period of time to watch and evaluate walk-on athletes. After a period of time — dependent upon the individual coaching staffs — they will let you know whom they choose to keep on as walk-ons.

Tryouts are your time to shine. During this time, you'll be required to practice with the team, execute plays, and show the coaching staff that you can work with the team and remember specific drills.

You aren't an official member of the team — yet. For the most part, you'll be used as a practice player. In football, for example, Texas Tech may be scheduled to play Missouri State. In the weeks prior to that game, coaches use the walk-ons to act as the Missouri offense, allowing the starting defense to run plays.

The coaches may take notice of your ability to retain information, learn plays, and be a viable member of the team. And you may be allowed to join officially.

Make each practice your best. Don't expect anything.

The promise: Talk of a future scholarship

Andy Carroll walked on at the University of Washington and proved himself to be a vital member of the team, playing as a running back, wide receiver, and member of special teams. According to Carroll, he was told that he was being considered for a scholarship. Through a series of rules changes, however, schools are now limited to 85 scholarships for 1-A football. Prior to 1977, there were no limitations on the number of football scholarships a Division 1-A school could offer, but with the new rules, Carroll had no chance. On May 19, 2004, Carroll filed a class-action lawsuit against the NCAA in U.S. District Court in Seattle, contending that major football teams violate antitrust laws by refusing to give athletic scholarships to all walk-on players. Although walk-ons are compensated for at least their tuition costs, Carroll maintained that he had been promised more and certainly earned more.

Walk-ons do not receive any form of scholarship, so to say they are compensated for their tuition is not accurate. They do receive equipment, apparel, and travel expenses for away games, but that is usually it.

This is but just one story of promises made of scholarships that never came to fruition. Whether a coach knows if a scholarship is actually available is hard to know, but student-athletes and their families are left feeing frustrated and used.

A scholarship is not a scholarship until you and your coach have signed a financial-aid agreement. We don't care how hearty the handshake, how great the promise, how fabulous your performance on the field — it is *not* official until it's a signed agreement. Until that time, have fun and continue to play for the very reason you walked on in the first place: to fulfill a dream. But do not bank on a scholarship and everything it has to offer until the actual agreement has been presented and signed.

Using the Recruiting Service

In the literary world, a writer should never have to pay for agent representation. In the modeling world, would-be models have to pay only for their head shots, not the agent representation. And in the sports world, a good recruiting service shouldn't have a price tag attached to it.

The entire process of college recruiting and collegiate sports is a business. And businesses require and generate money. So, although we *hope* you don't have to spend money in the recruiting process, you may decide that having someone else take care of the smaller, more-tedious expenses — such as postage, envelopes, faxes, and business cards — is worth your money.

In the following sections, we let you know why a recruiting service may be right for you, what services they offer, and how to choose the best one.

What a recruiting service can do for you

One of the biggest problems in facing recruiting deadlines lies with the high school coach. Although they're well intentioned, many high school coaches are simply too busy to help individual athletes through the recruiting process. That's where recruiting services come in. A good recruiting service can

- ✔ Help you write an athletic résumé
- ✔ Help you write an academic résumé

✔ Explain the recruiting timeline, including what to do when you're a freshman, sophomore, junior, and senior in high school

✔ Show you sample profiles, allowing you to see what college coaches are looking for

✔ Give you links to college Web sites

✔ Give you links to government agencies, including information on financial aid, scholarships for minorities, and Title IX

✔ Give you links to the NCAA, NJCAA, and NAIA

✔ Provide you with updates on rules of eligibility and recruiting rules

✔ Provide important information on SAT and ACT testing

✔ Share success stories about other student-athletes as they are recruited and signed by Division I, II, and III schools

✔ Offer help to parents, providing inside information from parents and student-athletes who have been there before.

This is a great time to ask yourself how busy you really are. Many families budget time — an hour a day — to send out faxes and bio sheets and to collect names and addresses so that they can do their own recruiting. But if your family's time is too limited, a recruiting service may offer the perfect solution.

Before signing on the dotted line, find out what you're paying for. Find out about what each recruiting service offers. For example, you should not pay $1,000 for a service of sending out faxes.

Beware of the guarantee

If a recruiting service guarantees a scholarship, walk away. Not even college recruiters can always promise — much less guarantee — a scholarship. Securing a scholarship involves all kinds of variables. Don't trust any agency that promises to land you a scholarship for a dollar fee.

Some services charge up to $3,000 for their guidance in the murky world of scholarships and college recruiting. And you figure if they're asking that much, they must be good, right? Wrong.

Being on a mailing list or becoming a client of a recruiting service only means that your name is being looked at (or sent out). Until a college coach actively calls you or comes to visit you, you are *not* being recruited.

Researching their records

If you're thinking about signing up with a particular recruiting agency, be sure to ask for the names and contact information of previous clients. Then be sure to follow through and ask those clients what their experience with the recruiting service was like.

How will you know how good the service is if you don't speak to those who have used it before you?

Here's a list of questions to ask former clients:

- ✓ **What did the service do for you that you couldn't have done yourself?**

- ✓ **Was the service personable?** Many student-athletes feel like they're simply a number and nothing more. If you're paying for a service, you need to know that someone will talk to you directly, answer your questions, and make you feel like you're an important client.

- ✓ **How much money did you spend?** Shopping around and comparing services is always a good idea.

- ✓ **Was it money well spent?**

- ✓ **Did the recruiting service follow through with what it promised?**

- ✓ **What was your best experience with the recruiting service?**

- ✓ **What was your worst experience?**

- ✓ **Did you end up doing some of the work yourself?** Many overeager parents and student-athletes sign on with a recruiting service, only to do much or most of the recruiting themselves. People usually don't realize how many contacts they actually had through club or select sports, coaches, or names they found through their own research. In the end, some families say they could have — and should have — done their own recruiting.

Many recruiting agencies simply offer to place your name and personal profile on their Web site, which they market to college recruiters around the nation. They can and will show you documentation of who they send profiles to, and they post letters of recommendations from happy clients. But the reality is, most college coaches do not browse the Internet looking for talent — they don't have the time.

What do college recruiters say about recruiting services?

Bigger-name schools with bigger budgets typically don't use recruiting services. Simply put, they don't need to. But smaller schools with smaller budgets may turn to recruiting services as a matter of convenience. They want to offer scholarships to gifted athletes but simply don't have the resources to visit high schools and actively recruit. For these schools, recruiting services offer a nice alternative to traveling to find talent.

Don't use a recruiting service that only puts your name and profile on *its* letterhead when writing to a coach. Your letters, information packets, and profile should always look as though they came from you. As impersonal as the entire process seems, coaches want to feel as though you're intimately interested in their program.

What questions to ask

As you begin to meet more college recruiters, take the time to ask them their thoughts on individual recruiting services. Not surprisingly, each recruiter will have his own opinion about recruiting services, but with carefully placed questions, you can find out how recruiting services may (or may not) help you.

Be sure to ask recruiters:

- ✔ **What is the most helpful information you get from recruiting services?**
- ✔ **How often do you look at the Web site of a recruiting service or look at the information it sends you?**
- ✔ **How important is a recruiting service in helping you find an athlete you're looking for?**
- ✔ **What are the five most important services a recruiting service offers a student-athlete?**
- ✔ **What are the five most important services a recruiting service can offer a college recruiter?**
- ✔ **What is the single greatest asset a recruiting service offers?**
- ✔ **What are the least important services offered?**
- ✔ **Do you pay more or less attention to an athlete who is represented by a recruiting service?** Does it matter whether the student-athlete has representation?

The biggest mistake athletes make

Lay it on a little thick. Sweeten the pot. It's just to get in the front door, right?

Making yourself sound better on paper than you are in person is not a practice we recommend and certainly not something a reputable recruiting service will condone.

A reputable recruiting service is not going to put its reputation on the line by exaggerating your abilities and successes. A good recruiting service relies on having and keeping solid relationships with schools and coaches. Credible recruiting services must operate on that basis alone: credibility.

No matter how tempted you are to pad your athletic résumé, don't do it.

Show them the money!

After you've decided to go with a recruiting service, you may expect someone to call you or your family to set up an appointment to talk about the service. By now, you should have searched the Web, talked to previous clients, and determined that you need the help of a recruiting service because you don't have the time.

The recruiter will sit down and explain how the recruiting service works and what it expects from you. Typically, 50 percent of people sign during that first appointment. But we recommend taking a few more days to discuss the fees of the recruiting service, reevaluate your schedule, and fully understand what the recruiting service is offering before signing.

What not to do

Recruiting services are gaining popularity as people's lives become more and more complicated, but there are a few potential pitfalls you need to be aware of:

- ✔ **Don't offer something in exchange for the services of a recruiting service.** For example, don't agree to promote the service or to arrange meetings between recruiters and coaches in exchange for a recruiting service. The arrangement should be purely business. You are being offered a service, and you pay for it.

- ✔ **Don't agree to give part of your scholarship money as a way to pay the recruiting-service fee.** This activity is illegal and could get you in big trouble. If you can't afford the service, this may indicate that you need to do the work yourself. Any service that asks to take a portion of your scholarship must be reported to the NCAA, NJCAA, and NAIA.

✔ **Don't believe endorsements from college coaches.** Because recruiting services rely upon the good word of happy clients to appeal to potential new customers, they often try to have college coaches put in a good word as well. Some recruiting services may have quotes by college coaches endorsing their particular service. *Beware:* The NCAA does not allow coaches to endorse such services. Be wary of recruiting services that boast personal endorsements by coaches.

Chapter 9

Recognizing College Recruiting Violations

. . . .

In This Chapter

▶ Understanding infractions

▶ Knowing how an infraction may affect your eligibility

▶ Determining the role of coaches and infractions

▶ Defining the boosters: Who they are and what they do

. . . .

*W*hen we're talking infractions, we're not talking about the newest mathematics. No, this chapter is about athletics infractions — everything you know need to know about recruiting violations and how to stay out of trouble.

Throughout the history of the NCAA, NJCAA, and NAIA, there have been many heartbreaking stories of student-athletes who unwittingly violated a rule that led to severe penalties and career-ending consequences. Here, the expression "Knowledge is power" certainly applies. This chapter gives you the knowledge — and power — you need to stay out of trouble.

Defining Infractions

An *infraction,* in basic terms, is a violation of a rule or rules. The problem from the student-athlete's perspective is that there are many rules associated with recruiting for college sports. Any mistake in this area *could* become an infraction. In some cases, the line is obvious — but in others, it may be pretty subtle.

Everyone knows that if you break a rule, you'll likely have to face some penalty. In the context of a recruiting infraction, the penalty may be probation.

The word *probation* strikes fear in the heart of every college administrator, coach, student-athlete, alumnus, booster, and fan of collegiate sports. A university or college that is placed on probation can lose thousands (sometimes millions) of dollars, and it gains a stigma that may last much longer than a financial penalty.

Since January 2005, probation has been applied against NCAA Division I institutions in response to 57 infractions. This does not mean 57 different schools — some schools are on the list more than once. Looking at the issue more broadly, since January 1990, 164 separate Division I schools have been placed on probation! The reasons for these probations range from recruiting violations by a coach to boosters providing currently enrolled student-athletes extra benefits.

One of the most publicized recent cases occurred at the University of Alabama. A booster allegedly paid approximately $150,000 to a high school athlete to induce him to sign to play football at the university. Moreover, the student-athlete's high school coach was also involved in the scandal, and he received about $90,000 of the inducement, leaving the athlete's family $60,000. The booster was eventually sentenced to six months in jail for his involvement. The high school coach pleaded guilty and testified against the booster to avoid jail time. Not surprisingly, the high school coach claimed that at least seven other Division I programs offered him cash and/or jobs to attempt to get him to persuade the prospect to sign with their schools.

In this case, the student-athlete was aware of some dirty dealings. But there have been instances when the student-athlete and his family took the word of a coach, believing everything to be legal. If the coach okayed it, that was good enough.

The questions you should ask yourself are: Could this happen to me? How can I find out if a school has had recruiting violations in the past? In the following sections, we give you the answers you need.

Major versus secondary infractions

Truthfully, making a mistake is easy. The 2005–2006 *NCAA Division I Manual* is 494 pages long. With that many rules and regulations, violations are bound to occur. Coaches, administrators, student-athletes, and boosters are all human, and some will make mistakes.

As a case in point, until 1995, it was technically against NCAA rules for a student-athlete to receive a ride back to his dorm or apartment from a coach after practice, even if it was 15 degrees and snowing! How many times do you think that rule was inadvertently (and most times justifiably) broken? Clearly, a violation like that is a heck of a lot less egregious than the $150,000 University of Alabama case we describe earlier. Yet minor and even egregious violations occur on a regular basis, and student-athletes and their coaches may pay.

Fortunately, there is recognition at the NCAA that not all infractions are alike. The main difference between a *secondary infraction* and a *major infraction* is one of intent. According to the NCAA Web site, "A secondary infraction is one that is isolated or inadvertent in nature, provides or is intended to provide only a minimal recruiting advantage, and does not include any significant recruiting inducement or extra benefit." In reality, while the major infractions grab all the headlines, the NCAA processes far more secondary violations. For example, during the five-and-a-half-year span discussed earlier, 8,220 secondary violations have been reported to the NCAA by Division I institutions. Although there are three leading categories of secondary violations, the biggest problem is in the area of recruiting.

Most secondary cases are self-reported (either by the institution or through a conference office). Secondary infractions generally result in minor penalties, and sometimes no penalty is assessed at all.

Anything that is not deemed a secondary violation is considered a major infraction, and these infractions are the ones that bring severe penalties for the college in question.

The "mother of all infractions" for any school is to be penalized for "lack of institutional control." The concept of institutional control is so important that the NCAA has created a document to define major infractions further for the college sport directors and administrative staff. If you're interested, you can find a summary of it by going to `www.ncaa.org/databases/regional_seminars/guide_rules_compliance/other_topics/oth_01.html`.

The most common infractions

Since January 2000, there have been 3,894 secondary violations in Division I that pertain to recruiting. That number is almost triple the number of violations reported regarding eligibility and extra benefits (the other two of the big three). In addition, 41 major infraction cases during that time period have been recruiting-related.

You may wonder, "Why there are so many more recruiting violations, and what are some examples?" Here are a few reasons:

✔ **The recruiting rules are very complex, and there are many of them.** The recruiting section of the *Division I Manual* is 47 pages long, and there are hundreds, maybe thousands, of interpretations regarding these rules.

✔ **The rules are constantly changing.** The membership has the ability to amend its rules annually (and sometimes even more often than that!). Imagine how frustrating it would be to play a sport in which the rules changed each year.

✔ **Coaches are competitive by nature and will push the envelope as much as they can to gain a recruiting advantage over other schools.** This is the main reason why there are so many recruiting violations.

Many of the recruiting violations are inadvertent and can be as simple as the head coach's calling a prospect on Monday and an assistant coach's calling on Wednesday without realizing that the head coach had used the one call per week.

Another common recruiting violation occurs when prospects make unofficial visits to campuses during designated dead periods and coaches meet with them. These visits are considered to be contact during a period when contact isn't permissible (even on the school's campus).

A *dead period* is a period of time when it isn't permissible for coaches to make recruiting contacts or evaluations on or off the college campus. Coaches can write and call prospects during this time, but any face-to-face contact is against the rules.

Paying the penalties

The Mustangs of Southern Methodist University were on the rise in the world of college football in the early 1980s. In 1980, the school received its first-ever ranking at #20. The next season, the Mustangs went 10-1 and won their first conference title since 1965. It only got better for the Mustangs when they finished #2 in the final polls in 1982. By all accounts, SMU was becoming a force in the world of football.

It all came crashing down when, in 1987, the NCAA handed down the first and only "death penalty" sanction to any sports program, forcing SMU to cancel the entire season and limiting it to a seven-game season in 1988. Only in 1989 was the school allowed to resume a full competitive season.

The reasons for these severe penalties are many, but here are a few of the highlights:

 ✔ Twenty-one football players allegedly received roughly $61,000 in cash payments.

 ✔ Boosters and members of the athletic department were involved in the payments.

 ✔ Payments ranged from $50 to $725 per month.

Because of these violations, the NCAA made an example of SMU, not only restricting their 1987 and 1988 competitive seasons but also placing a two-year ban on any bowl games. The NCAA also restricted the number of coaches the team was allowed to have (three fewer coaches than other schools were permitted). Finally, the college lost 55 scholarships over a four-year period.

How has all this impacted the football program with the Mustangs? Since the death penalty, the football team has posted one winning season, when it went 6-5 in 1997. In fact, the victory bell has rung a total of only ten times in the last four years.

The long-term impact of this ruling has forced the NCAA to do everything in its power not to hand down the death penalty again. Giving the SMU football program the death penalty has been compared to the United States dropping the atom bomb in World War II. The results and aftermath were so catastrophic that the committee on infractions will do everything in its power to avoid handing down the death penalty to another program.

In your everyday, run-of-the-mill violations, the penalties are not nearly so severe and are contingent on what the infraction was. For example, if a school exceeds the number of permissible games it is allowed to play in one year, the standard NCAA penalty is to reduce the number of contests the school may play the following year, using a two-for-one formula. In Division I soccer, a school is permitted to play a maximum of 20 games (not including conference or NCAA tournament games) during the fall season. So if a school inadvertently played 21 games in 2005, it would be limited to 18 games in 2006 using the two-for-one formula.

The bottom line: A school invariably pays the penalty for committing a violation. The severity of the penalty is determined by many factors but can range from losing a scholarship to not being able to recruit a prospect for a short period of time.

In the end, the moral of this story is clear. It's everything your mother ever taught you growing up: Play nice and obey the rules — or you're gonna get it!

Knowing the history

Why care about infractions? Because they could impact you directly. If a school has had a history of major infractions, it may be required to reduce the number of scholarships it can offer in the next few years or be banned from participating in postseason play (either conference or NCAA tournaments).

Take the case of Mississippi State as an example. In the summer of 2004, the school's football program was placed on four years' probation. The probation included a ban on postseason play (no conference championship or bowl game if the team qualified for one or both) and limited the program to 81 scholarships for both the 2005–2006 and 2006–2007 academic years (which is four fewer than the maximum 85 scholarships permitted).

Imagine that the school had been recruiting you to play football there beginning in 2005–2006. There may be a chance that the scholarship you were offered now no longer exists, due to the limitations placed on the program.

Although this is a very rare case, it happens. The possibility of not having a scholarship available may cause you concern and encourage you to start looking more closely at other schools that may be recruiting you. Even though the postseason ban was for only one year, such restrictions can make it even more difficult to qualify for postseason play for the next few years.

So we ask again: Why care? Because infractions may directly impact your chance to play.

Remember: You have the right to know if a school has reported violations on its own or had the NCAA impose sanctions on it in recent years that might affect where, when, and how you play. The NCAA Web site has a listing of every school that has had a major-infractions case since 1953. You can go to www.ncaa.org and click Major Infractions to find out more.

Playing (or Not) with an Infraction

Indeed, infractions can be confusing, if not scary, stuff. You've spent a significant amount of time, energy, and money to gather information, talk to college recruiters and athletes, review records, and visit campuses around your state or the nation. Then, in one instant, a mistake could ruin everything. And the mistake may not be yours. But by knowing the rules and understanding the importance of self-reporting and a coach's boundaries, you can save yourself and your family a lot of heartache.

When the coach violates recruiting rules

The NCAA imposes penalties for recruiting violations. Usually the penalties are levied on the coach or the institution, but occasionally they can impact the student-athlete's eligibility at that school. Case in point: Let's say a college coach is attending a golf tournament organized by your high school, and about an hour before you start your round, he visits with you and wishes you good luck. Because coaches aren't allowed to have in-person contact with prospects prior to competition, this is a violation.

Normally, when a violation such as this is reported to the NCAA, the college must declare the prospect ineligible to play there. At the same time, the school will request to have eligibility restored. Ninety-five percent of the time, the prospect's eligibility is restored at that school, but sometimes the prospect will not be eligible to compete at that school and will have to scratch it off his list. This situation may warrant special consideration to determine whether the violation was intentional or an innocent mistake.

If the violation does not involve the eligibility of a prospect, the general rule of thumb is the penalty will be "two for one." What that means is if a coach accidentally calls you twice in one week, the automatic penalty will be that the coach will not be permitted to call for the next two weeks.

When the college makes a mistake

Mistakes happen — and most mistakes are not deliberate but merely an oversight or a bad judgment call. A perfect example of this may be demonstrated by none other than co-author Pat Britz. While working as the assistant athletic director for compliance at East Tennessee State, Britz once told the women's basketball coach that she could go out and begin recruiting days before it was actually permitted.

To this day, Pat has no idea where he got the idea that she might go out early. Perhaps he was distracted or was looking at the wrong date on the calendar. But for whatever reason, she either trusted her assistant athletic director completely or didn't discuss her schedule with her colleagues. Off she went, making a home visit to a prospect. Another school, which was also recruiting the girl, learned that a coach from East Tennessee State had already been to see her.

The school called East Tennessee State and asked how this was possible. That's how they found out about the screw-up. Pat's coach was great about it and took it in stride, but he felt horrible. East Tennessee State reported it to the NCAA, and during the next contact period, they had to wait three days before their coaches could go out.

While Britz and East Tennessee State worked to restore the student-athlete's eligibility, the athlete wound up going to another school altogether. The best part about the whole story was how surprised and excited Pat's coach was that she was the first one to visit the girl in her home. The coach really had no idea she was violating any rules, and the family had no reason to suspect a problem because they were unaware of the rules.

Discovering the Wonders (and Horrors) of Boosters

If you're a sports fan, you've heard the term *booster* associated with various sports programs. Typically, boosters raise funds or donate sports apparel or equipment to an athletic program. If you're an athlete, you may be familiar with the term as it pertains to car washes, cookie sales, and making T-shirts.

But what is a booster, really? What does a booster do? And how can a booster be a problem for a sports program or an individual athlete? Just as well-meaning coaches, athletic directors, and parents can violate NCAA rulings, overzealous boosters can be a real headache for athletic programs.

Defining the booster

A *booster* is a person who makes a financial contribution to that particular program. According to the NCAA, however, a booster (or "representative of athletics interests," in NCAA language) is someone who has done at least one of the following activities:

- ✓ Participated in or been a member of an agency or organization promoting the institution's intercollegiate athletics program
- ✓ Made financial contributions to the athletics department or to an athletics-booster organization of that institution
- ✓ Assisted or been requested (by the athletic department staff) to assist in the recruitment of prospects

> ✔ Assisted or been asked to assist in providing benefits to enrolled student-athletes or their families
>
> ✔ Been otherwise involved in promoting the institution's athletics program

As you can see, there are several ways an individual can earn the label *booster* in the eyes of the NCAA. Some people have argued that simply purchasing season tickets for a college team can make someone a booster.

Another interesting fact about being a booster is that, after you become one, you're considered one indefinitely. Why? The main reason is to prevent an individual from moving back and forth from not being a booster to being a booster so that he can be involved in activities not otherwise permitted by the NCAA, such as recruiting.

How boosters are involved in the recruiting process

As we mention at the beginning of this chapter, involvement in the recruiting process by boosters can become a major headache for schools and the NCAA. For that reason, the NCAA has attempted to eliminate boosters from the entire recruiting process. This includes not permitting a booster to have in-person contact with, or even written or phone communication with, a prospect. In fact, one by-law in the *NCAA Manual* is specifically devoted to listing the restrictions against a booster's being involved in the recruiting process, while several other by-laws refer to it.

An interesting scenario that occasionally crops up, however, is when a booster is a neighbor of yours or a close family friend. Does this mean your neighbor can't speak to you because he's a booster? Fortunately, there is a provision that contains the term *pre-existing relationship,* which takes into account situations like this. The situation can get sticky, however, if the booster starts providing you and/or your family with benefits that are more extravagant than those you received prior to becoming a high school athlete.

For example, while you were growing up, your neighbor was always pleasant to you and supported your athletic pursuits as a fan and friend, but no gifts or favors were ever exchanged. After your sophomore year in high school, however, you've been named All-State in your sport, and the school from which your neighbor graduated has started recruiting you. All of a sudden, your neighbor starts asking you to attend games with him at his expense and gives you a sweatshirt with the school's logo on it. Because activities like this didn't occur prior to your becoming a prospect, the NCAA would not consider this okay under the pre-existing relationship exception.

What matters is that your relationship with a booster not change based on your athletic performance.

The role of a booster can be powerful, but the role of family should be even more so. A few years ago, one of the hottest names in college football was being recruited by colleges such as Penn State, Notre Dame, Ohio State, Michigan State, and Texas, to name a few. A booster of one of the colleges also happened to act as a surrogate father to this hot new prospect. Understandably, the athlete's single mother turned to the booster for help. What was the best school for her son? Which school offered the best athletic program and the best education?

It came as a huge surprise to many when the young athlete chose a different school from his surrogate father's alma mater, but the father/booster took it well, telling friends and family that he would respect the student-athlete's wishes. In truth, it was the booster who urged his surrogate son to choose a different school. His devotion to the boy overrode his connections to the school. His request that his name be withheld from this story is proof of how committed boosters can be and are to their schools. His concern was that despite the fact that the young athlete chose the school that was best for him personally, boosters and fans of the surrogate father's school would not care or understand. For many people, winning is everything.

Understanding that recruiting is serious business is important. You must always remember that even the kindest and most sincere booster, coach, or recruiter can make an innocent, deliberate, calculated, or unwitting violation to get what he wants.

When you hear the chants of "Rah, rah, team!", remember that you and your family are the critical team at this time. Make sure you understand the rules of the game and make sound decisions before moving forward. You have plenty of time down the road to hear the cheers of your fans, coaches, boosters, and teammates.

Part III
Making College Visits

The 5th Wave   By Rich Tennant

CLOWN COLLEGE

Oh, great! Probably got in on an athletic scholarship.

In this part . . .

Not only will you find out what to look for in a college, its facilities, and academics, but you'll also get some useful tips about what to ask when talking to fellow athletes, parents, and potential coaches and trainers. You'll discover both the positive and negative sides to recruiting, and you'll keep track of everything by taking copious notes.

Chapter 10

The Play-by-Play of College Visits

*Y*ou think you know what college you want to attend. Maybe you love it because of its team mascot or the school colors or because you have friends there. Maybe you want to attend a specific university because it has a winning record.

Whatever your reason, don't make a final decision until you've checked out the campus and facilities. You wouldn't buy a car you've never seen, and you don't want to commit to a school until you've walked the campus, talked to students who attend the school, read the college paper, and eaten the food. After all, the school you choose will be your home for the next four years. You want to be sure the school is a good fit with your wants and needs as a student-athlete.

This chapter shows you how to make the most of your official and unofficial campus visits, including knowing what to see, who to talk to, and whether to work out with the prospective team.

Visiting the Campus

The wonderful thing about campus visits is that you can browse, peruse, and investigate at your leisure — well, for 48 hours, anyway. By making both official and unofficial visits to college campuses, you can get a better feel for college life and social activities, as well as where you may live, eat, study, and train. In the following sections, we explain the difference between official visits and unofficial visits, and fill you in on how you can benefit from both kinds.

Taking official visits

Official visits are prearranged visits you make to a college during your senior year in high school in which the college may finance the entire trip or part of it. Official visits are a key component of the recruiting process, so if you're asked to make one by a school, chances are that you're high on the list of players the college program is interested in.

Although you can make official visits only during your senior year, you can prepare for your official visits earlier. Before you're a senior, start making notes on what you want to ask college officials, and begin thinking about what you'll take with you. See "Looking at a Typical Visit," later in this chapter, for ideas.

According to NCAA rules, an official visit is when you're invited to a college to check out the facility, coaching staff, academic environment, and geographic location at the college's expense. Most major Division I programs pay for your entire visit (for example, transportation, lodging, and meals). Some smaller Division I schools, and most Division II and Division III schools, can pay for only part of the trip or none of it (depending on how much money they have available).

Just because you're on an official visit doesn't mean the school will be paying for everything. The school may pay for your transportation, lodging, and/or meals. But you may receive an official-visit invitation from a university that can or will pay for only part of your trip. You'll be responsible for all other expenses.

Be sure you know what the school is paying for before you accept. If you can't afford to pay for the portion of the trip the school won't cover, be honest with the recruiter.

If you don't have the funds for lodging or meals, you can't hold a fund-raiser to raise money. Doing so may jeopardize your amateur status within the NCAA and NAIA guidelines. Your best strategy if you're strapped for cash is to be completely honest with the recruiter. Tell him that you'd love to come, but you simply can't afford the added cost of gas, travel, lodging, and food. If the school really wants you, it may be able to offer you an extra allowance for those things.

Prior to the 2004–2005 academic year, the NCAA passed a new ruling that seriously affects official visits for athletes. In the past, schools were allowed to fly prospects on private planes so that, for example, a football prospect was able to play in a Friday-night high school game, catch a private airplane to a college early Saturday morning, and then stay for the duration of the weekend. This practice was particularly helpful for student-athletes who lived in remote places or hoped to attend rural colleges with no commercial airport nearby. Under the new rules, you have to take a flight on a commercial airline — no more private flights on official visits.

Opting for unofficial visits

The NCAA defines *unofficial visits* as visits you make to a college at your own expense. That means you pay for everything. Rules do not limit the number of unofficial visits you can make to a school. If you want to visit the same school 15 times at your own expense, feel free.

Another key difference between official and unofficial visits: You can make an unofficial visit prior to your senior year of high school. Many prospects begin making unofficial visits as early as their freshman or sophomore year, and some students commit to a school by their junior year (that is, before even having the opportunity to make an official visit).

The only expenses a school can pick up for you on an unofficial visit are three complimentary admissions to any home athletics contest (these can be used by you and anyone who is with you, even if they aren't your parents) and transportation on campus. If, for some reason, the sport you play has a facility off campus, the coach can drive you to see that facility as long as it's within 30 miles of the campus. You must pay for any meals you eat while on the unofficial visit. You can stay in a campus dorm or apartment during an unofficial visit as long as you pay the institution rate for such lodging.

How many visits can you make?

In Divisions I and II, you're allowed a total of five official visits between the two divisions. Even though you may be interested in schools in both divisions, you can make a total of only five official visits. Although an official visit to a Division III school doesn't count in the five-visit limit, you may not make more than one official visit to any particular school in Division III.

For example, you can make three official visits to Division I schools, two official visits to Division II schools, and three official visits to a Division III school so long as you don't make more than one official visit to the same school in Division III.

Because you're allowed only five official visits, you must be selective about where you go. If you live within driving distance of a college that interests you, you may be better off making an *unofficial* visit to that campus and saving the official visits for more-distant colleges.

If you're a multisport athlete, you still get only five official visits total. For example, if you play baseball and football, you can make three official visits to schools for baseball and two official visits to schools for football — but not more than five total.

When can you visit?

Generally speaking, your first opportunity to make an official visit to any college is the first day of classes of your senior year in high school.

The summer before your senior year, make a list of the colleges you want to visit — officially and unofficially. You can create your own game plan — or traveling schedule — of when and how you'll visit these schools.

In all cases, for any sport, before the school can pay for your visit, it must have a copy of your high school transcript (the official document or a copy of it) and a standardized test score (PSAT, SAT, PLAN, or ACT). Your test score doesn't have to make you eligible at that point, but a school may be reluctant to spend the money to bring you to campus if it's concerned about whether you'll be eligible as a freshman — further proof that grades matter!

If, for some reason, you need to make an official visit after you've finished high school (for example, if you're transferring or have delayed enrollment, for whatever reason), you're permitted five *more* visits after October 15 (for Divisions I and III) or September 1 (for Division II). So you could make a total of ten official visits if you made five in high school and five after graduating. In addition, if you made an official visit to a college or university while you were in high school, you could make another visit to the same school as long as it was after one of the no-earlier-than dates listed.

Another limiting factor regarding official visits is that some Division I sports have restrictions on the number of visits they can offer to prospects. They are as follows:

- ✔ **Football:** 56
- ✔ **Basketball:** 12
- ✔ **Baseball:** 25

The reason for limiting the number of official visits a college may offer to prospects is simple: It prevents bigger, better-funded athletic programs from outspending everyone else . . . and getting a recruiting advantage.

How long can you stay?

Official visits are limited to 48 hours. Fortunately, the 48-hour clock begins to tick when you arrive on the campus, not when you start traveling.

If, for some reason, the coach picks you up at your home to travel by automobile, the 48-hour period begins when the coach begins transporting you to campus (that is, the moment when she has the opportunity to begin a recruiting pitch).

Unofficial visits impose no restriction on the length of your stay. You or your family can stay as long as you feel comfortable paying lodging, food, and other bills. For economic reasons, however, most unofficial visits last one or two days.

Who will be with you on an official tour?

Coaches, athletic directors, trainers, and professors generally make themselves available to meet you and to answer a few questions, but few have time to spend an entire afternoon with you and your family. Therefore, a student host is assigned to you to show you around campus and answer questions. A *student host* is usually an underclassman on the team (and a potential future teammate).

The student host's main goal is to make sure that you leave with a good impression of the school — not to give you a completely honest assessment.

Who pays for entertainment?

One of the most misunderstood parts of official visits is what type of entertainment is permitted during that visit. At most Division I schools, the student host is given $30 a day to entertain you, but the student host can't give you this money or buy you sweatshirts, hats, posters, and so on. This money is intended to take you to a movie, go get a pizza, play miniature golf, or provide whatever other entertainment floats your boat.

Unfortunately, this entertainment rule has been abused frequently in the past. But rules were made to be broken, right? Not with the NCAA. Any violation of NCAA rules, such as accepting gifts or buying nonregulated items with college funds, could make you ineligible at that particular school until the value of that so-called *extra benefit* is paid back. If you borrow money from the allotted $30 in order to buy a college T-shirt, the student host has to show that the money was borrowed, and you must pay it back. Even so, you've violated the NCAA prohibition on using entertainment money to buy something for a souvenir. And if you receive a benefit that exceeds $100, you may be permanently ineligible to compete for that school. Be careful, be aware of the rules, and insist that the host spend money on approved items only.

The good news is that during an official visit, the school pays for all meals for you and for your parents, legal guardians, and/or spouse. In addition, the school can provide you and your family admissions for any home athletics events. For this reason, most schools try to schedule official visits during a regular season or playoff home contest of some sort. You're permitted to receive three complimentary admissions for any home contests that occur during the official visit. These complimentary admissions, which are good for any sport, can be used by you and anyone else who may be accompanying you on the visit.

Schools may *not* provide you the three complimentary admissions to a conference tournament or championship the school is hosting during an official or unofficial visit. In addition, if the school is hosting an NCAA championship, you're on your own for tickets, even if you're on an official visit.

For other forms of entertainment (meals, movies, and so on), the school may pay only for you and your parents (or legal guardians) or your spouse. For example, if your little brother comes with you on the visit, and the whole family goes out to eat with the coach, you or your parents need to pay for the kid's grilled-cheese sandwich.

A recently adopted NCAA rule requires schools to have on file all policies related to official visits for prospects, student hosts, coaches, and administrators. The school must inform you that sex, drugs, alcohol, and gambling will *not* be part of the visit. If you engage in any of these activities during an official visit, you could jeopardize your eligibility at that school. If any of the forbidden activities occurs while you're on an official visit, the school has violated an NCAA rule and must self-report it. You don't need this kind of trouble.

Coaches talk to one another, and it does not take long for word to travel to different colleges about an athlete's behavior. Read the school policies; adhere to the rules; and conduct yourself in a mature, responsible fashion. You're a guest at the school, and it pays to behave like one.

Where do you stay?

You and whoever accompanies you will likely stay at a local hotel during an official visit. Many athletic departments trade out a certain number of rooms at a hotel in exchange for tickets, advertising space, and so on. The accommodations you receive must be comparable to typical student living. What that means is the school can't put you up in a suite that's three times the size of a dorm room and has a Jacuzzi and other special qualities. Also, keep in mind that the school is permitted to pay for lodging only for you and your parents, legal guardians, or spouse. If other family members or friends accompany you on the visit, they need to pay for their own lodging, or they all have to cram into your room.

If you make phone calls from the room or watch a pay-per-view movie, you're responsible for those charges. NCAA rules forbid the school to pay for incidental charges you may accumulate. Many schools ask the hotel to disconnect these services in order to prevent any potential problems.

Many coaches prefer that you spend at least one night in a dorm or apartment with your student host. This is an excellent opportunity for you to get the feel of what it would be like to be a student-athlete at the school. It also allows you to see what your life would be like on campus. You may find that you don't get along with the members of the current team or simply don't like the atmosphere at the school. You're better off knowing this before you commit to a college.

Just because you don't like one school doesn't mean there isn't a school out there that's right for you. You just need to look around for the right fit.

Deciding Whether Your Parents Should Make the Trip

Where to attend college may be one of the toughest decisions you'll make in your academic and athletic career. This decision will affect at least the next four or five years of your life — it may have an impact on your career or who you end up marrying!

The extent to which you want your parents involved is a matter of personal preference. Keep in mind that your parents may very well have attended college themselves, and they may have a lot of helpful advice to offer.

Wooing your parents

Many coaches recruit parents as actively as they do student-athletes. They understand that attending a particular college is often a family decision, and they hope to endear themselves to your parents. For this reason, it may be very important for at least one of your parents to travel with you on official visits.

A major drawback to having your parents go with you, however, is that the school is not allowed to pay for your parents' transportation if you're flying. If you're driving, the school may reimburse your mileage or gas, but the reimbursement must be made out to you, as the athlete.

 Be wary of coaches or a school policy that discourages parents from participating in an official visit. Although no hard rules require the presence of parents during official visits, schools should never *discourage* your parents from attending, asking questions, and being part of this important time in your life.

 If your high school or club coach drives you to an official visit in his own personal vehicle, you or your coach are not allowed to be reimbursed for mileage. You can be reimbursed only if your parents drive you.

Leaving them behind

Some people believe that because you'll be attending school alone, you should visit the campus alone — making the first of many important adult decisions by yourself. This decision is a personal one, but having another perspective on a big decision is very help-ful. **Remember:** No one will have your best interests at heart more than your parents.

If you and your parents do decide that they won't go with you, they can still be a vital part of the team effort. Together, you can come up with a list of questions you plan to ask the coaches, training staff, current athletes, and professors from your chosen major. You can also make a list of items you want to check on — the library, dorm rooms, laundry and training facilities — and your parents can remind you of things you've forgotten (or didn't even know about).

Leave copies of these notes and questions for your parents so that each night you're away, you can call or e-mail them and talk about them together. You can give your perspective of what you've seen and heard, and your parents can make their own notes based on what you tell them. This conversation will help you reiterate what you saw and heard during the day, giving you the opportunity to reflect on your own impressions.

You can also send digital pictures of the campus, dorm rooms, training facilities, and more. That way, your parents will get to "see" the campus along with you and be part of the experience.

Looking at a Typical Visit

A typical official visit will be structured so that you and your family have an opportunity to check out specific facilities, sporting events, faculty, and the dorms. Most likely, your official campus tour will be given by another student. Your guide will be able to answer ques-tions about college life, academics, and off-campus activities.

If you make an unofficial visit — for which you pay your own expenses — you may discover more-useful information by touring the facilities on your own. After all, the student host you'll have on an official visit is trying to put a positive spin on everything. You may be able to get a more-accurate picture by talking to students who aren't trying to woo you on behalf of the coach or team.

Whether official or unofficial, the trick is deciding when to go, who to talk to, and what to ask.

During *dead periods* (periods of inactivity for recruiters), coaches are not permitted to talk to you in person. Coaches may not speak with you on or off campus. They can, however, speak to you by telephone or correspond in writing.

But if you have any hopes of having a face-to-face meeting during this time, it can't happen. Therefore, when planning an unofficial visit, be sure it isn't during the dead period for that sport.

So strict are these guidelines that coaching-staff members may not even attend or speak at banquets in which a student-athlete prospect may be in attendance.

 Weekend visits are the most common for families hoping to find out more about a college — they usually fit in best with work and school schedules. If at all possible, we recommend making your visit during the week instead of on the weekend. Weekend, spring-break, and summer visits don't give you the complete picture. Campus life is considerably quieter. Although you may have full access to athletic facilities and the athletic dorms, you'll miss out on the feel of the college campus.

Walking the campus

 When you're walking around the campus, read bulletin boards, get a copy of the student newspaper, eat in the cafeteria, and talk to other students. If you're visiting a campus with your family, split up for a while, allowing each of you to check out the campus individually and take notes. When you get together later and compare notes, chances are that your parents, guardian, friend, sibling, or spouse will have a different perspective on the campus than you did, and you can use the information they found that you didn't.

 If you feel too embarrassed or intimidated to talk to students or athletes, let your parents help you out. While you're checking out the classes, your parents can talk to college students, asking their opinions on academic, athletic, and social issues.

Here are the questions you should be asking:

- ✔ What makes this college campus so special?
- ✔ What are the big issues being debated on campus?
- ✔ What's dorm life like?
- ✔ How large are the first-year/introductory classes?
- ✔ What do students do on the weekends?
- ✔ How does the team appear to get along?
- ✔ What's the athletic facility like?
- ✔ If you're a minority: What is the minority population on campus?

✔ What is the one thing you would change about this college?

✔ How are student athletes viewed by the general student body, and, in particular, how are members of the team you'll be playing on viewed?

You can check out the Princeton Review's *The Best 361 Colleges: The Smart Student's Guide to Colleges* to get an idea of what campus living is like at any college that interests you. This book even includes such topics as parking accommodations and how students rank the food. You can find it at major bookstores or at www.princetonreview.com/college/.

Sitting in on a class

When you arrange an official visit, you'll meet with faculty members who teach the subjects you're thinking about majoring in, and choose a few classes to sit in on. If you're not sure what you'll major in, you can meet with faculty who teach some of the courses that all freshmen are likely to take, like 100-level history or English courses.

Attending class is an important step in visualizing yourself on campus. While you're attending a class, you may want to get a copy of the *course syllabus* (which outlines all the course requirements and assignments) to get a better idea of what's expected of you academically. You can get a copy of the syllabus from the professor.

If you're visiting the campus unofficially, you can still discover a lot about the campus, coaches, students, and classes. With a few phone calls ahead of time, and perhaps the help of your school guidance counselor, you can probably arrange to meet with faculty members and attend a few classes. You can also check out the dorms and the academic buildings, and see where they are in relation to the rest of the campus. You can find out about transportation between where you would live, class buildings, athletic facilities, the student union, the library, and the health center.

Be sure to visit the campus library, and check to see how many computers are available to students, what kind of assistance is offered to new students, the hours of operation, and what kind of additional resources the staff may offer. If your schedule allows, check out the library on a Friday night. If there seem to be a lot of students around, chances are that the school has strong academic influences — or at least a segment of students who care about academics.

Touring the athletic facilities

Ah, yes. The reason for your being there — or so some people think. In reality, athletics is just one piece of the puzzle, albeit an important piece. During an official visit, you'll be introduced to the coaching staff and trainers, and you may even be given a personal tour by the coach.

For an unofficial visit, make arrangements in advance to meet the staff and have full access to the sports facilities.

Look at the condition of the equipment and field house itself. What kind of locker-room and weight-room facilities does the school have?

Passing the physical exam

During an official visit, be prepared for the coaching staff to have one of the athletic trainers give you a physical examination. This is a great time to talk to the trainers and discover more about the facility.

While you're getting your physical, you can check out the training room. Ask about the number of trainers per student-athlete and what kind of medical assistance is provided on campus, as well as the hours of operation and the availability of coaches and trainers in case of a medical issue.

What to expect

Before you buy the car, always kick the tires and take it for a spin. Your school of interest may feel the same way, wanting to check your medical history again before committing to anything long-term. Although the school has your transcripts, stats, and other vital information, the coaching staff always wants reassurances that you're as sound in person as you appear on paper.

Here's what you can expect:

- ✔ **Medical-history sheet:** You'll be asked to fill out a medical-history sheet, listing the dates, causes, and treatment of injuries such as concussions, surgeries, or prolonged illnesses.

- ✔ **Internal medical check:** The trainers may check your blood pressure, pulse, height, and weight, as well as investigate any problems that arise from the medical-history sheet, such as head injuries and/or surgeries.

Don't be surprised if you're also asked to submit a urine sample. More and more schools are locking down on substance abuse, including steroids, Creatine, and other muscle-building stimulants.

✔ **Orthopedic exam:** During this examination, the trainers will take a more-thorough look at your ankles, knees, shoulders, hips, and so on. This is their way of kicking your tires to be sure you don't have too many miles or any engine troubles before they buy in.

Play it smart, and bring with you as much information as possible, including:

✔ **An up-to-date medical history, including current personal history and vaccinations.**

✔ **A well-documented history of your medical injuries:** Trainers will be interested in how you injured your knee, what kind of surgery you had, and when it happened. More important, you want to be sure to include the kind of treatment or physical therapy you went through on your road to recovery. Trainers want reassurances that you took the injury seriously and were proactive in your physical therapy for a full recovery.

✔ **Phone numbers, addresses, and complete names of all the physicians, trainers, therapists, and/or coaches you've worked with.**

What to pack

You'll be meeting your potential training and coaching staff, and you want to appear prepared and eager to work. Even though you may not be asked to work out or fill out any medical history, you need to be ready for such tasks in case they do ask you.

Arrive with a small training bag in hand. Throw in:

✔ **A notebook:** Bring a notebook with questions you may have for the trainers and/or coaching staff. You may become overwhelmed by everything that's happening. By bringing a notebook, you'll appear organized — and you'll also get the answers to the questions you have.

✔ **Running shoes:** Pack athletic shoes that you can perform in, whether it's a cardio test on the treadmill or simply walking around the athletic facility.

✔ **Workout clothes:** If you're dressed in street clothes, you can change quickly and be ready to take any tests thrown your way.

✔ **Medications:** Pack any medications you may need while working out, such as your asthma inhaler.

Too many young athletes are hesitant to show their trainers their inhalers for fear that the trainers may think less of them. That simply isn't the case. Some of the greatest athletes in the world are asthmatics. Trainers want to see what kind of medication and what dosage you require. They'll be the ones handling the inhaler, so you need to have an open, candid discussion about your condition.

Playing with the team

You may be permitted to play a game of pick-up with the team on your official visit, so pack your bags wisely. Bring along your cleats, shorts, mouthpiece, or whatever sports-specific gear you own.

Not everyone gets to show her stuff in front of a coach. If you get this chance, here are the rules:

✔ **A coach may not arrange or be on hand to observe you while you're playing with the team.**

✔ **Playing with the team is only to allow you playtime — it isn't supposed to be a test of your abilities.** While you work with a trainer, he'll be assessing your physical conditioning and medical background. When you play with the team, no one is testing your abilities, but be warned: You *are* being tested. How well you work with others, your mental attitude, and how you mesh with the team will be noted — you can be sure of that. Always put your best foot forward, and show everyone a great mental attitude. Whining for water or declaring that it's too hot for practice is *not* a good strategy.

If you're visiting a Division II school, you can have on-campus playtime in which you'll be observed or tested by coaching staff, under the following conditions:

- The test or observation must take place on the college campus.

- Only a high school senior who is not in season for his sport may be observed by a college coach and/or staff.

- The two-year college student who has exhausted his eligibility status may also be tested by a coach/trainer.

- The four-year college student, following the conclusion of his season, may also test, as long as he has written permission from his athletic director and coach.

> ✔ **A medical examination may be given as part of the tryout process.** Be sure to have all your medical-history information with you.
>
> ✔ **The tryout or playtime should run no longer than a regularly sanctioned practice with the college.** It should be no longer than two hours.
>
> ✔ **The college may provide the gear you need for a competition or tryout, but be prepared, and bring your own gear.**
>
> ✔ **In the sport of football, you aren't permitted to wear a helmet or pads during this playtime.**

Looking at dorms and apartments

Your space is your space. Although it may sound ridiculous, space is one of the major reasons cited by college students for leaving a dorm, an apartment, or even a sports program. Keep this in mind as you tour your possible living quarters.

Despite what you may hear, not every college athlete lives in the athletic dorms. Some smaller colleges simply don't have dorm rooms designated for student-athletes, while others are so overcrowded that athletes may live off campus. Some student-athletes ask to live outside the athletic dorms for academic, work, or personal reasons, while other athletes could never imagine *not* living in the athletic dorms. For the latter group, living in the dorms is part of the whole college experience.

Where and how you live will greatly affect both your academic and athletic career.

How high can you jump?

If you think you have the talent to play at the Division II or NAIA level, but you haven't received much interest from or exposure to these schools, a tryout may be the answer to your scholarship prayers. It can give an opportunity to show a coach your skills.

The tryout may include tests to evaluate your performance as an athlete. You may be tested for strength, stamina, speed, agility, and sports-specific skills. Except for football, ice hockey, lacrosse, and wrestling, your tryout may include a competition. So bring your game!

For many college freshman, the first year away from home is a shock. Living with other people is even more shocking. As you consider where you might live, also think about *how* you might live. Try to tour the dorms when things are in full swing.

You'll want to consider even seemingly minor details before settling into dorm life. If you move into a dorm room, you need to consider the following:

✔ **How big is your bathroom, and where is it?** Many dorm bathrooms are down the hall, and you share the bathroom with the entire floor. Some dorms have private or semiprivate bathrooms, where you and your roommate may share a bathroom with another room of a couple people.

✔ **With whom will you be sharing closet space?**

✔ **Do you have a refrigerator, or will it be provided?**

✔ **Will you have to share a room?**

✔ **Where will you do laundry?**

Don't take a tour when a majority of the student body is gone (like on summer vacation or spring break). Be sure to view dorm living in the middle of the day and, if possible, in the evening. The sights, sounds, and smells of an active dorm are often the most important experiences in helping you make your decisions.

If you need to or want to live off campus, there are many questions you need to consider (and answer) before finding an apartment:

✔ Where is the apartment in relation to campus?

✔ Is there bus transportation to and from campus?

✔ How close are you to a grocery store? If you don't have a car, how will you transport bags of groceries?

✔ What was the landlord's or management's relationship with previous tenants?

✔ What is the landlord's or management's track record for fixing plumbing, air-conditioning, or heating problems?

✔ Would you need roommates? If so, how would you find responsible ones?

Contact campus and local police departments regarding safety and security on and off campus.

Being Watched: Putting Your Best Foot Forward

The whole idea of visiting a school is to check it out and see whether it's a nice fit for you, right? Not entirely. Remember that while you're looking at the school, the school is looking at you.

On an unofficial visit, you'll still want to look and behave your best. But you need to approach an *official* visit as you would a job interview. A coach and athletic director may meet you during an official visit, only later to withdraw his interest because you made a poor impression. Appearing cocky, overconfident, or ready to party on is not the way to wow a coaching staff.

Pre-interviewing

Before your visit, do some practice interviews with your friends and family. Have your parents, legal guardians, and high school coaches pose interview-type questions to you. For example:

✔ What do you expect to get from your experience at this school?

✔ What do you have to offer the team? The coaching staff?

✔ What kind of player would your current coach say you are? Are you a team player? What would she say about your work ethic?

✔ What would your teammates say behind your back?

✔ What are your greatest strengths? Your greatest weakness? How can you improve?

✔ Who is your role model, and why?

✔ How important are academics to you? How important have they been in high school?

Do some research on the school and its history. Then, while you talk to a coach, athletic director, student host, or trainer, you can mention something about the school's history, previous athletic records, a particular alumnus, or interesting facts about the school's founding. In other words, show an interest in the school beyond the fact that *they're* interested in *you*.

Selling yourself

You've heard that first impressions are everything. Many times, they *are*. The way you hold yourself; whether you look people in the eye; and how you walk, talk, and dress will carry a lot of weight with the coach and/or athletic director.

Schools invest a lot of money in scholarship athletes, so the coaches need reassurance that if they give you a scholarship, their money will be well spent. Will you turn out to be a discipline problem? A party animal? A slacker? A prima donna?

Read on for ways to make a good impression.

Arriving on time

You've made an appointment to meet someone at the college you're visiting, whether officially or unofficially. It doesn't matter whether the meeting is with the dean, coach, trainer, or student host: Be on time. If you're going to be late, call the person you're scheduled to meet with, and let him know.

Standing tall and being positive

Be confident, not cocky. This is your best opportunity to let the school meet you as a student, not just an athlete. Most likely, they know of your abilities on the court or field, but they'll have less understanding of your approach to academics. Use personal meetings with college officials as a time to let them know you, the person.

Remain positive when discussing teammates, current and previous coaches, and the recruiting process. Let it be known that you're both honored and excited about the opportunities ahead.

Dressing the part

You're a standout athlete, but you don't need to appear as though you just came off the court. Dress to impress and for success. No, you don't have to wear a dress or a suit and tie, but you do need to appear neat, clean, and appropriately dressed. Leave the excess jewelry, nose rings, and tongue piercing at home. If you have tattoos, cover them. Your school of interest wants to visualize a jersey with their school colors on your back, making them proud, not embarrassing them.

Your clothing and appearance make their own statement about who you are. Serious about your future? Arrogant? A team-oriented person? You can control the message you convey.

Staying grounded

Perhaps one of the best-loved athletes of all time was basketball sensation Michael Jordon. He was a marketing director's dream, a coach's fantasy, and a teammate's best friend. He was humble, sincere, hard-working, and honest. While you're being recruited, all the hype can be overwhelming. Instead of believing the hype, stay focused on the job at hand — closing the deal with the school you want to attend and the team you want to join.

You're visiting the school to be part of a team — not a standout.

Sending a thank-you note

As soon as you've returned home, send a thank-you note to the coach and athletic director. Whether you send an e-mail or a personal note, this is a great way to recap your meeting and remind people of who you are and how appreciative you are of their efforts. You can be sure that not all the prospects will take the time to say thanks — writing a thank-you note gives you another way to show everyone how special you are.

Chapter 11

Taking Your Turn to Recruit

● ●

In This Chapter

▶ Looking at the success rate of your school

▶ Researching your favorite programs

▶ Checking references

▶ Turning the tables: Interviewing the schools of your choice

● ●

*W*hat is college? Parties, independence, money, a road to success in business, a means to play upper-level sports, and — oh, yeah — education. Although we hope that education is first and foremost in your mind, everyone is driven by his or her own desire. Whatever your motivation and drive, understanding what you're getting into is vital — and that understanding will come only when you ask questions. Many questions. *Remember:* This is *your* turn to recruit the college of your choice.

MIT graduate and CEO Cristina Dolan believes wholly in research, particularly before any interviews. A standout in the world of technology, and president and CEO of WordStream, Dolan always turned the tables during job interviews on her way to the top. Her philosophy has always been to interview the company — rather than the other way around — to see if she wanted to work for them. She always asked potential employers two important questions: "Why would I want to work for you?" and "What do you have to offer me?"

You should be asking such questions of the schools you're considering attending: "Why should I attend this school and play for your team?" and "What do you have to offer me?" It shouldn't be enough for you that a particular college has great colors or a cute mascot. Take time to analyze what the college experience means to you and what you hope to gain from attending a school. Then research, research, research. In this chapter, we show you how.

Research, Research, Research

What if, since you were 10 years old, you've known that you wanted to play for a certain school? You love everything about that school: its traditions, its colors, its dedication to your sport. You love the students, the location, and even the mascot. Everything is perfect about that school. Why should you even bother looking around when you know this is what you want? Wouldn't researching other schools, taking notes, and thinking hard about the best choice just be a waste of time?

Don't fall into the same trap so many high school athletes do by assuming that your acceptance to your dream school is a sure thing. Researching and applying to other schools is the only way to avoid ending up empty handed. But let's assume that you're one of the few college-bound student-athletes whose acceptance to your dream school is a lock. Why should you continue to do research when you already know where you're going?

First of all, you still need to make a good impression with the faculty, admissions counselors, and coach/athletic-department staff of your college. You get only one chance to make a good first impression. And that first impression will stay with these people — people who have some degree of control over your life — for your entire collegiate career. So it's important to research your school to prepare for your entrance interviews. But there are other important, long-range reasons to do research. Here are some of them:

- ✔ Research opens doors, allowing you to make more contacts and talk to new people.
- ✔ Research will help you better understand the academic world.
- ✔ Research will help you better understand athletic scholarships and prevent you from making very costly mistakes.
- ✔ Research will allow you to have more intelligent, thoughtful conversations with coaches, faculty members, admissions officers, and directors.
- ✔ Research will open your eyes to new ideas and new traditions at schools other than the one you've loved since you were 10.
- ✔ Research will help you in making decisions.
- ✔ Research will give you confidence.
- ✔ Research allows you to be more open-minded.
- ✔ Research helps you think strategically.

✔ Research can give you a point of reference from which you can better view your future.

✔ Research will allow you to identify new problems to be considered.

✔ Research will allow you to identify new solutions to old problems.

Diving into college without proper research is a lot like diving into a bobsled for the first time: You're completely unprepared for the disasters to come. Flying headfirst at 80 miles per hour, you'd have to ask yourself (or, rather, scream to yourself), "What am I doing?! Why am I doing this?! Why am I here?!" No bobsledder with a lick of sense would simply jump into such danger without practice, training, and coaching. No extreme-sport athlete, from Nordic ski jumpers to professional bull riders, would. But college isn't the same as an enraged bull, right? Well, while you're not likely to be crushed by a speeding bobsled or gored by a mad bull on campus, a bad college experience can be even more painful than these extreme accidents. Bobsledders and bull riders generally lick their wounds, heal, and move on. But a bad college decision can mean a lost scholarship, failing grades, or a disappointing academic career.

Mercifully, there are much safer ways to find out about the college experience than just diving in headfirst.

Checking Up on Your Favorite Programs

At the beginning of this chapter, we asked the question "What is college?" Our next question is "Did you have an answer?" After all, your answer is imperative. Before you can determine where you should go, you need to truly understand what matters to you.

All-state champion pole vaulter Nick Frawley was heavily recruited by colleges from around the nation. By the time he was a junior, he knew that he wanted to fly planes for a living and continue jumping as long as he could. This immediately narrowed down the list of potential schools. Frawley was looking exclusively at schools with strong aerospace and fighter-pilot programs — and, obviously, good track-and-field programs.

The Frawley family arranged family vacations around nearby colleges with such programs. They visited Cornell, as well as the Naval and Air Force academies. At the same time that many schools were busily following Nick's athletic career, he was researching all the schools, looking for the best possible fit. Nick compiled a list of wants and needs that were high on his list: weather, geographic location, access to fly, academic records, and athletic facilities. As an honor student with an outstanding extracurricular and athletic résumé, Frawley knew what he would bring to a college. So his new questions, in Cristina Dolan fashion, became "Why would I want to go to that school?" and "What would they have to offer me?"

To focus your research as Nick did, talk to your school counselor to gather more information about specific schools according to your wants and needs. Although most experienced counselors agree that in-person visits are the best way to determine whether a school is for you, a variety of other avenues to research schools are available, including the following:

- ✔ **Seek the advice of friends and family who are in college or who have recently graduated.** What did they like or dislike? Did they go to a big school with 200 students in most classes? Did they go to a "suitcase school," where everyone went home on the weekends? Or was it a big party school? The key to remember is this: Schools are like snowflakes and fingerprints. Although they may *appear* to be similar, each one is unique. And, ultimately, it will be up to you to make the most of your college experience.

- ✔ **Make a list of potential schools, and check their official Web sites.** This is a great initial step. Just by browsing the Web, you'll find out about the history and achievements of each school. Remember that the official school Web sites are not only a way for the schools to let people know about them, but also an opportunity for the schools to post bragging rights. So the picture you get from looking at a school's Web site is a lot like looking at the Web site for your favorite athletic-shoe manufacturer — lots of hype and nothing negative. Still, you can get basic, important facts like location, student-body size, and academic and athletic reputations.

- ✔ **Attend college fairs.** These one- or two-day events allow schools to set up booths and have representatives from the school's admissions office on hand to answer your questions. College fairs are usually regional or even local, and they're a great way to get information and brochures on as many schools as you want, in addition to applications for admissions and financial aid. The National College Fairs Program, which sponsors about 35 college fairs around the country each year, sends information to local high school counselors. So ask your guidance counselor to tell you about college fairs near you or check the Web at www.nacacnet.org.

Identify some schools you want to investigate at the fair, have questions prepared for the college reps, and write down their answers with the pen and notebook that you bring. Ask questions about admissions and financial-aid application deadlines, the deadline for choosing your major, special placement tests that may be required of incoming freshmen, the school's enrollment and average class size, whether graduate students teach core classes, and so on. To prepare more for college fairs, visit the following Web sites:

- www.collegeboard.com

- www.petersons.com

- www.schoolguides.com/calendar.asp

- www.schoolsintheusa.com/college_fairs.cfm

✔ **Take virtual campus tours.** Although actually visiting a campus is the best way to find out about the school's environment, visiting isn't always possible. If you absolutely can't visit a campus in person, take a virtual tour of the campuses in which you're interested. Visit these Web sites to take virtual tours:

- www.campustours.com

- www.college-visits.com

- www.collegiatechoice.com

- www.ecampustours.com

✔ **Find the best schools and sports programs.** Research college and university rankings in academics and athletics to find out about scholastic achievements as well as athletic success, standout athletes, and the winningest coaches. *U.S. News & World Report* publishes an annual ranking of America's best colleges, from academics to athletics. (See www.usnews.com/usnews/edu/college/rankings/rankindex_brief.php and www.usnews.com/usnews/edu/college/sports/sportsindex.htm.) Princeton Review (www.princeton review.com/college/research/rankings/rankings.asp), the Riley Guide (www.therileyguide.com), and Yahoo! Education Directory (http://dir.yahoo.com/Education/Higher_Education/College_and_University_Planning) also rank schools annually, including such issues as academics, demographics, social life, and sports. Another helpful Web site that gives links to college ranking services as well as related articles and books is www.library.uiuc.edu/edx/rankings.htm.

✔ **Research college life online.** Got more questions? In addition to following the links in the Web sites listed earlier in this list, read articles posted online on topics from acing the admissions essay to the do's and don'ts of college life, from which schools are the biggest party schools to how to overcome homesickness your freshman year.

By researching on the Web, you'll find dozens of excellent resources to help guide you in a better direction to find out more about potential colleges; what they offer; and their relationships with government agencies, recruiting, academics, and athletics. Here are several such resources:

- www.campusdirt.com
- www.collegeanduniversity.net
- www.colleges.com
- www.collegesofdistinction.com
- www.decatursports.com
- www.fafsa.com
- www.findarticles.com
- www.makingitcount.com
- www.nacacnet.com
- www.nextstepmag.com

For many more helpful online resources, see Appendix B.

✔ **Research campus culture.** There's one more avenue of research you should pursue: specific cultures you may belong to or be interested in. It's just one more aspect of life that may make the college/campus experience more enjoyable for you. See if some of these Web sites interest you:

- www.collegenews.com (for student newspapers)
- www.hillel.org and www.jewish.com (for Jewish life on campus)
- www.greekpages.com (for the Greek life — fraternities and sororities)
- www.princetonreview.com/college/research/asklm/glbt.asp (for gay and lesbian life)
- www.hacu.net (for colleges with Hispanic populations)
- www.edonline.com/cq/hbcu (for historically black colleges/universities)
- www.infoplease.com/ipa/A0771723.html (for the top 50 colleges for black students)

Everyone has his or her own opinion about which school is best. No matter how well intentioned they are, your high school counselor, parents, aunts, uncles, or neighbors will want to weigh in on what is best for you. This is where your own personal research will help you make the best choice for *you* — not for Uncle Chuck from Kalamazoo.

By researching schools — their academic and athletic reputations, and their faculty and staff — you can make very informed decision. But be realistic in your research. Consider your grades, how great your athletic talent really is, and how hard you're willing to work before (and after) making the team. And be realistic about where you're going to be happy living (on a large campus or a small one? in a big city or a rural area?).

Bigger is not necessarily better

One of the most common misconceptions students have when choosing a school has to do with size. By sheer size, a university must be better than a small college, right? And Division I must be better than Division II. Certainly, there are advantages to being in a Division I school, but depending upon your needs, bigger does not necessarily mean better. In fact, many smaller Division II or NAIA schools are among the best academic universities in the nation. And if you're looking for more one-on-one interaction with your professors, smaller is usually better.

Big schools offer

✔ Well-known faculty and a large number of faculty members

✔ Diverse course offerings

✔ Diverse student body

✔ Excellent academic facilities (library, laboratories)

✔ Excellent recreational facilities (gyms, fields, courts) and extensive intramural program

✔ Big-time sports programs

✔ Lower tuition and fees (frequently)

But the disadvantages of big schools include

✔ Large and impersonal classes. (If you don't want to sit in a classroom with as many as 300 students, a big school may not be for you.)

✔ Graduate students (instead of professors) teaching lower-level or nongraduate classes.

(continued)

(continued)

✔ Difficulty getting into classes because of the large student body.

✔ More frequent standardized tests (true/false, multiple choice) in large classes, which can limit students' creativity.

✔ Limited housing on campus.

✔ Difficulty getting around or parking on campus.

The advantages of smaller schools include

✔ Excellent student-faculty ratios and easy access to senior faculty members. (You'll often see student-faculty ratios expressed as a number like 10:1, which means there are 10 students for every 1 faculty member. The fewer students per faculty member, the more one-on-one attention you're likely to receive.)

✔ Small classes and fewer standardized tests.

✔ Availability of offered classes.

✔ Availability of on-campus housing.

✔ Easier times getting around campus.

✔ Friendlier and more-personalized campus experience.

✔ More opportunity to play sports (potentially two varsity sports).

And the disadvantages of smaller schools include

✔ Less diversity in course offerings

✔ Less diverse student body

✔ Fewer faculty members and fewer well-known faculty members

✔ Fewer campus resources like computer labs, libraries, dorms, and dining halls

✔ Fewer recreational facilities and activities

✔ Smaller sports program

✔ More-expensive tuition (frequently)

Calling References: Don't Be Afraid to Ask

There is nothing like walking the campus, talking to students, and attending a few classes to get the feel of a school. But if you can't make the unofficial or official visit, or if you simply want more information, nothing beats picking up the telephone.

You can refer to catalogues for faculty and staff names or browse the Web site. Faculty members will almost always be very frank and open with you. They see students every day and are committed to helping them succeed. They don't want to see anyone get in over his head. You may also want to speak to someone in admissions, as well as the student-body president, the librarian, or even reporters at the school newspaper.

Talk to students

Here's a list of questions to ask *students* at the school:

- ✔ How many hours do you study for each class? How many hours a day? A week?

- ✔ How many pages do you have to read for a typical assignment?

- ✔ What is the average class size?

- ✔ Are professors accessible outside class, and how do you get in touch with them?

- ✔ Do you usually get the classes you register for?

- ✔ Do professors or grad students teach most of the classes?

- ✔ Are there any professors who are not native-English speakers who are difficult to understand?

- ✔ Is there a tutoring service on campus? How good is it?

- ✔ Is there a career counseling center on campus? Do many students use its services?

- ✔ Do most students live on or off campus?

- ✔ Do you like the surrounding town? Is it big or small? Urban or rural?

- ✔ Does the town have restaurants, movie theaters, nightclubs, museums, parks, a shopping mall?

- ✔ Are the dorms single-sex or coed? Quiet or noisy?

- ✔ Do the dorms have computer labs?

- ✔ How strict are the dorm rules?

- ✔ Are parties allowed in the dorms? Is alcohol allowed in the dorms?

- ✔ How good is the cafeteria food?

- ✔ What hours is the cafeteria open?

- ✔ Do most upperclassmen eat in the cafeteria or off campus?

✔ What is transportation like on and off campus?

✔ How frequently do school buses run, and where do they go off campus?

✔ Do you need to have a car to go to school here?

✔ Is there a waiting list for parking permits?

✔ Is there enough parking?

✔ Is there a grocery store within walking distance of campus?

✔ How safe is it on campus? Off campus?

✔ Where is the health center, and what are its hours?

✔ Does the health center have a good reputation? What about the campus police?

✔ What percentage of students are Greek (fraternity/sorority)?

✔ Are there many parties on the weekends?

✔ Are there many extracurricular activities on campus — intramural sports, student organizations, and so on?

✔ Why did you choose to attend this school?

✔ Do you have any regrets about your decision?

✔ What do you wish you had known before you chose to attend this school?

✔ What are some negative aspects about this school?

✔ What will you miss most about this school after you graduate?

✔ How are athletes viewed by nonathletes here? By faculty?

✔ Do athletes miss a lot of classes for games?

✔ How much studying time do athletes actually have?

✔ What is the coach's relationship with the team? What is he or she like?

✔ What is the coach's relationship with the school paper, the faculty, the president?

✔ How does the team get along?

Talk to faculty

Talking to professors is just as important as talking to students. What you want are good teachers who are interested in teaching. Unlike in high school, where teachers are there strictly to teach (and supervise), many college professors are actually there as much to do research as they are to teach. And with a few professors, teaching can sometimes take a backseat to research.

Many colleges flaunt the names of famous scholars or writers who are faculty members. But you may never see that high-profile personality in a classroom.

What you should be most concerned with is the quality of education you'll receive — not the impressive list of faculty you may never even meet.

As you begin to research the classroom atmosphere of your school of choice, have a prepared list to ask faculty members:

- ✔ What is the average class size?
- ✔ What is the student-faculty ratio?
- ✔ Who teaches more classes: faculty or graduate students?
- ✔ How many professors teach freshman courses?
- ✔ How accessible are you and other professors during nonclass hours?
- ✔ How good is the department in my major?
- ✔ What is the study load for students in your class? In other classes?
- ✔ How realistic is that study load for an athlete on scholarship?
- ✔ How do the students at this school compare with students at other schools where you've taught?
- ✔ What percentage of students graduate? What percentage of students graduate in four years?
- ✔ What percentage of athletes graduate? What percentage of players on scholarship graduate? How many graduate in four years?
- ✔ How many freshmen fall below a 2.0 GPA? How many of those freshmen are athletes?
- ✔ How many credit hours should I take in a semester in season and out of season?
- ✔ Is tutoring available?
- ✔ If I have a diagnosed, documented learning disability, what kind of academic services are available?
- ✔ Will I have an advisor to help me with scheduling?
- ✔ Who will be my faculty advisor?

✔ How does college work differ from high school work?

✔ Why do students leave this college?

✔ What are the most common complaints by students?

✔ Is summer school available?

✔ Is cheating a common problem at this school? How is it dealt with?

✔ What is the attendance policy?

✔ What is the reputation of athletes among the faculty?

✔ How lenient are faculty with athletes' conflicting schedules?

Looking at Graduation Rates and Academic Successes

Two-thirds of college students change their majors at least once, often twice, before graduating from college. Most graduates make a major job change within the first five years after graduating, pursuing a career that has little or nothing to do with their major. Nothing is ever as straightforward as it seems.

You're offered a scholarship; so you plan to attend the school, play hard, study harder, graduate, and move on to better things. Right? It seems so simple. But scholarships can be lost due to injury or poor academic performance. That's all the more reason for you to be sure that the school you attend is a good fit; that you're comfortable with the academic structure and core curriculum; and that you want to be there not only as an athlete, but also as a student.

Research what happens to students after graduation and how many actually graduate. Call faculty or administrators, check the Web site of your school, or visit www.collegeresults.org to find answers to the following questions:

✔ How realistic is the study load for students at the school, particularly for student-athletes?

✔ What the graduation rate of students in general?

✔ What is the graduation rate of student-athletes? How many graduate in four years? In five years?

✔ What percentage of graduates continue in higher education?

✔ What percentage of graduates get jobs? What kind of jobs do they get, and what are their starting salaries?

✔ What is the school's reputation among business leaders in the community?

✔ How proactively does the school career counseling center work with students?

✔ How does the college rate itself in terms of preparing students for graduation and life after graduation?

✔ How many student-athletes turn pro after graduation? (Continue asking this question throughout your academic career — the answer will keep your feet on the ground and remind you that getting an education is key.)

The Web site mentioned earlier, www.collegeresults.org, will give you graduation rates and other information for your college.

Paying attention to athletic success and coaching changes

Sometimes when you want something badly enough, you can easily overlook indiscretions or problems. People do this in personal relationships, in business, and when choosing schools. Don't let this happen to you. We've cautioned you to be sure that the school you choose is a match for you socially and academically. But you also need to be sure that the athletic program you're joining is one you'll be happy with.

You *can* check up on the athletic department of your potential school-to-be and make good decisions.

Visit the school's Web site, and check out its sports records. It doesn't matter what your parents, friends, or coaches tell you about how well this season or previous seasons have gone. See for yourself. For one thing, how well a sports program does or doesn't do may be a reflection of the coaching staff and, in many cases, coaching changes.

If a sports program does *very* well, certain members of the coaching staff may have the chance to move on to a different school and coaching position. A high turnover rate among coaches is not necessarily a bad thing, because success reaps rewards for coaches who start new programs at other schools. But if you notice that a sports program is continuously struggling and the coaching staff is always turning over, this may indicate serious problems within the athletic department of the school you're considering. And this is a red flag you shouldn't ignore.

Probing colleges on probation

Major-infraction cases are open to the public, and you can find information on them at the school's conference Web site. This is a valuable tool that allows you to type in the name of the school you're researching or a specific time frame. For example, you may want to know what major infractions have occurred in a certain time frame. By keying in this time frame, you'll discover all the schools that have been placed on probation.

Here are the Web addresses you'll need:

- **NCAA:** Go to www2.ncaa.org/legislation_and_governance/compliance and click Legislative Tools for the list of NCAA schools on probation.

- **NAIA:** Go to http://naia.collegesports.com/member-services/legislative.

- **NJCAA:** Go to www.njcaa.org and click NJCAA Office of Eligibility Probation List.

Research is the name of your game now. Even if you don't think there is a problem with your school of interest, check it out to be sure. There is no such thing as too much knowledge.

Chapter 12

Preparing for and Evaluating Each Visit

*Y*ou've narrowed down your list of the colleges you want to attend. Perhaps you've already visited them to get a lay of the land. But now you've been invited for an official visit and an interview. Now it isn't just about whether you would like to go to this school; it's about whether this school is interested in *you*. In this chapter, we help you prepare for a successful interview; we give you suggestions on what types of questions you should be asking school officials and what types of questions you should anticipate being asked by them; and we give you tips on how to be informed and professional in your interview. The rest is up to you!

Getting Ready for the Interview

At this point in the game, you should have already made your lists of what you need and want in a college. You also should have lists of questions to ask students and faculty at the schools you visit (see Chapter 11). Your questions will help you make decisions about the schools from both an academic standpoint (for example, does the school have a good department in the major you're considering?) and a social standpoint (for example, are you comfortable on campus?).

Now you need to make a list of questions to ask the coaches and athletic directors you visit so you can make informed decisions about the schools' athletic programs as well. In addition, you need to anticipate and write down the questions that these people will ask *you*.

After you have a list of questions, practice these question-and-answer sessions with someone (a parent, a high school coach, a mentor) who will give you constructive feedback and suggestions — you don't want to be surprised or confused by a question during your official interview.

The impression you make during your interview will most likely determine whether you receive a letter of admission or rejection. So be prepared: Practice, practice, practice!

When you've been officially invited to a college for an interview, research that school's history, traditions, its president, its faculty, its athletic department, its athletic director, and the coach of your sport. Be sure to get the correct names and titles of anyone with whom you'll be interviewing. (You can look up this information on the college's official Web site.) Getting a person's name or title wrong is a terrible way to begin an interview; it's disrespectful and tells that person that you aren't serious about going to her school.

Find out whether there have been any scandals, any NCAA violations, any student protests or accusations. You can find this information at the NCAA's official Web site:

1. Go to www.ncaa.org.

2. Click Legislation & Governance.

3. Under Helpful Links, click Legislative Services Database (LSDBi).

4. On the left side of the page, click Major Infractions.

   You'll be able to search the database for the school you're interested in.

In doing your research, your goal isn't to humiliate your interviewers by discussing unpleasant or embarrassing episodes in the school's history. Instead, your research will give you broad knowledge about the school's history, traditions, student body, and so on — knowledge that will help you make an educated decision about whether or not you want to attend this school, knowledge that will give you extra confidence in the interview (always a plus), and knowledge that will not go unnoticed by your interviewers.

If your research turns up some potentially negative information, you're entitled to ask questions and get answers — particularly about such issues as NCAA violations and potential probation or rumors that the head coach may be leaving. Don't be afraid to ask the coach, during your interview, how long he intends to stay with the school. Perhaps you wanted to go to this school because of this particular coach. By asking when his coaching contract ends or whether he's being seriously recruited by other schools, you may get information that leads you not to commit to this school. This method isn't foolproof (there's no law that the coach has to tell you everything), but it may at least give you a clue as to what your coach has in mind.

Your research also will demonstrate to school officials that you're seriously interested in their school. If the school you're visiting has special traditions (such as Texas A&M University's 12th Man or Notre Dame's Four Horsemen), you should know about those traditions, just as you should know what (or who) the school's mascot is. Also, many college buildings are named after people who are important to the school's history. If a coach or a faculty member makes a reference to a building or to a name, you should know about it. If you've obviously done your homework and know about the school, you'll impress the people with whom you interview. It shows you have a real desire to be there.

Asking the Important Questions

In the height of excitement of meeting new coaches, visiting new places, and being flattered by recruitment salesmanship, you can easily become overwhelmed and overlook what may later appear to be pretty big or obvious problems. If you come to your college interview with prepared questions in hand, you can head off many of these problems and make a more informed, intelligent decision about your future. In short, you can prevent decisions you may later regret.

More than 70 percent of college students have experienced varying degrees of such regret about their college choice and about their academic careers. Many of those students are athletes who suddenly wondered "Why didn't I see this when I interviewed with the coaches or college?" or "Why didn't I ask about this before I signed on?"

One student in this situation was a well-known athlete who was being heavily recruited by several high-profile Division I schools. As one of the hottest athletes in the nation, owning two national records and showing great potential as a two-sport athlete, she had her pick of colleges. But she had narrowed her choices down to two schools.

School A had an excellent academic reputation with renowned faculty in her major. Its athletic reputation was equally attractive, with a strong sense of camaraderie among the athletes and coaching staff. School B also boasted academic and athletic acclaim, but it was much closer to her home. Encouraged by her family, she chose School B, believing this was the wiser choice of the two. She and her family had been so enamored with the geographic location of the school that they hadn't paid attention to the relationship between the athletes and coaching staff.

Later, the discouraged athlete acknowledged that she hadn't even noticed the contentious relationship between the athletes and the coach — until it was too late. During her junior and senior years, many of her teammates transferred to other schools. This very tumultuous time stressed her out — both personally and academically. And it could have been prevented.

To avoid such undue stress and potentially damaging decisions, be sure to carefully think about (and then write down) the issues that are important to you in choosing a college — the questions you'll ask a college interviewer.

Following are several examples of questions you should ask. If you practice question-and-answer sessions in *mock interviews* (where you role-play with your parent or a teacher or coach), you'll go into each interview with greater confidence and impress your interviewers. Plus, if you have questions written down, you'll be sure not to forget important questions — and when you write down the answers, you'll be sure to remember everything you were told and impressions that you formed.

Bringing notes to an interview is a great idea. Rather than looking nervous or childish, you'll appear well prepared and eager to have all your questions answered.

Here are some important questions to ask the coach:

- ✔ What positions will I play on your team?
- ✔ Who else are you recruiting for my position?
- ✔ Will I be redshirted my first year?
- ✔ What expectations do you have for training and conditioning?
- ✔ How would you best describe your coaching style?
- ✔ When does the head coach's contract end?
- ✔ What percentage of players on scholarship graduate in four years?

> ✔ What percentage of students return after their freshman year?
>
> ✔ What is the student-to-faculty ratio?
>
> ✔ What is the typical class size?
>
> ✔ How much time will I be allowed for studying?
>
> ✔ Will I be required to live on campus throughout my athletic participation?
>
> ✔ How long does my scholarship last?
>
> ✔ What happens to my scholarship/financial aid if I'm injured?
>
> ✔ What happens to my scholarship if there is a change in coaches?

 You can find more questions regarding athletics, academics, financial aid, and college life by visiting the NCAA Initial-Eligibility Clearinghouse Web site. Go to www.ncaa.org, click Prospective Student-Athletes, and then click The Guide for College-Bound Student-Athletes. Appendix C of the NCAA guide has "Questions to Ask as You Consider Colleges."

 To keep your questions — and your thoughts — organized, write each question on a 3-x-5-inch note card. Be sure to leave space on each card to write your answers.

Giving Intelligent Answers to the Questions You're Asked

Being able to answer intelligently the questions coaches and staff ask you is as important as asking intelligent questions of them, because it shows that you care about your education and you care about attending the school you're visiting.

 Remarkably, one of the most common questions asked by athletic directors and coaches remains the biggest stumper among student-athletes: What are your needs, and how can our school provide for those needs? Coaches and staff want to see that you have the answers to those questions. They want to know that you want to be at *their* school. They need to know that you feel committed to what the school has to offer and are excited to be part of their team. Shrugging and saying only that you want to play doesn't inspire interviewers with great confidence about your dedication, and it certainly won't help you when the time comes for them to make the critical decisions about who to accept and who to deny.

Other questions to anticipate include the following:

- ✔ Why are you interested in this college?
- ✔ What are you interested in studying at this college?
- ✔ What are your postcollege goals?
- ✔ What are your strengths?
- ✔ What are your weaknesses?
- ✔ How do you handle adversity?
- ✔ What do you do in your spare time? What are your other interests?
- ✔ What was the last book you read?
- ✔ Who is your favorite author, and why?
- ✔ Tell me about yourself. How would your best friend describe you?
- ✔ In what ways have you served in your community?
- ✔ What are some of your concerns about the nation/world today? If you could change one thing in the world, what would it be?
- ✔ Why should I choose you over the other student-athletes competing for your spot?
- ✔ What are your plans if you're accepted at this institution?
- ✔ Do you have any questions?

Yes, coaches *will* ask you questions about your outside interests. They want athletes on their team who care about things other than just the sport they play. One reason for this is that student-athletes who focus only on their sport are more likely to burn out. Having outside interests makes you not only more interesting and appealing as a person, but also more reliable and solid as an athlete. To borrow from the movie *Jerry Maguire,* it completes you.

Nailing the Interview

When the big day comes, it's important to set the stage for success. You've put a lot of work into this interview, and you want to be sure to get out of it all the information you need. Still, there is no need to be nervous — as long as you're prepared and practiced. This is not a pass/fail test; it's just a conversation (albeit a somewhat formal conversation).

Come prepared to ask and answer questions, but be sure that your questions are appropriate for this college and not generic questions that you've simply memorized from sample question lists. Be prepared to talk about yourself, about your strengths and weaknesses. You want to be spontaneous and at ease, but not arrogant. *Remember:* There is a fine line between confidence and arrogance; you want the former, not the latter.

You can bolster your confidence through practice and moral support. If having your parents with you at the interview would give you more confidence, you can bring them — *as long as they allow you to do all the talking.* An interviewer shouldn't mind having an extra set of ears in the room — but well-intentioned parents can quickly become intrusive and disruptive. Your parents should be there only as moral support.

Even if you aren't sure that this is the school you want to attend, you should try to make a good impression in case you decide you do want to apply. And even if you're pretty sure that you *don't* want to attend this school, you should approach this interview — indeed, every interview — as an opportunity to perfect your interviewing skills.

To ensure that your interview is a success, here are a few tips:

- ✔ **Make sure you know exactly where the interview is being held.** Call before the interview to get directions (then make a practice run so there are no surprises), get the name and title of the person interviewing you, and find out how long you'll be there (again, no surprises).

- ✔ **Arrive on time.** In fact, you should arrive at least 15 minutes before your interview in order to give yourself time to unwind and relax (and to find a parking space). Also, check with the receptionist to be sure you know the proper pronunciation and title of the person interviewing you. (Mispronouncing someone's name is a big no-no.)

- ✔ **Be polite to the receptionist and any office staff.**

- ✔ **When you enter the interview room, introduce yourself, and greet the interviewer with a firm handshake and a smile.**

- ✔ **Maintain eye contact and body language that says, "I'm interested and alert."** Sit up straight, and lean toward the interviewer to show interest (but don't lean on the desk). Don't cross your arms; you'll seem bored or unenthusiastic.

- ✔ **Dress appropriately and professionally.** Men should wear a suit or a jacket and tie. Women should not wear short skirts or low-cut blouses. Don't wear too much cologne or perfume.

And don't wear lots of jewelry. (In the case of jewelry and fragrance, less is more.)

✔ **Don't eat, drink, chew gum, or smoke during the interview — even if you're offered something to eat or drink.**

✔ **Bring your questions on note cards and a pen to jot down answers and notes to yourself.** Be sure the pen has ink, and bring a spare just in case.

✔ **Don't place anything on the interviewer's desk.** This includes your notes; keep those in your lap or in a folder.

✔ **Speak succinctly, and use proper English.** Don't swear or use too much slang.

✔ **Relax!** Remember that a good interview is really just a good conversation. So don't just provide "yes" and "no" answers.

✔ **Be positive.** Highlight the good things from your past. If the interviewer brings up negative experiences, try to focus on what you've learned from your mistakes or from adversity. Remember that problems can be viewed as challenges.

✔ ***Always* be honest.** Lies will come back to haunt you.

✔ **Above all else, just be yourself.**

After Your Interview

After your interview, send a thank-you note to the person with whom you interviewed. This demonstrates that you're courteous and mature, and it reinforces the impression you made in the mind of the interviewer. *Remember:* The more interest you show in the school, the more interest the school will show in you.

Before you leave the interviewer's office, be sure to ask for her business card. This way, you'll have the correct spelling of her name and correct title to use in your thank-you note.

As soon as you return to your hotel room or home, review and rewrite the notes you took during the interview. By rewriting the notes right away, you can add notations about the impressions that are still fresh in your mind. Plus, when you're rewriting your notes, you may notice something that you missed before.

Now that you've interviewed with some school officials and visited some different campuses, you have the raw data — in your notes — to help you choose the school that's right for you.

You need to look first for a college that will allow you to accomplish your academic and personal goals. Some of the factors that may affect your decision include

- ✔ The academic major(s) you're interested in
- ✔ The school's academic reputation
- ✔ How prepared you'll be for graduate or professional school when you finish undergrad work
- ✔ The size of the school
- ✔ How close the school is to your hometown
- ✔ The setting of the school (urban, rural, small town, and so on)
- ✔ Campus life (for example, is there a big Greek system? do most of the students go home on the weekends or stay on campus? do they focus more on partying than on schoolwork?)
- ✔ Residential opportunities (dorms, apartments, and so on)

Ask yourself about your motivation to attend that school: Do you want to attend this school to have the chance to do something you've never done before, the chance to demonstrate your independence? Or are you just doing what is expected of you?

You also need to look for a college that will allow you to accomplish your athletic goals. You'll need to be honest with yourself when you assess your own abilities. You can consider other determining factors by asking yourself a number of questions (and being honest with your answers):

- ✔ Will I be allowed to play more than one sport at that school, if that's what I want to do? (Playing two sports would be a possibility in Division III, for example, but probably not in Division I.)
- ✔ Will I have a scholarship or financial aid?
- ✔ How do I relate to the coaching staff?
- ✔ How I describe the coaching style? How do I feel about that coaching style?
- ✔ How do I relate to the other student-athletes?
- ✔ What positions would I play on the team?
- ✔ Who are the other players competing for my position? Describe them. What years are they in?
- ✔ Will I be likely to play at the school? If not, is it more important for me to be part of a bigger, more prestigious program, even though I may ride the bench?

✔ What are the physical requirements?

✔ What is the time commitment required?

✔ What percentage of players graduate in four years? What percentage of players graduate?

✔ What is the academic support for athletes at this college?

✔ What is the typical day for a student-athlete? A typical semester?

✔ Will I be required to live on campus for my entire athletic participation?

✔ And the ultimate question: If I'm injured and can never compete again, will I accomplish the rest of my goals and be happy at this school?

Evaluate how you answered these questions. Look to see where your focus is. College is much like athletic training: You must be dedicated and passionate about the long-term goals. As an athlete, you want to hone your skills, make great plays, and be an asset to your team. As a student, you want to do the same.

Your successes on the field or court are seasonal, but your college degree will be with you for a lifetime.

Part IV
Committing to a School

The 5th Wave   By Rich Tennant

"I can see the advantage, but I'm pretty sure helium-filled shoes aren't regulation."

In this part . . .

You'll better understand the process of recruiting and signing a National Letter of Intent *before* you sign a financial-aid agreement. Before you sign *any* contract, you need to understand what you're signing. In this part, we remind you that, although this is an exciting time for you and your family, you need to consider a variety of issues before signing. Your parents should be a big part of this process — but, in the end, you're doing this for *you*.

Chapter 13

Negotiating a Financial-Aid Agreement

. . . .

In This Chapter

▶ Understanding the terms of a financial-aid agreement

▶ Knowing what kind of deals you may be offered

▶ Negotiating the best deal for you

▶ Talking to the right people

. . . .

This is it! You've been working and waiting for this moment. Being offered a financial-aid agreement between you and a college or university is a moment that should preview great things to come: an excellent education; more-intense competition; a possible platform for professional athletics; and, you hope, a financial break for you and your family.

In this chapter, we show you how to read a financial-aid offer and close the best deal for you and your family.

Reading the Agreement

Remarkably, every year, every season, nearly every minute, someone signs a financial-aid agreement without understanding the terms — and without reading the fine print. Even more remarkably, because an agreement is too long or too confusing, people often happily accept the school's watered-down explanation of what the agreement means.

"Here, just sign here. All this says is blah, blah, blah." And people sign. They sign because they want to believe they're being given the best deal possible and that they're being told the truth. But the stakes are too high simply to sign away a major component of your future — in this case, your education and athletic career.

Reading between the lines

Financial-aid agreements are not meant to be confusing, but legalities and the school's obligation to protect its interests (and you as the student-athlete) often require a lot of words.

Understanding the terms that are presented in the offer is critical. Here are some terms that may be in your financial-aid agreement, along with what they mean for you:

- **Cost of attendance:** An amount calculated by the financial-aid office at the school, using federal regulations. It includes the total cost of tuition, fees, room, board, books, supplies, transportation, and other expenses related to attendance at the institution.

- **Counter:** A student who is receiving institutional financial aid that counts toward the maximum financial-aid limitations in a sport.

- **Full grant-in-aid:** Financial aid that consists of tuition, fees, room, board, and required course-related books.

- **Initial counter:** A counter who is receiving countable financial aid in a sport for the first time.

- **Institutional aid:** All funds administered by the college or university. This includes, but is not limited to, any scholarship, grant, tuition waiver, or loan. It also includes any aid from the government or private sources if the school is responsible for selecting the recipient or determining the amount of aid.

- **Period of the award:** The period of the award starts on the first day of classes for a semester or quarter, or the first day of practice, whichever is earlier. The period of award ends at the conclusion of the period set forth in the financial-aid agreement, which is usually the last day of classes for a semester or quarter. The grant-in-aid may not be awarded for more than one academic year.

 Signing an agreement should be a time for serious thought and careful consideration. There should be no one but a trusted adviser whose first interest is your future looking over your shoulder as you read the agreement and make your decision.

Understanding what you're signing

The financial-aid agreement is the contract you sign that commits the school to providing you financial assistance to attend the college or university in return for your playing your sport. It is a legally binding document signed by you, the athletic director, and the director of financial aid at the school. Because it is a legally binding document, as soon as you sign it and return it to the school, it becomes official.

Before you sign anything, you need to know what the school is offering. For example, is the scholarship for one semester (fall or spring term only) or for one full year? Make sure you know what the scholarship will cover. Is it just tuition, fees, and books — or is it only room and board? Some percentage may go to pay for tuition and fees, and the remainder may go toward room and board — the agreement will spell all this out.

When the financial-aid agreement has been signed and returned to the school, the school can increase the value of the scholarship before the beginning of the semester or quarter, whichever is earlier, but the school may *not* reduce it — without just cause.

Your scholarship may be terminated. Specifically, under NCAA rules, your scholarship can be immediately canceled or removed for the following reasons:

- ✔ You become ineligible for intercollegiate competition.

- ✔ You fraudulently misrepresent *any* information on an application for assistance, a financial-aid agreement, or the National Letter of Intent.

- ✔ You engage in conduct warranting substantial disciplinary action.

- ✔ You voluntarily withdraw from your sport.

These negative outcomes will likely be listed on the financial-aid agreement, but keep them in mind in case they aren't.

It is also important to remember that coaches may have even more stringent rules about scholarships being terminated, even though they may not take effect immediately. Case in point: Some coaches have rules that strictly prohibit drinking alcohol during the season. If your coach has this rule, and if you violate the rule, you could lose your scholarship.

Some rules may not be in writing, so you must make sure you know the coach's expectations for keeping your scholarship. If your scholarship is reduced or cut, the school must inform you of this in writing and give you the opportunity to appeal this decision. The committee that hears the appeal must be made up of individuals outside the athletic department. This is important to know in case you feel your scholarship has been canceled or reduced unfairly.

Knowing what kinds of scholarships are typically offered

Everywhere you turn, it seems like a teammate or friend is being offered some kind of scholarship, but remember: Not all scholarships are the same. As we explain in Chapter 2, a scholarship offer is often based on what the coach is *allowed* to offer.

College sports are divided into two categories: head-count sports and equivalency sports (see Chapter 2). At most Division I schools, scholarships in head-count sports are often full scholarships, because even if you receive only a small scholarship in these sports, it counts as one of the maximum that is permitted. For example, in women's tennis, if a student-athlete receives a scholarship worth only $500, her scholarship counts as one of the eight scholarships permitted by the NCAA in that sport. For equivalency sports (such as track, swimming, and wrestling), full scholarships are rare — so rare, in fact, that scholarships in these sports are typically offered based on percentages so that the overall team limit can be accurately tracked and determined.

Typically, the coach works with a member of the school's financial-aid office to ensure the accuracy of the individual and team limits. If a school awards more scholarships than are permitted, it can be slapped with penalties that will require scholarship reductions in the future.

For a complete explanation of the difference between head-count and equivalency sports, refer to Chapter 2.

Identifying what you want or need in terms of financial relief is important. You may vie for books rather than training, for a specific degree rather than board. You and the college recruiter may be able to reach an agreement (in terms of financial aid) to cover your academic costs.

Talk to your recruiter and high school counselors about what you want. You never know what may be available until you ask.

Head coaches are sometimes like general managers of professional sports teams. ***Remember:*** The overall financial-aid team limits apply to each sport (for example, Division I baseball = 11.7), and each student-athlete is limited to a certain amount of financial aid. (See Chapter 2 for more info.) Imagine that the overall financial-aid team limit is the salary cap for the particular team and that the scholarship that the student-athlete is receiving is his own salary. The scholarships the players receive cannot be for more than one year, so the financial-aid agreement can be equated to a contract. Each year, the head coach has to sit down and figure out how much of the "salary cap" he has returning for the next year and how much can be allocated to new players via "contracts." And the negotiating begins. . . .

Understanding the Rules of Negotiating

If you're receiving multiple offers for a full scholarship, this section probably won't apply to you because you won't need to negotiate. A full scholarship is the most you're able to receive.

According to the dictionary, *negotiate* means "to confer with another or others in order to come to terms or reach an agreement." You may not think this definition applies to the world of athletic scholarships, but believe it or not, it does. If you've had the privilege (or the challenge) of purchasing a car, you may get a similar feeling during this process.

The negotiating process may occur every year for you, because the scholarships are renewed each year. For example, you may improve as a player each year and, based on your performance, every off season you can negotiate with your coach to receive more financial aid.

Honing a poker face

With the increased popularity of poker on television these days, you may think that a poker face includes sunglasses, a hat pulled way down, and earphones connected to your iPod. In the world of college scholarships, however, it means keeping your cool and not negotiating with emotion.

More often than not, a coach is going to offer you less than what you (or your parents) think you deserve, because that's human nature. Don't show your disappointment if this happens. If a coach offers you a 25 percent scholarship, and you feel you deserve at least 40 percent, be prepared to explain exactly *why* you feel this way. Don't simply ask, "Can you make it 40 percent?" Give the coach reasons you should get a better deal.

Here are some common reasons that you might request more athletic aid:

✔ I play a skill position that deserves more.

✔ I can play right away and help the team improve.

✔ I'm a local player who is well known in the community.

✔ I'm out of state, so the cost for me to come here is greater.

You and your parents will want to discuss these suggestions and other points to make about your special skills in case you feel you're being undervalued by the offer.

One more thing to remember: Because the coach probably has gone through this process a lot, don't expect him to be easily persuaded. In some cases, the coach simply may not be able to give you a bigger scholarship because of the NCAA limits.

You and your family need to know what you want and should expect from a recruiter before you move into the negotiating process.

Separating fact from fiction

You and your family meet with a recruiter to discuss your possible scholarship. He offers you a partial scholarship, but you've done your research. You know this school needs an athlete of your caliber, playing your position. You know from previous conversations that this particular school is very interested in you, and from your recent official on-campus visit, you believe that you would fit well with the team and coaching staff. Yet, the recruiter can offer only a partial scholarship.

You've seen this routine before on television, where the car salesman claims to be on the side of the consumer but says he just needs to check with his boss about the deal you and he just made. As the camera follows the salesman, we see that he merely goes around the corner; eats a doughnut; drinks some coffee; checks his watch; makes some random slashing marks on his pad of paper of facts and figures; and, after some time, returns to the buyer, making claims of being overruled by the nonexistent boss, who has a counteroffer —always a higher price.

We like to think this is how all salespeople operate. But the reality is that your scholarship — or its availability — may already be determined by NCAA rules and regulations.

We talked to coaches, recruiters, parents, student-athletes, and athletic directors about negotiating financial-aid offers, and some common themes came up again and again. Consider this your reality checklist:

✔ **Recruiters can't always make the final decision.** Many times, the offer they give is the only one they're permitted based on the amount of scholarships they have to give. One of the biggest complaints we hear from recruiters is how often they've made a scholarship offer only to be told later by their own department that there is no such money. Sometimes, even the recruiter is unaware of the financial allowances for the college.

✔ **Just because you're the best in high school doesn't always mean you're the best in college or, for that matter, the best for a particular team.**

✔ **Listen to a few trusted allies — such as your parents, high school counselor, and other athletes who have done their own research or have been through the system.**

✔ **If you don't like an offer, it's okay to ask to renegotiate.** Recruiters will respect this process. However, be sure to act respectfully and intelligently.

✔ **Keep in mind that money isn't everything.** Some of the best scholarships offer education (in the form of books and tuition fees) as the selling point.

✔ **Scholarships don't have to be strictly athletic scholarships.** A good recruiter can help you work with the financial-aid department to cover other costs.

Mentioning what other schools are offering

Let's say you've gotten an offer from School B for 25 percent, but you feel you're worth 40 percent. If School A has offered you 40 percent, you may want to tell the School B coach that you want to attend his school, but because of finances, you may have to choose School A because School A has offered you more athletic aid.

Chances are the coach will react in one of the following ways:

✔ Tell you that the offer he made to you is as high as he can go, and you need to make a decision based on that

✔ Increase your scholarship amount to match what School A is offering you

✔ Negotiate with you to increase your scholarship offer, but not quite to what you wanted

✔ Wish you well at the other school and take back his original offer (leaving you no choice but to go to School A)

Using this other-offer strategy is very much a gamble and could backfire on you, so make sure you're comfortable mentioning another school's offer to a coach.

Keep in mind that coaches talk to one another a lot, and if you aren't being honest about an offer from another school, there is a very good chance you could be found out. Just as you expect a coach to be honest with you regarding other athletes he may be recruiting, you have to be honest with him when it comes to discussing scholarship offers from other schools.

Resisting the Pressure

You've done the research. You've selected your team of trusted advisors. You know what colleges you want, the degree you hope to earn, and the direction you want to move in. It's all laid out in front of you, and you feel pretty secure about your decisions. Then comes the pressure.

Suddenly, a coach with an excellent track record and a background of championships and experience is telling you how things should go, what you should do, how you can make things happen. But what he's saying isn't the way you had planned it, and suddenly, you and your family are very confused.

Everything looks great on paper. But now you're talking to a seasoned coach who knows what he wants — and it's another matter altogether. What do you do when the coach puts on the pressure? Read on for answers.

When the coach pressures you to sign

Several years ago, the NCAA membership was looking for a way to cut costs within their athletic departments. This was a few years before multimillion contracts for coaches became run of the mill. So, to cut recruiting travel costs — and to the delight of express-delivery companies all over the country — the NCAA passed a rule prohibiting schools from delivering the National Letter of Intent (NLI) or an athletic-scholarship agreement to a prospect in person. Although reducing costs was the initial rationale, there was another reason for the NCAA's travel prohibition: to reduce a coach's ability to pressure a student-athlete into signing an agreement.

This prohibition applies only to in-person delivery *off campus*. The coach can give you an NLI and/or financial-aid statement in person if you're visiting the campus. You can even sign it right there, if you want. (Many administrators, however, frown upon this practice because the implication that the coach pressured you to do so is tough to defend.)

Although it has never been publicly addressed, coaches pressuring athletes to sign has been a huge problem. Over the years, families have claimed to have been bullied or tricked into various agreements. So, while the NCAA ruling appeared to be a logical solution, the problem remains.

You may be saying to yourself that you would never allow a coach to pressure you into signing with a school before you were ready.

Are you committed?

The 1994 documentary *Hoop Dreams* is an example of the kind of intimidation we're talking about in this chapter. In one scene, the student-athlete, William Gates, is at his home, and the then–head coach of Marquette, Kevin O'Neill, is making an in-home recruiting visit, trying to persuade Gates to commit to Marquette.

O'Neill basically tells Gates that he is recruiting six or seven student-athletes for three spots, but if Gates tells the coach that he is coming to Marquette, O'Neill will stop recruiting the other players at Gates's position. He goes on to say that if Gates doesn't commit and the other players he's recruiting go elsewhere in the meantime, O'Neill will have to answer to his athletic director and president if the team struggles. This discussion takes place in front of Gates's mother and brother (a former college basketball player himself).

O'Neill didn't tell Gates anything inaccurate, and the head coach is definitely under pressure himself to win and put fans in the stands. But telling a 17-year-old or 18-year-old that if he doesn't commit to a particular school, his decision may impact the coach's job is giving a young athlete information that's tough to deal with. That pressure is the kind the NCAA tries to prevent.

Ultimately, Gates did sign with Marquette and lettered for three years, but he never became an NBA star, as he had hoped. He did, however, graduate from Marquette with a degree in communications and now works in a ministry in his hometown.

Remember: Understanding your rights as a student-athlete is essential. You should not be pressured to make your final decisions in the presence of a coach. Had William Gates's story taken place today, he would have been allowed to review the scholarship offer alone with his mother and brother. Who knows what his ultimate decision might have been?

But you might think differently if the coach says, "If you don't commit to me by such-and-such date, I'm going to have to offer your scholarship to someone else."

If you're feeling pressured by a coach, and you aren't ready to make a commitment, the best advice we can give you is to be honest and let the coach know you need some more time. Even though you run the risk of the coach's withdrawing the offer, you'll at least know you won't be making a rushed decision. (Chances are that if this is your situation, you have other offers on the table, which is why the decision may not be an easy one.)

If you don't commit, will someone else get your slot?

Recruiting is often a game that involves sales and timing. If a coach is recruiting more than one person at the position you play, your slot may be taken by someone else who commits before you.

A volleyball coach may need only one setter for her team, but she may be recruiting *four* girls she thinks can play that position. More often than not, the coach will meet with each recruit separately, letting each one know that there are four girls being recruited for the setter position and that whichever one commits first is the one the coach will go with. When that commitment has been made, the other three will no longer be recruited.

This strategy is also a risk for the coach. If one of the girls commits, and the coach stops recruiting the other three, what happens if the committed recruit changes her mind? The three whom the coach stopped recruiting may have already committed or signed with other schools, and the coach may be back to square one.

This is why the recruiting process is sometimes compared to the game of chess, with the coach and recruit trying to determine what the other is thinking or what the next move will be.

If the school sends you a National Letter of Intent and/or a financial-aid agreement, you're guaranteed a scholarship (even if you sign it on the very last permissible day to sign), regardless of how many others have signed ahead of you. The school's athletic director is responsible for making sure that the program does not exceed the overall financial-aid limits for that sport.

You'll be asked to make many decisions, and knowing which option is best is difficult. But this is why you have to do your research. You have to know where you want to go to school and, most important, why. When you know that you want to go to medical school and that playing with State U. will make this possible, or that you want a degree in business *and* your chance to play in the big leagues, you can be more comfortable about your future. You're not going to a specific college just because someone else wants you to or because you like its colors. You have a plan. You foresee a future.

With that said, why wait? Signing your National Letter of Intent or financial-aid agreement is your best way of ensuring a scholarship. This is your contract. Go for it!

Chapter 14

Making the Verbal Commitment

*N*ot all student-athletes are asked to make a verbal commitment. Sometimes, the process moves so quickly that there is
no time for a verbal commitment. It may be that the next thing you
know, you're signing on the dotted line. Others make a verbal commitment to more than one school. It happens — and there's nothing improper about that.

Because a verbal commitment is just that — verbal — there is no
binding contract between you and the institution. Such verbal
agreements are more common in football and basketball, but they
may occur for athletes in any sport. For that reason alone, you
need to understand what verbal commitments are about and how
you should handle them. In this chapter, we fill you in.

The Big Decision: Making Your Choice

What are your long-term goals? In Chapters 10 and 11, we show
you the importance of researching schools to determine which is
the best one for you. In the middle of this process, many of your
goals, and even decisions that you thought you had already made,
may change when you're face to face with a recruiter. Suddenly,
here is a person who is excited about you and what you have to
offer her program.

Recruiting college athletes is a business. Recruiters and coaches are excited about you as an athlete, not so much as a person. They aren't happy for you because you're a swell guy or gal, or because you worked so hard and deserve this great opportunity. In reality, you represent a better future for their sports program. You promise new strength or talent. Although you may have a clear idea of where you want to be in four years, the recruiter's enthusiasm and finely tuned sales pitch can suddenly alter everything.

For this reason, before that recruiter arrives at your door, get out the old pen and paper again, and create a list of questions you need to answer for yourself — this list will prepare you for the surprise offer that may lie ahead. *Remember:* To answer these questions fully, you'll need to discuss them with your family, friends, and coaches.

Think of yourself as an incoming freshman student-athlete at College X, and ask yourself the following questions:

- **How prepared are you for college academics?** Will the demands at College X, with its reputation for academic excellence, be too much? Would you fit in better at a less demanding college?

- **Are you really ready to play college sports in light of the added pressure of a scholarship, demanding coaches, and the need to make the minimum grades to remain eligible?**

- **Are you able to compare College X to other colleges?** If not, you need to do some more homework.

- **When you're able to compare College X to other schools, have you assessed the sports and academic records of each school on your short list?** Have you tried to identify the school that offers you the best balance given your academic record and commitment to your sport?

- **Is it time to look again at your short list?** Maybe you need to investigate other schools in search of the best academic and athletic balance. Have you considered creating a second-choice list?

- **Have you considered your financial position?** No matter how attractive College X may be, it has to be affordable. *Remember*: Not everyone gets a full ride — you may receive only a partial scholarship. Will a partial scholarship work with your available resources?

- **Looking beyond graduation, does College X offer you a clear path toward what you want?** Do you hope to play pro ball? Do you want to pursue a particular profession? How will College X help you achieve your goals, whatever they are?

Answering these questions will give you a better idea of where you hope to be in the three, four, or five years ahead, when you graduate. With a carefully designed plan for what you want, you'll have confidence when talking one on one with a recruiter.

Getting advice

Before a decision-making meeting with a recruiter, supplement what you know about College X and other schools on your list with information from those who have been in your shoes, especially athletes you know from playing your sport. You'll get your best information from athletes who know you on the field, on the court, or in the pool.

While you were making your official visits, you asked about the positives and negatives of each school. But you can't realistically expect the host (athlete) to dish out the dirt. A better strategy is to talk to alumni or to find a potential teammate during the off season to ask questions about the program.

Perhaps the best question-and-answer we've heard came from a top, nationally ranked track-and-field athlete, whom we'll call Joe. Joe began asking other track athletes about a smaller Division II school. He asked them, "What if the program was dropped? Would you still want to come to this school?" They told Joe, "No way." They didn't like the geographic location and weren't that interested in the school itself (because of its traditions and academic reputation). With that in mind, Joe refocused his search.

Can I commit to more than one school?

Because the verbal commitment isn't binding, you can commit to one, five, even ten schools. But what is the fallout from this strategy? Although you may be thinking you don't want to rule out any school, is it okay to say yes to so many? Technically, yes, you can — but coaches talk, and if you commit to more than one school, the coaches may not trust you.

Be forthright with coaches. *Remember:* This is their profession. You want and need coaches to speak openly and honestly with you. And you should do the same with them in return.

Reviewing your notes

Recruiting is business. Let there be no mistake: Providing scholarships and making dollars work is serious business in college athletic departments. Looking for evidence? The hiring and firing of coaches based on personal performance, recruiting, and success are business decisions. So, in your decision-making process, you should think like a business major. Whether you plan to major in physical education, liberal arts, or engineering, you need a business plan for yourself.

By answering the questions you developed earlier in this chapter, you automatically began creating a "business plan." When you initialize the first stage of your "business plan" (by selecting the school you hope to attend based on the information you've gathered), you can feel more confident about the path to and beyond graduation.

The business plan requires information that you've gathered about those colleges that meet your academic interests and that have a strong program in your sport. You've also factored in your criteria for geographic and social considerations. Finally, you've researched their scholarship offers, and you can reasonably believe that these colleges will be willing to work with you.

You've also acquired essential information about the process of being recruited from those who went before you. There shouldn't be any surprises in terms of how the recruiter will do his business. You can game it out: He says this, and I say that.

So, you know what you want. But you need a plan that will let you achieve your goals. The best way to carry out your plan is to have a specific list of items to be discussed with a recruiter, who may be a coach:

- ✔ Ask about the recruiting statistics for the recruiter/coach talking to you.

- ✔ Ask about the success of the coach's current and past teams.

- ✔ Be ready and willing to discuss scholarship options.

- ✔ What can you learn from the recruiter about the coaching staff's view of the school's academic standards? Are there tutors to assist athletes who need extra help?

- ✔ Do the athletes on the team you may join generally manage to maintain eligibility?

- ✔ How committed is the coach to giving and getting you a scholarship?

Although this strategy will help you stay on course as you, the coach, and your parents discuss your possible future in college, any promises made are not guarantees! There is nothing legally binding about what you're discussing.

Now it's time to put the plan into effect. Using 3-x-5-inch index cards, write out all your questions, and number them. No matter how silly or insignificant they may seem, if you wondered about something that the recruiter should be able to answer, put it on a card to make sure you remember to ask about it.

Have a backup plan — a Plan B. What is the backup plan? It's your insurance policy. Recruiters will sometimes overpromise regarding scholarships, and it may turn out that the school they represent will not fulfill their promises. In reality, sometimes even a gifted athlete with a strong academic record has a scholarship offer pulled out from under him for reasons that are beyond his control. That's where the backup plan becomes essential. Yes, you're excited about meeting a recruiter to discuss a verbal commitment, but you remember that this is not a binding contract. Therefore, you're more comfortable because your Plan B has a list with two or three other attractive schools on it.

Recognizing that not all that glitters is gold

One of the key elements of your business plan is marketing you, which requires that you maintain communication with the key players. In particular, you must respond to phone calls, e-mails, or letters from the academic and/or athletic side of the school in which you're interested. Don't put off responding if there is a question about your commitment or your potential spot on the team.

According to the former NAIA athletic director of Northwood College, Shawn Winget, prospects often take the recruiting process for granted. In early 2000, Winget recruited a young talent, offering a scholarship. What happened next was unfortunate and unavoidable. "Sometimes, there are cutbacks. I hadn't talked to the kid in six months, and then all of a sudden he calls. I said, 'Who? Eric? Oh, yeah . . . but that was in December. This is June!'" There had been a change in the available funding, and Winget had to call the prospect's father to explain that there was no longer a scholarship offer on the table.

In other cases, there is no gold at all. Overly aggressive recruiters may simply offer something that does not exist. Sadly, not all coaches are completely honest about scholarship money. Although the NCAA, NAIA, and NJCAA do their best to watch out for this kind of behavior, honesty is not the only policy in the recruiting game.

Fortunately, most recruiters are honest and have the best of intentions for the prospect and their families. But even with the best of intentions, a deal can go sour. For example, a head coach in track and field knows that she has three scholarships to offer. She also knows that just because she makes an offer to a student-athlete, it doesn't mean the athlete will accept. Therefore, a more-aggressive coach may offer those three scholarships to as many as six athletes, knowing she won't get every one of them. But what happens when that same coach strikes gold, and all six athletes accept? Someone — maybe you — loses out.

Every year, the NCAA and NAIA investigate claims by disgruntled parents and athletes who claim to have been misled by a recruiter or coach regarding a scholarship — and, indeed, many have. So, how can you protect yourself in all this?

Do your homework. Research the recruiter or coach who is looking at you. Understand his previous record, talk to former athletes, and get whatever you can in writing. When you've decided on the college you want to attend, notify the school right away — and remember, it's not a deal until a scholarship agreement is signed (see Chapter 15).

Going with your gut

Let's talk business strategy again: You've done everything we've covered to this point in the chapter. You've made the lists, done the comparisons, thought hard about what you want to do after graduation, and you're ready to meet the recruiter.

So, the rest of the decision-making process will be a snap, right? Well, maybe and maybe not. You can strategize and strategize, but eventually you'll have to do something about it.

The trick is to stick with your plan, including using those 3-x-5-inch cards.

As we spoke to athletes and parents, we asked about their number-one regret, if they had one, following their face-to-face meetings with a recruiter. They said that, even though they had more questions for the recruiter, they were afraid to ask because:

- They didn't want to appear stupid or uneducated.
- They didn't want to monopolize the recruiter's time.

> ✔ They didn't want to admit they didn't fully understand the process.

Instead, they thought they would figure it out later. Most often, they reported, they didn't — at least not until it was too late.

When you meet with a recruiter or coach, this is your time to clarify concerns, dispel myths, confirm information, and educate yourself about the entire process. Rely on your gut feeling. If this isn't a person you feel comfortable talking to, perhaps this is your clue that you need to find another school.

In particular, if you're talking with a coach from your potential team, you need to feel good about her. You don't want to tie your athletic — and to some degree your academic — future to someone you're not comfortable with. Trust your gut!

Of course, we aren't saying that a coach has to be perfect. Here are some tips to help you make a judgment:

✔ **Coaches should be professional and knowledgeable.** This doesn't mean, however, that they have to know everything. If you ask a question that a coach is unable to answer, this can be a good thing. How quickly and earnestly your coach or recruiter tries to find an answer for your question speaks volumes. She should go that extra mile and do whatever it takes to answer your questions and meet your needs.

✔ **Coaches should be good communicators.** You don't need a fast-talking coach who leaves you with more questions than answers. What you do need is a coach or recruiter who can and will take the time to outline what she wants of you and where she sees you on the field and with the team (both short and long term).

✔ **Trustworthiness and caring are critical qualities.** Your potential coach should leave you with the feeling that this is a person you can later talk to about any problems. Ask yourself, "Will I want to talk to this person about something that's highly personal and that's affecting my ability on the field?"

The Tough Calls: Phoning Your Second and Third Choices

Congratulations! You've made your choice, and you're ready to make the verbal commitment. Now you need to inform the other schools that you've indicated strong interest in another college.

You don't have to tell them before verbally committing to your first choice, but keep in mind that the word will get to them pretty quickly. You want to tell them *before* you commit to your number-one school. By doing this, you show respect and give the other coaches time to reevaluate their own recruiting processes. You also earn respect for yourself as a thoughtful athlete.

Let's face it: No one looks forward to saying, "I've thought about it, and you're not my first choice." That's true whether we're talking about a date to the senior prom or choosing a college. Still, it needs to be done, and your grandmother was right: Honesty is the best policy.

So, what do you say? Try to cover the following points (if they relate to you):

- ✔ I'm calling to tell you that, after a lot of thought, I've decided to accept an offer from College X.

- ✔ I really appreciate the time you've given me. I had a hard time choosing between your program and the one at College X.

- ✔ I would happily recommend your program to any of my teammates — it's a great one. The offer from College X just fit really well with my needs.

- ✔ If the situation changes for some reason, I hope that you'll still consider me for your program.

The last point is especially important, because things can change. Your second and third choices were likely part of your Plan B, and it's in your best interest to leave open the possibility that you'll come back to them. You never know what may happen at College X down the road. . . .

Your reputation as a reliable straight-shooter will be important for the rest of your life. How you handle a difficult task such as making these phone calls is likely to become an important part of your reputation.

Your Last Call: Making the Verbal Commitment

You're assuming that saying "yes" to your first choice will be an easy call. Not always. It depends on various factors, including how much College X wants you, how much attention your decision-making process is getting, and the desires of your new coach. If the recruiting process has been low key, you may only need to call the coach to say, "Thanks for your offer. I accept!"

For the majority of athletes, a local paper will be the only news outlet running the story — after the fact — when the announcement of your college choice is made. In many ways, this is a good thing. It relieves you of the added pressure from family, friends, coaches, and perhaps the general public that comes with making the "right" decision about exactly the "right" college and program.

On the other hand, if for any reason your decision is a big deal, you may decide to have your parents, a coach, or a recruiting service announce your decision. Whoever makes the call, it should be courteous. Assuming that you've already told your second and third choices of your decision, you'll want to acknowledge the other great schools and programs you looked at, whether you name them or not, and make the point that it was a hard choice to make. Needless to say, you also want to be humble in commenting on the contributions that you'll make to the team: "This is a great team, and I just hope that I'll be able to help the program."

Again, remember that a verbal commitment is simply a verbal commitment. There is no *obligation* to let other schools know (although we recommend that you do), just as schools may continue to recruit you. Not until you've signed the National Letter of Intent must coaches stop communicating with you (according to NCAA guidelines).

Whether yours is high profile or a private family affair, it's an exciting opportunity that few get a chance to experience. By communicating openly and honestly with everyone, you respect the entire process.

Planning the Next Steps

You've probably seen TV coverage of some hot new prospect making the announcement in front of a room full of reporters, coaches, and family. "I choose . . ." and the athlete dons a cap with his choice's logo, underlining his intention. Hurray! There is a gasp, applause, and a burst of flashes as photographers record the moment. The work is done, right? Baseball legend Yogi Berra's comment that "It ain't over 'til it's over" is worth remembering.

In reality, the verbal commitment is just a gesture of good faith. Not until you sign on the dotted line does the commitment become official. Before you sign, you still have the opportunity to look at other schools, review your offers, and revisit the checklist we cover earlier. (If you decide to actually visit other schools that interest you, turn to Chapter 10 for more on the rules for visiting schools.)

Keep your "business plan" close by. Continue reviewing your options, focusing especially on the Plan B schools that you've identified. Discussions with your trusted advisors, family, friends, high school coaching staff, and others can be helpful in various ways — for example, helping you get through the waiting.

Also seek their advice on your Plan B thinking. For all you know, your thinking about your career objectives may change, and you may decide you actually prefer another school, whether for the academics or the athletics.

At the same time, you need to stay in touch with College X while their decision-making continues. You don't want them to assume that, because they haven't heard from you, you aren't really interested.

Chapter 15

Understanding the National Letter of Intent

*O*ver the past decade, the first Wednesday in February has almost become a national holiday. In certain parts of the country (the Southeast, for example), this notion may not be too far from the truth. For many, this day calls for a celebration, inviting family, friends, and the press.

So, what is this day? The first Wednesday in February each year is the national signing day for college football. Internet traffic on that day can be compared to major gridlock in Los Angeles because of all the college-football fans scouring the Web to see who signed with their favorite schools and if their local high school stud decided to play close to home or take his talents to a university across the country.

The National Letter of Intent (NLI) is, as they say, big doings around the nation. But what is it? Exactly what is the purpose of this signing, and how will it benefit you? In this chapter, we fill you in.

What Is a National Letter of Intent?

The National Letter of Intent (NLI) is a commitment between you (the prospective student-athlete) and a collegiate institution. An NLI is not issued to a prospect without a scholarship. An individual who has been invited to walk on to a team, but who has not been offered an athletic scholarship, is not permitted to sign an NLI.

The point of the NLI is to bring assurance to the recruiting process. Even though the nuances of the NLI can be complex, its premise isn't that complicated. If you're admitted to a school, and eligible for financial aid and competition per NCAA rules, the school agrees to award you an athletic scholarship for one full academic year. In return, you (the prospect) agree to attend that school for no less than one full academic year.

Some coaches allow a prospect to sign an NLI without an athletic scholarship and then the coach doesn't file the NLI with the proper authority (usually the conference office) because the NLI is invalid. Why? Because many student-athletes think of the NLI as a prestigious thing — and the coaches don't want their nonscholarship athletes to feel slighted. If you don't have a scholarship, and the coach asks you for your NLI, it's just for show — you can sign it or not, whichever you prefer.

Understanding the fine print

The NLI is not associated with the NCAA. It is a form that was created by the Collegiate Commissioners Association as a protection for the universities.

Just as the athletic scholarship you sign is your protection that the school must offer you the scholarship for the specified period of time (not for more than one academic year), the NLI is the school's protection that you'll attend that particular institution for at least one full academic year.

NCAA rules do not permit schools to offer athletic scholarships for more than one academic year. However, that scholarship can be renewed each year for no more than five years.

After you've signed an NLI with a particular school, other colleges and universities that participate in the program are no longer permitted to recruit you. Likewise, you're no longer subjected to recruiting phone calls and contacts, and you aren't allowed to make any more official visits.

The NLI program is *voluntary* for schools — however, more than 500 Division I and Division II colleges and universities participate in the program. The Ivy League, the National Service Academies (Air Force, Army, and Navy), and some of the schools in the Patriot League are Division I schools that do *not* subscribe to the NLI. No Division III schools, NAIA institutions, or junior colleges participate in the NLI program. You can find a complete list of NLI member schools and conferences on the NLI Web site (`www.national-letter.org`).

If you're under the age of 21, your parent or legal guardian is required to cosign the NLI with you. This rule applies even if you don't currently live with your parent or legal guardian.

What if your parent or legal guardian lives in a different location from you? Not to worry. You can get the signatures by faxing the NLI to your parent or legal guardian and have him or her fax it back to you. Be sure to make three copies, and send all three to your parent or legal guardian. When all three copies have been signed, you should keep one for your records and send the other two back to the school. The institution is responsible for forwarding at least one copy to the conference office.

The NLI is a binding document. Before you sign it, make sure that attending this school on this scholarship is what you want. By this time, you and your family should have made a long list of pros and cons. You should have discussed all your options and feel strongly about the school you're going to attend before signing on the dotted line.

If you do sign a NLI, you can meet the obligations of it in one of two ways:

- ✔ **Attend the institution with which you signed for at least one full academic year.**

- ✔ **Graduate from a junior college if you signed an NLI during your senior year in high school or during your first year of junior college, as long as it is not the year you are scheduled to graduate.** What that means is if you sign an NLI during your senior year in high school or during your first year of junior college, you can attend a different college that participates in the NLI program without penalties *if* you graduate from a junior college first.

You are not required to sign an NLI in order to receive a scholarship. However, most coaches will want you to sign one because the NLI binds you to the school for at least one full academic year. Don't sign just because you think this is something you have to do — if signing an NLI doesn't feel right to you, don't do it.

Although you may have a verbal offer from and/or make a verbal commitment to a school, verbal agreements are not legally binding, and they're often broken — both by the schools and by the athletes — prior to the actual NLI signing process.

Letters of intent outside the NCAA

What if you sign a letter of intent with a junior college or an NAIA school? Only NCAA Division I and II schools are members of the NLI program, so you can sign an NLI with a Division I or Division II school even you previously signed a letter of intent with a junior college or NAIA institution.

There is not a national letter of intent program for the NAIA; each school determines its requirements if it chooses to have a letter of intent. The NJCAA does have a letter of intent program and its requirements and penalties are similar to the NLI program. You can find a sample NJCAA letter of intent and scholarship agreement form at the following Web site: `www.njcaa.org/njcaaforms/050823_4_Letter ofIntent%20Compressed.pdf`.

If you do sign a letter of intent with either an NAIA school or a junior college, make sure you understand the differences between these letters and the NLI program before you sign more than one letter.

In most sports, when a verbal commitment has been made by the prospect, coaches from other schools may no longer recruit the prospect — this is very common in volleyball and soccer. High-profile sports such as football and men's and women's basketball, however, usually have a slightly different philosophy. When a prospect makes a verbal commitment in those sports, other schools *increase* their recruiting efforts and try to persuade the athlete to change his mind.

You are not permitted to sign a second NLI if you decide to transfer from one four-year school to another. You are permitted to sign only one NLI during your athletic career, and if you decide to transfer to another school, you would be permitted to sign only a financial-aid agreement with the second institution.

Knowing what you're committing to

The NLI is a legally binding document, and as soon as you sign one, other schools are not permitted to recruit you. For many athletes, signing an NLI is a relief — it means no more phone calls, letters, or heavy recruiting from other universities. And no more agonizing over which college to attend — the decision is made.

You are signing the NLI with an institution, not a specific coach or athletics program. If the coach leaves, you are not released from your obligation. Many times, a student-athlete who is excited about training and playing under a specific coach learns only after he or she has signed an NLI that the coach will be leaving the institution for greener pastures (or fields). The document is binding, and you will be expected to attend that school for at least one year, regardless of the coaching staff.

Failure to meet your obligation to the NLI could result in severe eligibility penalties if you want to transfer to another NLI school. See the nearby sidebar "A deal is a deal" for a real-life example.

Where do you turn if you have questions about the NLI? The answer is the Southeastern Conference (SEC). The SEC handles the daily administrative duties of the National Letter of Intent program on behalf of the Collegiate Commissioners Association. The phone number at the SEC is 205-458-3000, but the NLI Web site (www.national-letter.org) is the best place to start.

A deal is a deal

In November 2002, four highly recruited prospects all signed National Letters of Intent to play basketball at the University of Kansas starting in the fall of 2003. In April 2003, however, the longtime, successful head coach at Kansas decided to leave the school and become the head coach at his alma mater, the University of North Carolina.

All four of the recruits were shocked by the coach's departure, and three readily admitted that their main reason for choosing to sign with Kansas was the opportunity to play for the now-departed coach. Because the four had signed NLIs, they were obligated to attend Kansas for one full year. Their other options were to attend a junior college and then transfer to another Division I school or request a mutual release agreement from Kansas.

Three of the four were named to at least one high school All-American team, and all four were star players who could have chosen to attend a number of schools, so Kansas was reluctant to grant any relief from the NLIs that they signed. All four eventually attended Kansas for the 2003–2004 academic year, and all played on the basketball team.

After the 2003–2004 year, one transferred to the University of Louisville, while another transferred to the University of California at Berkeley. Both were required to sit out during the 2004–2005 season according to NCAA transfer rules and are eligible to play in 2005–2006. The remaining two stayed at Kansas during the 2004–2005 season, but only one is left now — the other recently transferred to the University of New Mexico and will have to sit out until the 2006–2007 season.

What would have happened if those basketball players decided not to attend Kansas and wanted to go to another school that participates in the NLI program?

(continued)

(continued)

They would have lost one year of eligibility and would have been required to serve a year of residence (sit out one year) at the second school. The same penalties would apply if they didn't fulfill the terms of the NLI completely (for example, they didn't attend the school with which they signed for at least one full year).

Of course, there are extenuating circumstances or situations beyond your control that may force you to not meet the obligations of the NLI. These could range from family emergencies to financial hardships. If you're unable to fulfill the terms of the NLI, the penalty can be waived or reduced by sending a Release Request Form to the athletic director at the school where you signed the NLI, requesting a complete release. If this request is denied, and you don't receive a complete release from the NLI, you may appeal to the NLI Steering Committee. The Steering Committee has the ability to grant a complete or partial release from the NLI.

You have other options if you choose not to attend the school at which you signed a NLI. You can attend any other school that does not participate in the NLI program (for example, an NAIA school or a junior college) without incurring any of the penalties we mention earlier. However, if you ever transfer to another school that *does* participate in the NLI program, the penalties will be applied at that point unless you received a waiver.

Knowing When and Where to Sign

Because the NLI is based on recruiting, the NCAA does have some rules regarding when it can be signed, and those rules vary depending on your sport. In the following sections, we help you navigate these waters in a way that works for you.

Deciding whether to sign early

Your coach may encourage you to sign your NLI early, during what's called the *early signing period*. In fact, athletic programs commonly offer and spend most of their available scholarship money during the early signing period. For example, if a basketball program has five scholarships available, more often than not, at least four of those will be offered and usually accepted during the early signing period.

If a coach hasn't received commitments from the prospects he wants the most, the coach may opt to save a spot (or a few spots) rather than offer it to a player he thinks may not be as good. More spots often open after the early signing period because players already on the team become ineligible, quit, or redshirt.

If the sport you play has an early signing period, there are advantages and disadvantages to signing at this time.

The advantages to signing early

The biggest advantage: After you sign the NLI, the recruiting process is over. You've made up your mind, and you've been guaranteed a scholarship for the next year at your college. You're now free to focus on your final year of high school (or junior college). If for some reason you haven't met the eligibility standards, you can concentrate on that so you don't lose the opportunity you just received.

Another advantage to signing early may come if you've had a less-than-stellar season. The senior slump can hit hard, causing your usually excellent performance on the field or court to lag. What with the pressure of school, scholarships, the recruiting process, and family, it's a wonder you can even play. Many student-athletes are relieved to know that, despite a so-so season, their scholarship is safe after they've signed the NLI. Your college coach may not revoke a scholarship offer simply because you didn't have a great senior season.

The disadvantages to signing early

Signing early is a disadvantage if you aren't ready to make a commitment. Numerous student-athletes have signed an NLI with a school because they didn't think they would have another opportunity or simply wanted to end the recruiting process. After a great senior year, however, several bigger or more prominent schools started showing interest — but because the athletes had already signed the NLI, they were locked in. They couldn't be recruited by other schools.

If you've already signed an NLI, and you're still being recruited, the right thing for you to do is tell the recruiters that you've already signed an NLI. Trying to back out of a signed NLI could cost you at least one season of competition and force you to serve a year in residence at another school.

Signing an NLI during the early signing period can be a gamble, so make sure you're 100 percent sure that you're making the right decision *before* you sign your name on that dotted line.

Knowing the signing date for your sport

Table 15-1 outlines the signing dates for the 2006–2007 recruiting class. The dates change every year, but they're usually close to these dates. (Check the NLI Web site at www.national-letter. org or call 205-458-3000 to find out what the dates are for the year you'll be starting.)

NLIs must be signed after 7 a.m. (local time) on the initial signing date or any time prior to the final signing date.

In Table 15-1, the *early period* is a week-long period in November that allows you to sign an NLI, while the *late period* is a longer period of time in the spring when it is permissible to sign the NLI. The sports that do not have an early signing period have a *regular period,* and this period is the only time it is permissible to sign an NLI.

Table 15-1 NLI Signing Dates for the 2006–2007 School Year

Sport	Initial Signing Date	Final Signing Date
Basketball (early period)	November 9, 2005	November 16, 2005
Basketball (late period)	April 12, 2006	May 17, 2006
Football (midyear junior-college transfer)	December 21, 2005	January 15, 2006
Football (regular period)	February 1, 2006	April 1, 2006
Field hockey, soccer, men's water polo*	February 1, 2006	August 1, 2006
All other sports (early period)	November 9, 2005	November 16, 2005
All other sports (late period)	April 12, 2006	August 1, 2006

*These sports do not have an early signing period.

Setting up a signing location

The signing of the NLI can be as private or public as you want it to be. You can sign in your own home or in a public setting.

If you want to set up your own press conference to announce your signing of an NLI, remember that your future college coach (or a booster from that university) is not allowed to be present for this press conference. In addition, the college is not allowed to give you or let you borrow any apparel for the announcement. If you and/or your parents want to sport the colors of the school of your choice, you must buy those items in the same way that the general public would get them.

You may work with your club or high school coach to arrange the press conference. Again, this setting can be as formal (renting a banquet hall at a local hotel) or informal (sitting at a table in your school's gymnasium) as you see fit. You may want to make this your chance to pay tribute to all the coaches, teammates, and family members who helped and supported you.

 After you've determined a time, place, and location, you need to create a press release to send to the media in your area. A *press release* is generally a one-page letter stating your name, the school you've been attending, and your athletic statistics. If the local press has been following your high school athletic career, they'll most likely know all they need to know about your highlights — but don't be shy about listing your stats. To have a strong press conference, you need to generate interest — but keep the information to one page.

 It never hurts to invite as many friends and family as you can to cheer you on as you announce your commitment and sign the National Letter of Intent. ***Remember:*** The camera loves a good crowd.

If you're a big-time, blue-chip prospect, members of the media will generally already have asked you or your parents what time and where you will sign the NLI, so asking them to cover the signing is not an issue.

 If you're less prominent, or you don't play a major sport, have your high school coach or athletic director contact the local media. The media generally takes these requests more seriously than they do similar requests from parents. Having a representative from your high school call the media won't guarantee that they'll show up to cover the event, but it never hurts to ask. Who knows? You may be more popular than you thought!

Some student-athletes choose to have a quiet ceremony in their home with little fanfare. If this is more your style, you can still take the opportunity to thank family, friends, coaches, and teammates.

Knowing who needs to be present at the signing

For an NLI signing, most student-athletes have their parents and other members of their family (sister, brother, grandparents), high school coach and/or athletic director, friends, and teammates at the signing. Who you invite is your choice, but for most student-athletes, the NLI signing is a momentous occasion, one they want to share with those who are closest to them.

The NLI signing is not the place for your new coach or recruiting staff. You'll see them soon enough — and the rules don't allow them to be present.

Part V

When You're in the Big Leagues: For Existing College Students

The 5th Wave   By Rich Tennant

BY IGNORING HER ACADEMIC STUDIES AT DOG WALKING SCHOOL, MONA'S ATHLETIC SCHOLARSHIP WAS ABOUT TO COME TO AN END.

In this part . . .

We give you specific solutions on how to handle the most common problems student-athletes face as they begin their collegiate careers. Maintaining your eligibility, focusing on academics, working with your team and coaches, and dealing with the day-to-day predicaments of college life are all covered here.

You'll find out how to make smart and careful decisions, adhere to the rules, and focus on the task at hand — college graduations and playing time.

Chapter 16

Maintaining Your Eligibility

* *

In This Chapter

▶ Keeping up your grades and maintaining your amateur status

▶ Holding on to your scholarship when you're injured or pregnant

▶ Fighting for your rights

* *

*A*fter you've earned an athletic scholarship for college, your work is not over. In fact, it's just begun: There are plenty of rules about maintaining your academic and athletic eligibility, and you have to know those rules and abide by them. You also need to know your rights in case you're sick, injured, or pregnant and your collegiate athletic career is interrupted. Knowing whom to turn to and what to do could save you not only your scholarship, but also your eligibility. In this chapter, we give you the information you need.

Keeping Your Scholarship

In order to keep your scholarship, you must

✔ Maintain your academic eligibility by progressing toward a bachelor's or equivalent degree as determined by your school

✔ Maintain your amateur status as defined by the division or association for which you compete

If you're eligible, you're qualified and in compliance with all NCAA, NAIA, or NJCAA requirements to compete in intercollegiate athletics — and if you're not eligible, you can't compete.

You're responsible for establishing and maintaining your eligibility — nobody else will do this or watch out for this on your behalf. To be eligible to practice and compete, you must comply with all the applicable provisions of NCAA, NAIA, or NJCAA legislation (whichever association you belong to) and follow the rules and regulations of your institution and conference. We cover those basic standards in the following sections.

Maintaining your academic eligibility

Each year you progress through college, the standards for compliance or maintaining eligibility are somewhat different. Following are breakdowns of those eligibility requirements by division or association *after* the freshman year. (The requirements for your freshman year — initial eligibility requirements — are listed in Chapter 4.)

Rules and regulations change, and these rules are current as of this writing. Always be sure to check the current regulations for your school and your athletic association.

In NCAA Division 1

For eligibility in NCAA Division I athletics, you must meet the following progress-toward-degree regulations:

- ✔ **Sophomore year:** To be eligible your sophomore year, you must have successfully completed 24 semester (or 36 quarter) hours of credit between the opening of classes in the fall of your freshman year and the end of the summer session immediately before your sophomore year. Of those 24 semester hours, you must have completed 18 hours during the regular academic year (fall and spring semesters). Therefore, you can use only a maximum of 6 semester or 9 quarter hours of summer school to meet the 24-hour requirement.

- ✔ **Junior year:** To be eligible your junior year, you must have successfully completed 18 semester hours of credit between the opening of classes in the fall of your sophomore year and the end of the regular academic year (usually around May if you're on the semester system or June if you're on the quarter system). By your fifth semester of enrollment (halfway through your junior year) or seventh quarter (after the first quarter of your junior year), you must declare a major and have 40 percent of the course requirements for your degree program completed.

  Note: When we say "fifth semester" or "seventh quarter," we're not talking about summer sessions — though any coursework you do in your summer sessions obviously does count toward that 40 percent number.

- ✔ **Senior year:** In order to be eligible your senior year, you must have successfully completed 18 semester hours of credit between the opening of classes in the fall of your junior year and the end of the regular academic year (usually around May if you're on the semester system or June if you're on the quarter system). You must have must have 60 percent of the course requirements for your degree program completed prior to the beginning of your fourth year of enrollment, which is usually your senior year. If you do go a fifth year, you have to have 80 percent completed prior to the start of that year.

✔ **Fifth year:** In order to be eligible your fifth year, you must have successfully completed 18 semester hours of credit between the opening of classes in the fall of your senior year and the end of the regular academic year (usually around May if you're on the semester system or June if you're on the quarter system). You must have completed 80 percent of the course requirements for your degree program prior to the beginning of your fourth year of enrollment, which is usually your senior year. If you do go a fifth year, you have to have 80 percent completed prior to the start of that year.

Note: You must successfully complete at least six semester hours in the previous regular academic term of full-time enrollment to be eligible to participate in the next regular academic term.

Included in these rules are minimum GPA requirements that place you in good academic standing as established by the college you're attending. Most schools have a minimum GPA requirement of 2.0 in order to graduate. By NCAA guidelines, you must have 90 percent of a 2.0 (1.8) by your second year, 95 percent (1.9) by your third year, and 100 percent (2.0) by your fourth and fifth years.

Under NCAA regulations for Division I, you must complete four years of playing eligibility within five consecutive years of your first day of class. Division II and Division III student-athletes have ten full-time semesters to finish four years of eligibility (these do not have to be completed consecutively, as in Division I). (Medical-hardship waivers and pregnancy exceptions may apply to Division I, II, and III student-athletes for an extra year of competition. See "The rights of the student-athlete," later in this chapter, and also refer to Chapter 17.)

A waiver of the minimum full-time enrollment requirement may be granted if you're enrolled in the final term of your bachelor's degree program. Also, you may represent the institution while enrolled as a graduate or professional student or while enrolled and seeking a second bachelor's degree at the same institution.

In NCAA Division III

For eligibility in NCAA Division III athletics, you must meet the following three requirements:

✔ Make satisfactory academic progress toward a recognized degree

✔ Be enrolled as a full-time student (taking an average of at least 12 credit hours per semester)

✔ Be in good academic standing (maintaining a minimum grade point average of 2.0 or however "good academic standing" is defined by your school)

NCAA Division III rules state that you have ten full-time semesters to finish four years of eligibility. (You may be granted an extra year of competition if you're ill, injured, or pregnant and meet the NCAA's criteria for a medical hardship— see "The rights of the student-athlete," later in this chapter.)

In NAIA colleges

For eligibility in NAIA schools, you must fulfill the following requirements:

✔ **Be enrolled as a full-time student (taking at least 12 credit hours per semester or 9 credit hours per quarter).**

✔ **Be certified as eligible in the spring based on the previous spring and fall terms.** For example, a baseball player may not be eligible at the beginning of the fall 2006 term if he did not complete 24 hours between the fall 2005 and spring 2006 terms. However, he may be eligible at the start of the spring 2007 season if he passed 24 hours during the spring 2006 and fall 2006 terms.

✔ **Maintain a minimum GPA that places you in good academic standing, as established by the school for all students who are at an equivalent stage of progress toward a degree.** According to NAIA regulations, you must — upon reaching junior academic standing as defined by your school — have a cumulative grade point average of at least 2.000 on a 4.000 scale as certified by the institutional registrar.

✔ **Complete competition in a sport within ten full-time semesters.** You may be granted an extra year of competition if you're ill, injured, or pregnant and meet the criteria of the NAIA for a medical hardship (see "The rights of the student-athlete" later in this chapter).

In NJCAA

To be eligible in NJCAA institutions, you must fulfill the following requirements:

✔ Be enrolled as a full-time student (at least 12 credit hours per semester)

✔ Maintain a GPA of at least 1.75 on a 4.00 scale during the first semester or quarter and a GPA of 2.00 after that

✔ Have passed, prior to the second season of competition, a minimum of 24 credit hours with at least a 2.00 GPA

Maintaining your amateur status

Although maintaining at least a minimum GPA and making satisfactory progress toward a degree are essential for every college student who plans to graduate, these requirements are not enough for the student-athlete to maintain amateur status and remain athletically eligible to participate in intercollegiate sports. As you'll soon discover, as a student-athlete, you must abide by all kinds of regulations in order to maintain your eligibility.

For example, you can represent a college or university in one sport and play a different sport professionally (for money) as long as you don't receive financial aid from the university in the second sport. If you're no longer involved in professional athletics, you're not receiving any remuneration from a professional sports organization, and you have no active contractual relationship with any professional athletics team, you can receive financial aid in a sport in which you were formerly a pro. You cannot, however, represent a university in one sport and play a different sport as an amateur (for no money) if you receive any endorsements to pay for the amateur sport training. (See the "NCAA versus USOC: Must athletes choose between college athletics and the Olympics?" sidebar.)

At the beginning of your first academic year and each subsequent year, the NCAA requires you to sign two statements in order to participate in intercollegiate athletics:

✔ **NCAA Student-Athlete Statement (or Buckley Amendment):** By signing this statement, you agree to disclose information related to:

- Eligibility

- Recruitment

- Financial aid

- Amateur status

- Previous positive drug tests

- Involvement in organized-gambling activities related to intercollegiate or professional athletic competition

✔ **NCAA Drug Testing Consent Form:** By signing this form, you consent to be tested for the use of drugs banned by the NCAA.

If you don't complete and sign both of these forms, you won't be eligible to participate in practice and competition. (You must sign the drug consent form prior to practice or competition in Division I and Division II sports in which the association conducts year-round drug testing, and prior to competition in all other sports in Divisions I, II, and III.)

But these forms, and the accompanying required physical examination, are just the tip of the proverbial iceberg. Following are NCAA guidelines for maintaining amateur status.

Be sure to check with your head coach or athletic director regarding any questions you have about eligibility and before making any decisions regarding outside athletic participation. These guidelines are current as of this writing, but like any rules, they're subject to change.

You cannot, within your sport:

✔ **Accept payment or a promise of payment (in cash, prizes, or travel) for participation in your sport.**

✔ **Enter into an agreement of any kind to compete in professional athletics.** You cannot negotiate a verbal or written professional contract.

✔ **Request that your name be put on a draft list for professional sports, try out for a professional sports team, or consent to a medical examination by a professional sports team during the academic year, including all school vacations.**

✔ **Use your athletic skill for payment.** You cannot be employed on a "fee-for-lesson" basis.

✔ **Play on any professional athletic team (under your own or an assumed name).**

✔ **Have your athletically related financial aid determined by anyone other than the university.**

✔ **Participate on teams other than those fielded by the institution you attend during the season.** This includes exhibition or tournament games.

You cannot, in *any* sport (including ones you don't play for your school):

- ✔ **Agree to have your picture or name used to promote a commercial product.**

- ✔ **Accept things such as gifts, meals, and loans of cars or money from athletic interest groups or individuals in the athletic program at the university.**

- ✔ **Be represented by an agent or organization, including a coach or member of the athletic staff at your institution, to market your athletic skills or reputation.**

- ✔ **Agree to be represented by an agent in the future.** You may not agree to be represented by an agent until after your eligibility has already ended, including during your team's post-season competition.

- ✔ **Receive any benefit not available to other students at the university.**

- ✔ **Participate in a summer basketball league not approved by the NCAA (if you're a basketball player at your school).**

- ✔ **Play on a nondepartmental athletic team during the academic year without permission from your head coach and faculty athletic representative.**

- ✔ **Knowingly take any banned substances.** Don't assume that banned substances relate only to street drugs or performance-enhancing drugs. Banned substances also include prescriptions and over-the-counter medications such as cold medications and nutritional/diet supplements.

- ✔ **Knowingly provide information to individuals involved in organized-gambling activities concerning intercollegiate athletic competition; solicit a bet on any intercollegiate or professional team; accept a bet on any team representing the institution; or participate in any gambling activity that involves intercollegiate athletics or professional athletics, through a bookmaker, parlay card, or any other method employed by organized gambling.** *Remember:* Gambling includes nonmonetary material items that have tangible value.

- ✔ **Retain professional services (legal advice) for personal reasons at less than the normal charge.**

You also cannot

- ✔ Receive special discounts, payment arrangements, or credit on purchases (for example, airline tickets or clothing) or services (for example, laundry, dry cleaning, or tailoring)

✔ Receive loans of money in any amount

✔ Receive guarantees of bond

✔ Receive the use of an automobile

✔ Receive a free meal or service at commercial establishments

✔ Receive free transportation to or from a summer job

✔ Receive a benefit connected with off-campus housing (for example, individual TV sets or stereo equipment, specialized recreational facilities, room furnishings, or appointments of extra quality or quantity) that is not available on the same basis in the housing provided to at least half of the other members of the student body living in on-campus housing

✔ Sign or cosign a note with an outside agency to arrange a loan

✔ Sell or give a student-athlete ticket to athletic, university, or town events

✔ Receive the use of someone else's personal property (for example, boats, summer homes, cars, or stereos)

✔ Make or bill long-distance telephone calls using college telephones

✔ Use copy machines or fax machines at no cost

✔ Have course papers typed at the athletic department's expense

Generally, the preceding restrictions apply to all divisions in all three intercollegiate associations (NCAA, NAIA, and NJCAA).

Although NCAA Division III and NJCAA may not award athletic scholarships, their students are still expected to uphold certain ethical responsibilities. Additionally, individual schools, conferences, and associations may have their own conduct requirements. So be sure to check the academic and athletic requirements not only for the association in which you compete, but also for the conference, the division, and the individual institution.

For example, most institutions have policies restricting the use of alcohol at university events, as well as the use of tobacco products (including smokeless tobacco). All these institutions have policies regarding class attendance. And all have policies requiring that you not only adhere to the preceding restrictions, but also report unethical or illegal behavior such as gambling or involvement in violations of NCAA, NAIA, or NJCAA regulations.

Knowledge is your greatest tool. Know the rules.

NCAA versus USOC: Must athletes choose between college athletics and the Olympics?

Sometimes the eligibility rules for college athletes are hard to understand — not because the language is complex, but because the logic is confusing.

Take Jeremy Bloom's eligibility, for example. Jeremy was a standout wide receiver (he still holds a school record with a 94-yard scoring reception) and punt returner for the University of Colorado at Boulder. He was named both first-team Freshman All-America and Big 12 Freshman All-Conference team for special teams in 2002 and second-team Big 12 All-Conference for special teams in 2003.

Bloom also is one of the world's top moguls skiers. A member of the 2002 U.S. Olympic ski team, he holds several World Cup championships in moguls skiing and is, as of this writing, training as a member of the 2006 U.S. Olympic ski team.

The NCAA allows student-athletes to compete in and receive payment for professional sports other than their collegiate sports. (This rule has been used mostly by several college football players who tried their hand and failed at professional — Minor League — baseball and then returned to college football and their full scholarships.)

The NCAA does not allow athletes, however, to receive endorsement money for the sports they play, which leaves amateur athletes, such as Olympic skiers like Bloom, in a bind, because they receive no salaries from their amateur sports. Instead, they rely on endorsements to pay for expensive training and travel costs (and coaches', trainers', and physical therapists' salaries).

The U.S. ski team, for example, pays only for in-season training; athletes have to pay for the rest of the year's training, for the costs of trainers and coaches, and for travel and housing out of their own pockets. For competitive freestyle skiing, that means at least $100,000 per year.

Before attending the University of Colorado, Bloom received endorsements to fund his ski training. But under the NCAA's strict rules to keep its players "amateur," Bloom couldn't have both endorsements and a spot on the Buffaloes' gridiron. The NCAA also proclaimed that Bloom would have to give up the modeling and TV careers he had been offered.

So that he could continue to play football for the UC Buffaloes, Bloom turned down the endorsements for skiing, the modeling career, and the TV career. But, after unsuccessfully lobbying Congress to allow some compensation for college athletes, Bloom filed a lawsuit against the NCAA, seeking permission to keep his ski sponsorships. He argued that his endorsements were from skiing, not football; had absolutely no impact on football; and were necessary to support his Olympic dream, because skiers (like all amateur athletes) depend on endorsements and not salaries

(continued)

(continued)

as a source of income. He also argued that the NCAA's rules on sponsorship are unfair, considering that the NCAA itself makes hundreds of millions of dollars from sponsorship endorsements, TV contracts, and apparel licensing (including the thousands of UC shirts with Bloom's number sold for profit, none of which went to Bloom).

In asking that an exception be made to the rule about amateur status or that the rule be changed, Bloom also cited an example of the NCAA's making exceptions to its own rules. In 1999, Tim Dwight was allowed to retain his NCAA eligibility and compete for the University of Iowa's track team after paying back endorsement money he received as a wide receiver for the NFL's Atlanta Falcons in 1998. Another recent example of the NCAA's exceptions to its own rules is the organization's decision in 2004 to waive the mandatory sit-out year for Division I transfers after a number of Baylor men's basketball players left for other universities after one of their teammates was murdered and their coach tried to cover it up.

After forgoing two seasons' worth of sponsorship money, Bloom announced in 2004 that he could no longer afford to pay for his ski training and that he would have to accept endorsements. Also, in April 2004, the General Assembly of Colorado appealed to the NCAA in a joint resolution "to review its rules that prohibit Jeremy Bloom from successfully competing in both collegiate football and competitive skiing and make changes or exceptions to these rules to allow for Jeremy Bloom to continue competing in both sports." Bloom had shown he could excel in both sports, and he was sure the NCAA would support him.

He was wrong.

Not only did the NCAA reject the Colorado General Assembly's request, but in August 2004, a judge also ruled against Bloom. The rationale in both decisions was that a precedent for endorsements would endanger the core principle of amateurism in college football. So, unable to follow two dreams, Jeremy chose his quest for Olympic gold. The Buffaloes now have to play without their star wide receiver, and many of Colorado's citizens wonder about the NCAA's logic — but many also wonder whether the NCAA's regulations discourage potential Olympians from getting college educations. If these would-be ambassadors for the United States have to choose between full scholarships to college or endorsements to supplement their amateur training, are they getting the full support they should be getting for their Olympic dreams — dreams that inspire and excite us all?

If you also have dreams of Olympic and collegiate glory, you need to be aware of these conflicts. The moral: The NCAA, NAIA, and NJCAA are there to support and protect student-athletes, but the rules don't always work for you. Be sure you know exactly what the rules mean and how they apply to you.

Injury or Pregnancy?

So what happens if — despite keeping your grades up, taking a full load each semester, making satisfactory progress toward your declared degree, and following all the rules about maintaining your amateur status — life interrupts your athletic pursuits? In the real world, student-athletes do get hurt during their athletic careers. In some cases, injury can put those athletes' eligibility in question.

Unexpected pregnancy also can happen, and it too can adversely affect a student-athlete's athletic activities, just as an injury or illness can. Again, eligibility could be at risk.

You hope that you won't be injured or get pregnant, but hope is not a plan. You need to know what your rights are and what rights the college has. You need to know how you can be sure that your scholarship will be protected while you're sitting out for a semester or two. Read on to find the information you need.

The rights of the student-athlete

So what are your rights as a scholarship athlete if you become injured, get sick, or become pregnant? The first thing you need to know are your association's, conference's, and university's policies on injury/pregnancy and scholarships.

In case of injury or illness

In case of injury or illness, you'll need to be familiar with the medical-hardship waiver for your university, athletic conference, and athletic association. The medical-hardship waiver is supposed to determine how much opportunity to compete you've lost. If the waiver is approved, you may be entitled to an additional year of eligibility.

Illness can include anything from cancer to chemical dependency to psychological illness — anything that requires treatment.

In **NCAA Division I,** you can apply for a medical-hardship waiver if a season-ending injury or illness occurs in the first half of the season. You must not have participated in more than two contests or dates of competition, or more than 20 percent of the institution's scheduled contests — whichever is greater. So, for example, if your school has ten games in a season, you can play in two of those, and they have to be two of the first five games. But under NCAA rules, any number with a "point" after it is bumped up. So if the school has 11 games in the season, you can't play in 2.2 games; instead, you can play in 3 games — games 1, 4, and 5, for example — and still qualify for a hardship waiver. If you compete in the second half of the playing season, you're not eligible for a hardship waiver.

In **NCAA Division II,** you can apply for a hardship waiver no matter when a season-ending injury occurs, as long as you haven't participated in more than two contests or dates of competition or 20 percent of your school's scheduled contests — whichever is greater.

In **NCAA Division III,** you can apply for a hardship waiver no matter when a season-ending injury occurs, as long as you haven't participated in more than three contests or one-third of your school's scheduled games.

In the **NAIA,** you can apply for a medical-hardship waiver if both of the following are true:

✔ Your illness or injury is beyond your control and/or your coach's control and incapacitates you from competing further in the season.

✔ You haven't participated in more contests or dates than the association's allowable number in any sport recognized by the NAIA during the school year. (Check with your school for the allowable number in your sport.)

In the **NJCAA,** the criteria for a medical-hardship waiver are generally the same as in the NCAA and NAIA. Check with your school for the number of games allowable.

In all the associations and divisions, specific and up-to-date medical documentation from a physician and the institution's athletic training staff is required in order for a medical-hardship waiver to be approved. You can't participate in sports (even practice) after being examined by a physician and before receiving your written medical clearance — if you do, your hardship consideration will be nullified.

If you participate in any outside competition during the second half of the playing season, you won't qualify for a hardship waiver.

The nature and extent of your injury will determine whether you may be eligible for insurance from the college or from the association itself. Your college may have what is called *secondary and catastrophic injury insurance.* You won't have to pay a premium, but the insurance usually has a deductible of about $250 (which means the first $250 of your medical care comes out of your pocket and then the insurance kicks in).

Make sure you already have primary health insurance that covers intercollegiate athletics — that insurance should be in place before you even start school.

Although statistically, most waivers submitted are approved, that doesn't mean getting one is easy. In fact, many athletes don't get approved. They often lose their scholarships — the schools revoke them because the athlete isn't playing.

The fact is that you're at the mercy of your school when you're injured, which is why getting everything about your injury documented (and submitted to the conference office) quickly is so important. Don't do anything to jeopardize your waiver status — like trying to participate in a practice or playing in a little pickup game with some friends.

If you have questions, discuss your rights with your school's athletic director, and request written copies of the rules and policies. Again, make sure you keep copies of all medical records.

In case of pregnancy

In case of pregnancy, you also need to apply for the medical-hardship waiver. If the waiver is approved, you could be entitled to a sixth year of eligibility. Although pregnancy is specifically mentioned (once) in each of the NCAA's division manuals and in the NAIA manual, getting waiver approval can still be difficult.

It is called the *pregnancy exemption,* and the **NCAA Division I** Manual states

> A member institution may approve a one-year extension of the five-year period of eligibility for a female student-athlete for the reasons of pregnancy.

The **NCAA Divisions II and III** manuals state

> A member institution may approve a two-semester or three-quarter extension of this 10-semester/15-quarter period of eligibility for a female student-athlete for the reasons of pregnancy.

The **NAIA** Official Handbook and Policy Handbook states

> A female student will be granted a two-semester or three-quarter, one-time extension of the ten-semester rule due to pregnancy. The requirement for the extension period of time will be processed as an exceptional ruling to a standard rule.

The **NJCAA's** hardship provision does not mention pregnancy specifically. Instead, it says it is

> available to students who are unable to complete a season of competition or did not satisfy one of the eligibility rules as a result of an injury, illness, or some type of emergency beyond their control.

Because the NJCAA's hardship waiver does not mention pregnancy, it is up to individual schools (or conferences) to establish rules regarding pregnancy in student-athletes.

Why is the pregnancy hardship waiver often so difficult to get in all the associations? Because scholarship awards are made at your coach's discretion, and because scholarships can be taken away if you decide to drop or quit the sport you were given the scholarship for.

Voluntarily dropping out of participation is the number-one reason in all three associations that pregnant student-athletes lose their scholarships (see the "And then there was baby . . ." sidebar). Because young women often don't know what is safe to do athletically when they're pregnant (and because many schools don't offer this sort of counseling and education), these athletes feel forced to quit the sport entirely rather than risk injury to their unborn children. In fact, it is widely considered safe to do any exercise up to the 14th week of pregnancy (and some forms of exercise are safe even after 14 weeks). If you're pregnant and concerned about this, talk with your obstetrician.

If you feel like you have to choose between your pregnancy or your athletic scholarship:

- ✔ **Find out what the rules concerning pregnant athletes are for your association, conference, and school.**

- ✔ **Talk to your head coach and athletic trainer.**

- ✔ **Talk to your doctor (preferably an obstetrician).**

- ✔ **Do your own research about what you should and should not do during each stage of your pregnancy.** Go to www.womens sportsfoundation.org for articles and advice on this issue. And for an extensive study of what is and what is not safe to do during all stages of your pregnancy and after (including advice about nutrition), read *Fit Pregnancy For Dummies,* by Catherine Cram and Tere Stouffer Drenth (Wiley).

The rights of the college

As you've probably figured out by now, you're not the only one who has rights if you're injured, sick, or pregnant. The college also has rights — as well as lawyers to interpret those rights — which is why you have to be sure to abide by all rules and document any medical conditions to the satisfaction of your school and conference.

And then there was baby . . .

Becky Ledbetter was one heck of a softball player, playing second base and short-stop in Cedar Hill, Texas. By her sophomore year in high school, she was already getting recruiting letters from universities and colleges around the nation. So she began dutifully filling out and returning their forms and filing copies in her scholarship box. But she already had her heart set on one university.

"I wanted to go to Baylor," Ledbetter says. "It was my childhood dream."

So when she got an acceptance letter from Baylor, she felt like her life was on track. Still, she continued filling out and returning forms from other schools, just to be safe (a wise strategy).

Ledbetter understood that questionnaires or letters of interest are important because college coaches can't follow you through your high school and club-ball career if you don't correspond with them (unless you're among the top 1 or 2 percent of athletes in your sport in the nation — and you shouldn't count on it even then). When coaches know about upcoming club games, they can come out to watch.

By her junior year, Ledbetter was receiving e-mails and letters from coaches who were expressing intense interest in her playing abilities. "You could always see them [recruiters] in the stands," she said. "They kind of stood out with their college shirts and colors. They would carry briefcases and wear their school hats, and you could just tell they were recruiters and not parents." It was an exciting time for Ledbetter.

The national championship tournament, the biggest tournament of the year, was just two weeks before her senior year. Ledbetter should have had nothing on her mind but that tournament. Instead, she had something to worry about. "I had suspicions that I was pregnant," she said. "I was late. And, you know, as an athlete, you're pretty regular. So I just knew." Standing under the night lights on the field, she would feel faint.

At first, she tried to deny what was happening. "I tried to dismiss the whole thing. Ignore it, and it'll go away," Ledbetter said. It didn't.

Her team was very successful; it finished eighth out of more than 80 teams. When the tournament was over and the rest of the team was celebrating, Ledbetter took a pregnancy test. The results: pregnant.

She couldn't ignore the problem anymore. "What was I going to do?" Ledbetter wondered. She was an honor student, played three varsity sports, and had every intention of playing — on full scholarship — at Baylor. That was her dream.

She continued to stay quiet about her pregnancy, but people around her began to figure out what was going on. She refused to return phone calls and dodged her club coach. When the club coach finally pinned her down, Ledbetter told him, "Oh, well, coach, I can't come back." She said, "I was too embarrassed to say I was pregnant, and so I just said I couldn't play."

(continued)

(continued)

When her high school coach heard the rumors floating through the halls, he confronted her. Ledbetter admitted the rumors were true, and the coach simply "wished [her] the best."

This deflated Ledbetter. People were telling her now that she had blown it, that her scholarship chances and her college career were over. And now her coach's reaction seemed to confirm her worst fears.

"I let all the [recruiting] letters drop, and that was that." She dropped out of both high school and club softball, even though she continued to get letters from colleges around the nation. She never responded to Baylor, which eventually gave up and offered a scholarship to another athlete.

When Ledbetter's twin girls were 4 months old, she got an invitation to try out for Abilene Christian College's softball team. But by then, she had listened to too many naysayers. She didn't even bother to try.

Today, at age 20, Ledbetter plays pickup games and also plays in a slow-pitch coed league. She works as a teacher's aide at a private school. And she regrets giving up on her softball dream.

Her advice to other young women who might find themselves in this predicament: "Don't give up." Ledbetter knows from experience that when teenage girls get pregnant, "so many girls think this is it; it's all over. You're a teenager, and you think it's the end of the world, but it's not."

When asked how she would handle her situation differently today, Ledbetter said, "I would have found a way to take advantage of playing again. At the time I had the girls, I still had a year left of eligibility to play. I could have tried to go to college later." But with few people supporting that idea, it was hard for her to try again.

Unfortunately, Ledbetter's experience is far from unique. And her coach's reaction — simply writing her off at such a young and impressionable age — did a tremendous amount of damage to her psyche. This also is not unusual. But if others can learn from Ledbetter's mistakes, she feels she will have accomplished something.

"Maybe I could have played at Baylor; maybe not. It took me so long to realize that this was not the end of my dreams. I wish other girls could know you can still accomplish your dreams."

Your school will require you to take several steps from the day you step on campus as a student-athlete in the hope of preventing injury or, at least, preparing for it. You must

- ✔ Sign an acknowledgement of your assumption of risk injury
- ✔ Provide proof of primary insurance

> ✔ Provide a medical history and a release for the college to obtain medical information about you
>
> ✔ Pass a medical exam

But when the unfortunate *does* happen and illness, injury, or pregnancy occurs, the athletic department and the college itself will demand that you:

> ✔ Provide proof that any claimed injuries occurred at the school or at a sanctioned athletic event where the coach was present
>
> ✔ Give evidence that the college has been appropriately notified
>
> ✔ Comply with time limits set by the college for seeking treatment and submitting medical bills
>
> ✔ Provide other appropriate medical documentation from a physician who provided care at the time of the injury or illness
>
> ✔ Show statistical evidence establishing that you competed in the required number of scheduled contests

 You need to be certain about your responsibilities for informing the college and meeting its other requirements concerning your injury. Check with your head coach, the athletic training staff, and even your athletic director if you have questions or concerns. Don't assume you have all your bases covered. You could end up with no insurance, no scholarship, and no eligibility.

Fighting for Your Rights

What if hope fails, and your eligibility is revoked because of your injury, illness, or pregnancy? What are your rights? What can you do?

 The most important thing to find out is why your eligibility has been revoked. Perhaps you didn't report the injury promptly to your school, which can relieve the school of all liability. Perhaps you sought medical attention from a doctor not approved by the school, which also can relieve the school of liability. Perhaps the conference didn't get all the medical data it required to consider your medical-hardship waiver. If not providing the medical documentation to the conference is the fault of the school, you don't have to worry — but if that's *your* fault, you do.

 The bottom line: If your school determines, for any reason, that you're ineligible under the provisions of the constitution, by-laws, or other regulations of the association you belong to (NCAA, NAIA, or NJCAA), the school is obligated to withhold you from all intercollegiate competition.

If your hardship waiver has been denied, or if you've been denied eligibility pending an investigation into either academic or athletic misconduct, you have the right to *appeal* (fight the decision). If your school agrees with you that you've been wrongly denied, the school may appeal on your behalf for restoration of your eligibility. The burden of proof rests with you and the school.

We hope that you never find yourself the subject of any institutional, conference, or association investigation. If you do, be sure to do as much research as possible about your options, and talk to as many experts as possible.

The best and most obvious course of action is to avoid *any* prohibited or questionable behavior or action. If you have questions about whether something is permitted, ask your head coach or athletic director — even if it seems like a small thing, even if it seems like a dumb question. You cannot be too careful about your collegiate athletic eligibility and scholarship. Too much is at stake, and you've worked too hard up to this point to throw it all away.

Chapter 17

Redshirting

. . . .

In This Chapter

▶ Understanding what redshirting is

▶ Deciding whether and when to redshirt

▶ Knowing the rules of the game

▶ Looking at graduation

. . . .

*Y*ou can't help but come across the term *redshirting* when you listen to sports shows, watch professional drafts, or read sports magazines. It's even a common term in the fantasy-sports leagues. But what is it? Figuring out the meaning and rules behind redshirting is as important as knowing the guidelines of the NCAA, NAIA, NJCAA, and different divisions if you ever intend to transfer or (temporarily) step out of sports during your academic career.

More often than not, student-athletes who redshirted never thought they would do such a thing, much less need to know the terminology. But as an athlete, you know that things don't always go as planned. Having a new game plan is always a wise idea. In this chapter, we tell you what you need to know.

Is My Shirt Really "Red"?

No, but it's highly likely that the term *redshirting* was derived from the use of a red jersey. During the 1950s and 1960s, college football players wore off-white practice uniforms and cotton vests, typically red, to distinguish the scout players from the starters in scrimmages. Referring to a scout player as a *redshirt* picked up among players and coaches.

Although the term is as commonplace as any other sports terminology, you won't find it anywhere in the NCAA by-laws. Officially, the term *redshirting* does not exist. But it's so widely used that the term needs to be defined.

Simply put, the term *redshirt* is used to describe a student-athlete who doesn't participate in competitive sport for an entire academic year. If you don't compete in a sport for an entire year, you don't use a season of competition.

So what's a season of competition? The NCAA says that *competition* is participation against outside competition (for example, another team from another college). This doesn't include things such as practices and intrasquad scrimmages. In fact, as a redshirt, you'll be expected to practice every day, and you'll probably be an integral part of intrasquad scrimmages; more than likely, you'll be on the scout team and help prepare the starters for the upcoming game(s).

Many athletes report that playing or practicing with the squad is an essential tool to coming onboard as a redshirt.

Why Redshirt?

Redshirting sounds complicated. You may feel as though there are all kinds of rules involved. Or you may have heard that problems are often attached to redshirt athletes. So, you're probably wondering why anyone would *want* to redshirt.

Here are the two main reasons you may want to redshirt:

- ✔ **You or your coach feels you need an additional year to prepare for actual intercollegiate competition.** This kind of redshirting usually occurs during your freshman year.

- ✔ **You've been injured.** You may hear this referred to as *medical redshirting,* though the official term is *medical-hardship waiver.* If you get injured during a season, you may be granted an additional season by the conference office or the NCAA (if the school does not belong to a conference) due to the "hardship" you've suffered.

You aren't by any means guaranteed a medical-hardship waiver, and your school must appeal for this waiver on your behalf and present contemporaneous medical documentation to support the appeal. You must meet certain criteria in order to be granted a medical-hardship waiver (and again, even if you meet all the criteria, you may not get a waiver). See the "Handling a medical hardship" sidebar for more information.

Redshirting automatically indicates that you'll be in school for five years rather than the traditional four.

Redshirting may require you to attend graduate school or pursue a second bachelor's degree if you graduate prior to your fifth year. Of course, it takes many students four and a half to five years to graduate anyway, so you could also simply continue to take undergraduate classes during your fifth year and receive your bachelor's degree.

Handling a medical hardship

The criteria you must meet in order to qualify for a medical-hardship waiver vary from division to division in the NCAA. Here's the lowdown.

No matter which division you play in, the injury (or illness) must occur during one of the four seasons of competition, and you must be incapacitated by the injury for the remainder of the year.

If you're a **Division I** athlete, you can apply for a medical-hardship waiver if you're injured in the first half of the season and you haven't participated in more than two competitions or 20 percent (whichever is greater) of your school's scheduled or completed competitions.

If you're a **Division II** athlete, you can apply for the hardship waiver at any time (not just in the first half of the season), as long as you haven't participated in more than two competitions or 20 percent of the school's scheduled contests (whichever is greater).

If you're a **Division III** athlete, you can apply for the hardship waiver at any time (not just in the first half of the season), as long as you haven't participated in three or one-third of the school's scheduled contests (whichever is greater). Although Division III does not allow redshirting, you may apply for a hardship waiver to gain another year, provided that you meet the medical-hardship criteria.

As little as a decade ago, coaches could simply submit a letter stating the condition (or the injury) of an athlete, and that was sufficient. Today, regulations require that your injury be fully documented by your team's trainer and physician, and be verified by the coaching staff. Letters must be on official letterhead from both the university and the attending physician's office.

Not only is this process a way to deter fraudulent claims, but it's also viewed as an injury surveillance system. By thoroughly documenting your injury — be it a torn anterior cruciate ligament (ACL) or a swollen knee requiring an ice pack — viable statistics regarding the health and welfare of college athletes can be collected.

Note: According to regular redshirt guidelines, you're permitted to practice with the team. However, by *medical*-hardship regulations, you have no business on the field or court. By simply tossing a ball around or taking a few swings, you could jeopardize your hardship waiver.

The bottom line: If you're injured, talk to your coaches and trainers and, together, come up with a plan that feels right for all of you.

Another reason student-athletes redshirt has everything to do with personality conflict and little to do with sport. Redshirting is part of college sports because the collegiate sports world is filled with dynamic personalities. Sometimes, those personalities clash, and the coach/athlete relationship just isn't working. We've interviewed countless athletes, parents, and coaches who talked about the need to transfer (and redshirt) when that coach/athlete relationship began to unravel.

Whether it's a difference in coaching style, a question of work ethic, the Saturday-morning lineup, or team responsibilities, sometimes the best option is for the student to transfer to another school. Transferring can force you to sit out of competition during your first year at the new school, which is generally used as your *redshirt* year.

Talking about the Timeline

Various rules having to do with time govern your play as a college athlete, and redshirting can affect each of them. In the following sections, we spell it all out.

The five-year rule

At the Division I level, you have five consecutive years from the time you initially become a full-time student to complete your four seasons of competition (assuming you were a qualifier). This is commonly called the *five-year clock* or *five-year rule*. The five-year period is relevant because, even though you may redshirt one year, your five-year clock is still ticking. So if you redshirt during your freshman year, you have to complete your four seasons of competition during the next four consecutive years.

A *qualifier* is someone who is immediately eligible to play his freshman year at a Division I or II school based on his GPA and test scores.

At the Division II and Division III levels, there is no consecutive five-year clock. The principle is the same with the *10-semester/ 15-quarter rule* at those schools, which says you have 10 semesters or 15 quarters of full-time enrollment to complete your seasons of competition. Unlike the 5-year clock in Division I, if you aren't enrolled as a full-time student for a semester or quarter, it does not count toward your 10-semester/15-quarter clock.

Here's an example of the five-year rule in action: Let's say you come in as a freshman, and your coach decides that you'll redshirt that year. You then play during your sophomore year, but during your junior year, you suffer an injury in the second game of the season that incapacitates you for the remainder of the year. You recover from the injury and then play your senior year and your fifth year, but you want to try to regain that season that was cut short due to the injury. Unfortunately, in this scenario, even though you may meet the criteria for a medical-hardship waiver, you have no more time left on your five-year clock.

We cannot begin to tell you how many waiver requests like this the NCAA receives — and almost every single one of them is denied, because the decision to not compete during freshman year was not beyond the athlete's control.

The NCAA rules and regulations on these matters are hard to accept at times. They're also very clear. But because each situation is different, we recommend that you contact the director of compliance at your school or the NCAA directly if you have any questions.

You may be wondering whether you can redshirt if you play only a few minutes in a season and then get injured. If the game clock was ticking, that time counts, and you can't redshirt the year. This rule is a tough one to accept for athletes who were inured in the first three minutes of the game, but according to NCAA regulation, any amount of time counts as one of your seasons of competition in that sport. Even if you run out onto the field or court for the last two minutes and never touch the ball, you'll be charged with one season of competition.

The Atlantic Coast Conference (ACC) recently proposed legislation to allow student-athletes in the sport of football to have five seasons of competition and to eliminate redshirting and medical-hardship waivers. The proposal didn't receive a lot of initial support, so the ACC withdrew the proposal, but don't be surprised if a similar proposal is submitted in the near future.

The 21-year-old rule

Another Division I rule that could impact redshirting in addition to the five-year rule is the *21-year-old rule.* Don't worry — this doesn't mean that, when you turn 21, you become ineligible to play college sports. This rule applies to you only if you haven't enrolled as a full-time student by the time you reach the age of 21.

If you haven't enrolled as a full-time student by the time you turn 21, and you participate as an individual or as part of a team in *organized competition,* you'll be charged with a season of competition for each 12-month period this occurs prior to your enrollment.

Clear as mud? Here's an example: Let's say you're a golfer and, for whatever reason, you don't enroll in college as a full-time student right out of high school. You still haven't enrolled full time by the time you turn 21. Your birthday is in June and, a month after you turn 21, you play in your local club championship.

At this point, you've used a season of competition. You could play in any number of organized events during this 12-month period (until your 22nd birthday), and you would still be charged with only one season of competition.

If the same situation occurred after your 22nd birthday, you would be charged with another season of competition. So if you enroll in college in August after you turn 22, with the intention of playing for the college golf team, you'll have two seasons of competition remaining (because every athlete gets a total of four seasons of competition, and you've used two) and five years in which to complete them.

In order for a competition to be considered *organized,* one of the following has to exist:

- ✔ Competition is scheduled and publicized in advance.

- ✔ Official score is kept.

- ✔ Individual or team standings are maintained.

- ✔ Admission is charged.

- ✔ Teams are regularly formed or team rosters are predetermined.

- ✔ Team uniforms are used.

- ✔ A team is privately or commercially sponsored.

The 21-year-old rule may be a factor when you're deciding whether to redshirt or even attend college. This rule tends to impact international student-athletes more than domestic ones, because international students often don't start college immediately after high school and most international universities don't sponsor intercollegiate athletics (so student-athletes may want to attend college in the United States, where these rules exist).

This rule is more stringent if you're a tennis player, a swimmer, or a diver, so if you're an older prospect, discuss this rule with the coach who is recruiting you or contact the NCAA directly.

At the Division II and III levels, a similar rule applies only if you don't enroll in college at the first possible opportunity upon graduation from high school (that is, August/September if you graduate high school in May/June) *and* if the competition you participate in involves compensation or is with a professional organization.

Timing the playtime

A recent rule change at the Division I level allows student-athletes to participate in preseason scrimmages or exhibition games against outside competition during their initial year of enrollment without using a season of competition. Beware, however, that this allowance does not apply to all sports, because not every sport has preseason scrimmages or exhibitions.

In Divisions I and II, if you play women's volleyball, men's or women's soccer, field hockey, or men's water polo, you may compete against outside competition during the nonchampionship season (spring) without being charged with a season of competition as long as *both* of the following apply:

✔ You didn't compete against outside competition during the championship season (fall).

✔ You were academically eligible during this time.

Changing the game plan and playing instead

What if you (and your coach) planned on your redshirting, and then your coach asks you to play in a game? Although not a very common occurrence, this situation has happened, and you need to be aware of the rules and the consequences.

Here's the scenario: You and your coach had planned that you would redshirt, but suddenly faced with lots of injured players, your coach is desperate for a player and turns to you. Let's say, for example, you're a football kicker. You have a great future with a good school, and you've planned your future (and place on the roster) with the coach. But in the final minutes of the last game of the season, the final outcome of the game hinges on a possible national title, and the kicker is injured. This situation is particularly bad because the first-string kicker was injured earlier in the season — so this most recently injured player is the team's second and only backup kicker. The team doesn't have anyone else who can kick field goals or extra points, so the coach turns to you.

If the coach puts you in, and you play those last few minutes, you're now considered to have played a full season of competition — even though you essentially sat out the whole season except for those last few minutes. Some players who are redshirting even dress for games just in case this situation arises.

If you're tempted to think of this situation as unfair — after all, this goes against everything you and the coach have discussed — remember that you're part of a team, and your main purpose is to help that team win.

Redshirting history among coaches

If you think you may be interested in redshirting, or if the coach has a history of redshirting players, you'll want to discuss this topic during the recruiting process.

Some coaches recruit several players to come to their school knowing full well they plan on redshirting a lot of them — but they don't tell the players until they arrive on campus and start school. Don't let this happen to you. Make an informed decision when you decide to redshirt, and make sure it's the right choice for the program *and* for you.

Graduation and Redshirting: How One Affects the Other

Good news: Redshirting doesn't affect graduation. In other words, you won't be penalized for redshirting or moving to another school. Assuming that you stay on track academically, you may expect to graduate on time.

If you're moving to another school, be sure to speak with an academic counselor to make sure your credits transfer. Basketweaving 101 may not transfer from one college to another, but your standard college classes should transfer easily.

Statistically, very few college athletes move on to the professional athletic arena. And too many are suddenly left without a real plan. Without a job in the pros, college graduates find they have little interest or life skills in anything but ball.

Still, consider graduation as you discuss the idea of redshirting with your coach. Ask yourself:

✔ **What are your interests beyond your sport?** Redshirting to a different school where you know the coach and athletic program is helpful. But you must have reasons beyond sports for changing schools. If you're interested in medicine, attending an engineering school may not be your best move. As you begin to look at different schools, consider what they have to offer academically.

✔ **Where do you see yourself in five years?** This question is an important one — and a difficult one to answer. Although you may *hope* to continue in sports, playing professional ball, you'll need a backup plan. Perhaps you envision yourself working as a pro-team trainer, a physical therapist, or a business owner. By taking a hard, realistic look into your own future, you can make a better decision about the school you hope to move to. Again, consider the academic courses a new school offers and how it fits into your own personal plan.

✔ **Are you ready for more academic demands?** At this stage in your game, you have two things to consider:

- **Will all your courses transfer to the new school?** Talk to an academic counselor at the new school to figure out your academic standing and to be sure what courses transfer and what do not.

- **What will the new core curriculum be?** If the idea of becoming a sports nutritionist or veterinarian appeals to you, but you don't like the sciences, you have a problem. Consider what academic demands will be placed upon you when choosing your future career.

✔ **What other studies are you interested in?** We love this question — it's an important question that is rarely asked of student-athletes. Throughout the recruiting and college visiting process, you've been asked or will be asked to identify just one major (or career) that interests you. How many people do you know who had one job or one career throughout their lives?

There is no hard-and-fast rule that says you must have one career choice. If you know you want to be a fighter pilot or dental hygienist, good for you. If you've determined that you'd really like to be both a fighter pilot *and* a dental hygienist, even better! This narrows your field considerably when choosing a good college, but it also opens new and exciting opportunities and studies for you.

As you move forward, train for your academics with as much dedication and passion as you train for sport.

Chapter 18

Transferring

- -

In This Chapter

▶ Understanding the rules of transferring within the divisions

▶ Assessing your reasons for transferring: Looking before you leap

▶ Talking to coaches about a possible transfer

▶ Getting out of your scholarship

▶ Finding a new home

- -

*Y*ou may be considering leaving your school for any number of reasons:

✔ You may have a personality conflict with a coach or teammate.

✔ Your grades may be in the toilet.

✔ You may not have enough money to continue at your current college.

✔ You may be homesick.

✔ You may be overworked — or underworked.

Whatever your reason, you need to understand the rules and regulations of transferring, as well as the effect transferring will have on your college athletic career.

NCAA rules and regulations are complex, so it should come as no surprise to you that the transfer rules can be confusing and the process difficult. In this chapter, we walk you through the rules of transferring. For even more information, check out the NCAA Transfer Guide, available at www.ncaa.org.

In this chapter, we tell you the rules regarding transferring from a two-year college to a four-year college, transferring from one four-year to another four-year, and transferring from a four-year school to a two-year school and then back to a four-year. Who knew you had so many options?

Looking at the Rules

The grass may seem greener on another college campus, but before you can move on, you need to make an honest assessment of your status at your current college. (In this section, we fill you in on what to look for.)

Additionally, you need to determine your eligibility standing. Generally, you aren't eligible to participate at an NCAA school you want to transfer to unless you would have been eligible at the college from which you're transferring.

If you're interested in transferring to an NAIA school, you can go to www.naia.org/local/transferguide.html for more information about their regulations. Even if you're working with a coach, always double-check the institution's rules and regulations to avoid any mistakes or miscommunication.

Transferring from a two-year college to a four-year college

Even if you initially enrolled in a two-year college, your status with the NCAA Initial-Eligibility Clearinghouse still matters if you want to transfer to a four-year school.

If you never register with the clearinghouse, you're automatically considered a nonqualifier! (See Chapter 4 for more details.)

The good news: It's never too late to register with the clearinghouse. Even if you're in your second year of school at a two-year college, the clearinghouse can review your high school records and determine your qualifier status. This situation is common for students who had no definite plans to enroll in a four-year school immediately upon completion of high school. (Turn to Chapter 4 to determine whether you meet the standards of an NCAA Division I, II, or III school, or NAIA regulations.)

Transferring to a Division 1 school

Check out Chapter 4 to figure out whether you qualify based on your high school records. If you're a qualifier based on your high school records, you still have to meet other specific requirements to transfer from a two-year college for Division I:

 ✔ **You must have completed one full-time semester or full-time quarter at a two-year college.**

✔ **You must have 12 hours of transferable credits to a Division I school.** *Remember:* Not all classes are transferable. Talk to your academic counselor to be sure all credits will transfer to a Division I school.

✔ **You must have at least a 2.0 GPA.**

If you don't meet the preceding requirements, you won't be allowed to compete during your first year at the four-year school, but you *will* be able to practice and receive an athletic scholarship.

If you are *not* a qualifier based on your high school records, you may still transfer as a partial qualifier or nonqualifier and be immediately eligible to compete or practice at a Division I institution. Before you transfer from the two-year school, you must meet the following requirements to be permitted to practice, compete, and receive a scholarship:

✔ **You must graduate from the two-year college.** Note that if you attend more than one two-year college, at least 25 percent of your credit hours applied to your degree must be earned from the two-year college that awarded the degree.

✔ **You must have attended a two-year college as a full-time student for a minimum of three semesters or four quarters.** This rule excludes summer sessions.

✔ **You must have completed at least 48 semester hours or 72 quarter hours of credits that you can transfer to the Division I school.** You may need to speak to an academic counselor about the number of credits you earned during summer sessions, because this may affect your accredited transfer hours.

✔ **You must have at least a 2.0 GPA.**

Most Division I schools have academic counselors solely devoted to working with student-athletes. Your athletic counselor at your new school will probably work with you and the coach to ensure that you meet these requirements after transferring — whether you were a qualifier or not.

Transferring to a Division II school

Whether you're a qualifier, a partial qualifier, or a nonqualifier, you must have certain credentials from a two-year college before you'll be allowed to practice, compete, or receive athletic funding immediately after transferring to a Division II school.

You must have attended a two-year college as a full-time student for at least two semesters or three quarters, and at least *one* of the following must be true:

✔ You must graduate from the two-year college, and 25 percent of your credit hours needed for your diploma must be earned at the two-year college from which you graduated.

✔ You must have a 2.0 GPA and must have completed an average of 12 credit hours per semester or per quarter, transferable to any degree program at the Division II school.

The NCAA guidelines stipulate that all two-year transfer requirements must be completed before you transfer to an NCAA school. If, however, you transfer to a Division I or II school as a full-time student before you've completed such requirements, you must complete one academic year (attending full time) at the NCAA school before you're eligible to compete — even if this means transferring back to the two-year college to complete the stated requirements.

If you were a qualifier or a partial qualifier, and you don't meet these requirements, you'll be able to practice and receive institutional financial aid (including an athletic scholarship) during your first year at the Division II school, but you won't be permitted to compete against outside competition.

If you were a nonqualifier, and you don't meet these requirements, you won't be able to receive an athletic scholarship, practice, or compete during your first year at the Division II school. You will, however, be able to receive institutional financial aid that is not from an athletic source.

Transferring to a Division III school

The general guideline for transfers from a two-year college to a Division III school is this: You aren't eligible to compete until you've completed one year at the Division III school.

The NCAA guidelines offer some exceptions to this rule. You are eligible to compete immediately at a Division III school if you meet *one* of the following qualifications *before* you transfer from a two-year college:

✔ You haven't previously competed or participated in intercollegiate sports.

✔ You haven't practiced or competed in intercollegiate competition for a consecutive two-year period prior to the date on which you began practicing and/or competing at the Division III school.

✔ You've participated in intercollegiate sports, and you would have been academically and athletically eligible if you had stayed with the two-year college.

If you don't meet one of these exceptions, you may still practice and receive financial aid during your first year of residence as long as you're enrolled as a full-time student and meet applicable conference and institutional regulations.

Division III schools don't offer athletic scholarships.

Transferring from a four-year college to a four-year college

If you're enrolled in a four-year school, you need a release from your current school's athletic director before you can begin contacting other four-year schools about transferring. This rule applies regardless of who makes the initial contact — you, your parents, your high-school coach, or the coach at the college in which you're interested. If you get permission from the four-year school you're currently attending, all applicable recruiting rules apply. For example, the coach at the school you want to transfer to can call you only once a week, and you have a limit on the number of official visits you can make, just as when you were in high school. (For more on the rules of recruiting, check out Chapters 7 and 10.)

If you're a student at a Division III school, and you want to transfer to another Division III school, you may issue your own release — called a *self-release* — and talk to that new Division III school about transferring. If you want to transfer to a Division I or Division II school, however, you'll have to get a written release from the athletic director.

The first thing you should do if you're thinking of transferring is talk to your coach and see if he's willing to release you to talk to other schools about transferring. You should do this even though the release technically must come from the athletic director, because the athletic director is usually going to make her decision based on what the coach wants to do. More often than not, the coach will grant you permission to talk to other schools. But if you're on scholarship and/or a key player, the coach may have some reservations and say no.

If you don't get permission to talk to the other school, you have the opportunity to appeal that decision to a committee made up of members outside the athletic department.

If you're transferring to a Division I or II school, you must complete one year of residence at the second school before being eligible to compete. This applies regardless of when you transfer (at the end of the year or in the middle of a semester).

There are several exceptions to this rule, but the most common is the *one-time transfer exception*. You are eligible for this one-time transfer exception if:

✔ **You want to transfer to a school for a sport other than Division I football, basketball, or men's ice hockey.** However, you may qualify for the one-time transfer exception if you're transferring from a Division I-A football program to a Division I-AA football program or from a Division I-AA *scholarship* program to a Division I-AA *nonscholarship* program.

✔ **You have never transferred from another four-year institution.**

✔ **You are both academically and athletically eligible at the school you're transferring *from* as well as the one you are transferring *to*.**

✔ **The school from which you're transferring releases you from the one-year residence requirement.**

All the exceptions are listed in the NCAA Transfer Guide (available at www.ncaa.org), but what follows is a list of some examples where you may be eligible to compete immediately after transferring:

✔ Your first school discontinued or never sponsored the sport in which you participate.

✔ Your first school discontinued your academic major.

✔ You've just returned from at least 18 months of active U.S. military service or an official church mission.

Moving from a four-year college to a two-year college and back again

Let's say you began your academic and/or athletic career at a four-year school. Then, for a variety of reasons, you transferred to a two-year college. Now you want to make the move back to a four-year institution. You probably won't be surprised to find out that there is a separate set of rules for that situation.

If you choose to attend a Division I school and be immediately eligible your first year there, you have to meet the following qualifications:

- ✔ You must have completed 24 semester hours or 36 quarter hours of transferable degree credits with a minimum GPA of 2.0 at the two-year college.

- ✔ You must have earned your two-year degree at an accredited school. If you've attended more than one two-year college, be sure that at least 25 percent of the credit hours received were earned from the college of your graduation.

- ✔ You must wait one calendar year after transferring from a four-year school to be eligible for play.

The preceding criteria aren't necessary if you decide to return to the four-year school you previously attended, directly after the two-year school — unless you have an *unfulfilled residence requirement* at the time you left the NCAA school. You are considered to have an unfulfilled residence requirement if you weren't eligible to compete at a school and you left before you completed two consecutive full-time semesters (or three quarters).

In Division II, the preceding rules apply, whether you attend one or more four-year colleges before your full-time status at a two-year college.

But what happens if you played at a four-year school, transferred to a two-year school, and then want to go to a Division III school? You must be both academically and athletically eligible to have continued your education (and play) at the four-year school, or you must have completed 24 semester credit hours or 36 quarter credit hours that can be transferred from a two-year college.

Looking at Reasons to Move On

Transferring from one school to another is a long process that involves research and comparison of academics and athletics, as well as location, cost, and personal needs. Before transferring, carefully consider all these issues and weigh your options. Ask yourself why you want to transfer, and be sure that transferring is the answer.

Following are some reasons you may want to look at transferring to another school.

Your second choice doesn't cut it

For many student-athletes, settling for second best becomes the only option. Maybe the school of your dreams wasn't interested in you or didn't have the scholarship offer that another school did. Reluctantly, you accepted the second-choice school, hoping you would learn to love it. But you never settled in — it just doesn't feel right, and you want to transfer somewhere else.

Before you go through the trouble of transferring, be sure you give your second-choice school a fair chance. Try to make it one school year before you transfer. Many students find the freshman year difficult — whether they're athletes or not. You may find that by the end of your freshman year, you *do* like the school you're attending.

You're not getting enough playing time

Playing time, or the lack of it, is the most common reason student-athletes transfer.

But before you transfer because you don't feel you're getting enough playing time, talk to your college coaches, your high school coaches, your parents, and your teammates. Try to figure out what the problem is. And be realistic. Talented athletes sometimes sit the bench their freshman year, for a variety of reasons. Maybe you're just having trouble getting used to being a smaller fish in a bigger pond.

If you move from school to school, continuously dissatisfied with the kind of coaching you're receiving, people will start to think of you as a difficult athlete. Some coaches see this as the behavior of a prima donna they don't want or need.

You don't have enough money, or you're not happy with the scholarship

You know that a promise is nothing more than a verbal commitment. Even a written financial commitment to an athlete doesn't always hold. Because an athletic scholarship is only a one-year, year-to-year contract, it is subject to change. You may feel overlooked or unappreciated as promises for scholarship dollars go unfulfilled. At some point, you have to ask yourself what you want from your school, what you expect of your coaches and yourself, and what you believe you are entitled to.

Student-athletes often transfer simply because they can't afford to attend that school anymore. If your scholarship is reduced or cut

School ties

When high school quarterback Adam Lybrand finally finished the recruiting process, he and his family thought they had been through the recruiting wringer. A series of misunderstandings, an unscheduled hand surgery, and open promises led Lybrand to a smaller school. Because Lybrand did his research, and because he worked from an active list of what he wanted from a college (Lybrand felt that he needed to be in a Christian environment), he was willing to wait for and win the quarterback position.

Harding University in Searcy, Arkansas, had also heavily recruited Lybrand, so after much deliberation, he asked his then-coach for a release. With the proper NCAA release, Lybrand was granted eligibility status to redshirt as a freshman and was set to play at Harding the following year.

Upon his arrival at Harding, however, no scholarship money was offered. Lybrand studied the plays and prepared himself for the next year of eligibility, continuously working out and training with the team. By his sophomore year, Lybrand had proven to be a valuable asset to Harding, yet he was given only a small scholarship — nothing that would pay his room and board, much less tuition.

Lybrand spoke directly to his coaches regarding his scholarship status and was told that, when current seniors graduated, there would be money available. Yet the money was slow in coming. Lybrand was willing to wait it out. Because of his ability, persistence, and loyalty to the team, he did earn a scholarship that would cover all his tuition and some room and board.

Lybrand knew what he wanted. Other athletes may have opted to transfer again, but he stuck it out. During the third game of his sophomore year, the first-string quarterback was injured, and Lybrand went on to start seven games. By his junior year, Lybrand was the starting quarterback and setting records for Harding. In 2004, he set records for pass attempts and completions, and was in the top five for passing yards, passing touchdowns, and total offense. He also holds the record for 2003, establishing himself as one of the outstanding quarterbacks in Harding history. Still, he was not granted a full scholarship — something that was difficult for his family to accept and very frustrating for Lybrand, especially as new recruits came onboard with scholarship money.

So, why did he stay? Lybrand became part of the system and believed that he could help his team. He developed a sense of loyalty to the school and honed the strong work and play ethics with which he had been raised. With his new leadership role, sense of family, and the community on the Harding campus, the issue was about more than money.

for whatever reason, or if your financial-aid package doesn't cover the tuition increase, you may be forced to look elsewhere, even though you really enjoy attending the school. Not all student-athletes transfer because they don't like the coach or aren't getting enough playtime.

The school is too challenging academically — or not challenging enough

Although transferring to pursue a more challenging education is always commendable, many student-athletes transfer to *avoid* tough classes. Some students change schools because the academics seem too hard or because they hope to avoid the hassle and stress of studying at an easier college.

 If you're thinking about transferring, be sure you aren't running away from bad grades. The problem may be more about your study habits or social calendar than about how much you're able to learn and retain. Before leaving for academic reasons, give yourself a chance. Speak to your coach and guidance counselor, arrange for a tutor, or request a study group. Make sure you give yourself every opportunity to succeed.

You have personal or social reasons for transferring

Your reasons for leaving one campus to go to another may range from lack of friends to too much partying to family problems or a personal crisis. Whatever the reason, be sure that you aren't running from the real problem by changing your location.

Talking to Coaches

While you're enrolled as a full-time student at a four-year college, a coach from *another* college is not allowed (by NCAA rules) to communicate with you. Chatting or politely acknowledging a phone call — however brief — is not okay. A college coach or any member of an athletic department may not speak to, write to, phone, or e-mail you, your parents, or your guardians without written permission from your school's athletic director.

If you don't have the permission of your athletic director to talk to other coaches, no further communication between you and the other school may take place. And the second school shouldn't in any way encourage you to transfer.

Even with permission and a successful transfer, you may not receive any financial assistance for one full academic year as an NCAA recruit.

If you move from a non-NCAA or non-NAIA institution to a Division I school, you're free to communicate with other coaches. You won't need written permission for contact. You can issue your own _self-release,_ a term used in Division III that means you're free to contact and transfer to another school.

Seeking a Release from Your Scholarship

Your athletic scholarship is a yearly gift from your college. If you decide to transfer, your scholarship doesn't transfer with you. You'll have to voluntarily withdraw from your sport and relinquish your scholarship.

Talk to your coach, athletic director, and guidance counselor if you're thinking about transferring. To meet various legal and financial requirements, your coach and/or athletic director may choose to hold a hearing to weigh your reasons for leaving the school and withdrawing from your financial-aid award. You may want to request an official letter of withdrawal from your coach.

Starting the Recruiting Process Over Again

When you decide to transfer, it is — as Yogi Berra said — déjà vu all over again. You've been through this process before. It may have been a pleasurable experience for you — you understood the process and played the recruiting game well throughout. Or maybe you learned things the hard way — no one told you about the importance of playing club ball, promoting yourself, or getting your name out by your freshman and sophomore years. Throughout the recruiting process, you always seemed behind the eight ball. Or maybe you did everything you were supposed to do, yet despite your great efforts and researching, things went wrong.

Deciding to stay put

Why *wouldn't* you transfer if you were unhappy where you were? Particularly if your scholarship were stripped from you? Outsiders ask this question with complete sincerity. Why would anyone want to stay in a bad situation?

But in the athletic community, the loss of a scholarship means one thing: You're damaged goods. Right or wrong, this is the consensus among many athletes. Athletes feel embarrassed and unworthy when they lose their scholarships. This feeling is so powerful that many athletes give up the game and simply stay on as full-time students.

In many cases, the scholarship is lost through no fault of the athlete — and coaches understand this. Losing a scholarship may mean more than feeling disillusionment or anger — it usually has financial implications. If you lose your scholarship, you need to talk to the coaches and counselors about what the future holds. No scholarship doesn't necessarily mean no playing. And if it does, it's time to look for other opportunities — other schools, a more-academic focus, other interests.

An old Chinese saying applies so well to the dramatic, unexpected, and often unpleasant events in our lives: Whenever a door closes, another one opens. And that is one thing that sports teach — to watch for an opportunity to score and take it! When something goes wrong, look for that open door.

Use this book as your refresher course throughout the process. Continue to question yourself about what you want from the college experience. Is it just about playing ball? What about academics? How important is the scholarship?

You'll find some differences in the recruiting process when you transfer. For example, there is a good chance the coach at the school has already seen you play at your current college or remembers you from your high school days. Therefore, the questions "Can you play for this coach, and are you good enough to play for the program?" may already be answered.

The best advice we can give you if want to transfer is to make sure that this is the right *school* for you. If you want to transfer again, chances are you'll be forced to sit out another year from competition and lose a season of eligibility. More important, however, each transfer generally results in a loss of academic credit, putting you farther behind in the real reason for attending college: to earn your degree.

Part VI
The Part of Tens

The 5th Wave   By Rich Tennant

"Oh great! The one part of the interview process I
didn't practice for!"

In this part . . .

The rest of this book covers everything you need to know about scholarships, different college divisions, recruiting rules and regulations, press kits, college visits, and maintaining eligibility. What could be left?

Here we offer a few more tips on the recruiting process and making the final decisions.

Just as with every part of this book, this part is designed to give you only the information you need and to help you avoid some of the most common mistakes student-athletes make.

Chapter 19

Ten Things Not to Do during the Recruiting Process

*E*ven though this book is full of helpful information on how, when, and where to follow recruiting guidelines, you may still fall into certain traps along the way. In this chapter, we call them out for you, naming the ten don'ts college recruiters would like you to know about.

Don't Overestimate Your Ability

Assuming that you're better at your sport than you truly are is easy to do. Very often, student-athletes (and their parents) think they'll automatically be recruited — and they simply wait for the letters to start pouring in, the phone to ring off the hook, and their e-mail inbox to be constantly full. This mistake is a common one in the recruiting process.

Family, friends, and teammates can either help or hinder you in the recruiting process. What you *don't* need are a bunch of yes-men — people who tell you no one is better than you, that you're the greatest, that you deserve and will get the best when there are actually equally gifted athletes around you.

During the writing of this book, we met many athletes who told us they believed the hype. They didn't bother to recruit themselves because they figured the recruiters would be standing in line, waiting to sign them on. In many cases, they were simply left out or overlooked.

Never overestimate your abilities. If you keep in mind that there is always someone bigger, faster, and stronger, you'll maintain the right perspective.

Don't Underestimate Your Ability

You don't have to be the best player on the team and be named all-conference or all-state to get a scholarship. If you have some skill and a good attitude and work ethic, you can earn some scholarship money — even if you have to ask for it!

In 1994, athletes filed into the hallway of the United States Olympic Training Center in Lake Placid, New York, to see the latest posting of those who had made the cut. It was during the trials of the U.S. women's bobsled team, and athletes had come from all over the United States. Among them were strong, agile athletes from the sports of soccer, field hockey, and track. Among that group was author Alexandra Allred.

Alex had just had a baby and was still struggling to return to her competitive shape when she was invited to attend the U.S. trials. What she lacked in conditioning, she made up for in enthusiasm, energy, and the undying quest to learn all the ins and outs of bob-sledding — a highly technical sport.

To the surprise of many — including Alex — she made the cut while some of the most physically gifted athletes were sent pack-ing. When Alex asked how she made the cut among such strong athletes, she was told it was her strong work ethic, positive atti-tude, and willingness to work with others — an important trait for bobsledders — that set her above the rest.

There will always be someone bigger, faster, and stronger than you. But you can always have something else to offer. Your attitude, combined with your willingness to learn, listen, and be a team leader, will take you farther than fast feet and good hands.

Don't Count On Receiving a Scholarship

A common misconception among parents and student-athletes is that a scholarship will justify all the time and money they've put into their athletic career. Even though you may have attended sev-eral camps and/or showcases and had your own personal coach, you may not get an athletic scholarship — and you don't have to get a scholarship from a Division I or Division II school to make all your effort worthwhile.

In fact, many athletes opt for a Division III school because they want smaller class sizes, because they want a more one-on-one educational experience, or because the Division III school allowed them to play as they always had — with joy for the sport and free of pressure. Many athletes who later went on to become professional athletes or Olympians believe that a Division III school was the best choice they could have ever made.

Don't Think You're Being Recruited Just Because You Get a Letter

If you get a letter from a college, don't make the mistake of thinking that the school is now recruiting you. Athletic programs send out hundreds and sometimes thousands of letters to "introduce" themselves to potential prospects. More often than not, the students who receive these letters may never again hear from those schools.

According to the NCAA, a prospect is not considered to be a recruited individual unless a coach calls him more than once; the prospect makes an official visit; or the coach makes an off-campus, in-person contact with the prospect.

Think of the letter you've received as the first of many exciting steps.

Don't Downplay the Importance of Academics

Just because you're the star of the team or the best athlete in your high school doesn't guarantee you an athletic scholarship — especially if you don't have the grades and test scores to be eligible.

"Yeah, but Shaquille O'Neal did it," we can hear you saying. This is true. A small number of athletes have successfully moved to the pros with limited education.

Recently, we were attending a recruiting conference when we heard a conversation between a young athlete and his mother. He had used O'Neal as an example of an athlete who skipped out on higher education for a chance at the pros. Statistically, his chances of sharing O'Neal's on-court experiences could be likened to winning the lottery.

But we were struck by another fact: After all his successes, after all his wealth and accomplishments, O'Neal went back to school to earn his master's degree at the University of Phoenix, lending the message that nothing beats a solid education. When asked why he went back to school, O'Neal said he wanted to ensure his future in business after retiring from the sport.

Don't Devalue a Partial Scholarship

Full athletics scholarships are very rare. Unless you're going to play football or basketball at a major Division I school, the chances of your receiving a full ride are remote. A few other sports (women's volleyball and tennis, for example) at the big-time schools may offer full scholarships, but if you swim, run track, or play golf, for example, don't be offended if you get only a partial scholarship.

Don't Believe Everything You Hear

Be careful who you take advice from. Many people think they know a lot about the recruiting process when in reality they know very little. You can appreciate their support and encouragement, but be leery of their recommendations unless you're sure they understand the recruiting process. On the topic of "What Other Athletes Wish You Knew," numerous athletes and parents talked to us about this very issue. Well-meaning friends, family, and teammates offered them advice that did more harm than good.

Your best information will come from research. Follow the NCAA guidelines. Talk to recruiters and coaches firsthand. Check out college Web sites, and review their history on recruiting, championships, coach turnovers, scholarship offers, and degrees offered. Read blogs so you can find out what alumni have to say about the school.

No matter what school you're thinking of, you'll find people who will praise the school and others who will bad-mouth it. Talking to other people is always a great way to find out more about the school you're interested in and investigate claims you've heard — but the key here is research, research, research.

Don't Ignore Your Gut Instinct

Just like most things in life, your first instinct is usually the best one when it comes to the recruiting process and which school to attend.

 Money complicates things. Family complicates things. What your friends and teammates think will also muddle your initial feelings. In Chapter 10, we suggest that you take notes on the things you see, what you hear, and how you feel. Refer to these notes often — they're important.

Don't Be Afraid to Ask Questions

Throughout the recruiting process, you'll be bombarded with questions from coaches, family, friends, and others. Because you'll be the one most affected during the process, make sure *you* take the opportunity to ask questions that will help you make the right decision.

Don't Trust a Cheater

 If a school or a coach has been in constant trouble with the NCAA, be careful when considering that school. The old adage "A leopard does not change its spots" may come to mind here. Your college playing career may not be as enjoyable if your team or school is always under the NCAA microscope.

Again, research, research, research.

Chapter 20

Ten Considerations When Choosing a School

As letters and phone calls come in, you can easily get excited about an athletic-scholarship offer and forget everything you said you wanted in a school. In this chapter, we remind you of ten questions to ask yourself before you make the final decision.

Is the School Right for You Academically?

Not many high school students are 100 percent sure what their major will be in college, but most at least have an idea what subjects interest them. If you're a female lacrosse player, and you're interested in majoring in sports management, your options for a college that offers both that major and that sport could be narrow.

When you're choosing a school, you have to consider not just your athletic ability, but also the quality of the school's academics and the diversity of majors available.

College is a time of exploration and discovery. Don't limit yourself by the majors and careers you've heard about in high school. No matter what school you attend, you're sure to find out about majors and careers you never even knew existed — and one of those may be perfect for you!

Is the School Right for You Socially?

If you're from a rural town in the Midwest, attending a school like Temple (in downtown Philadelphia), St. John's (in New York City), or the University of Southern California (in Los Angeles) may be too much of a culture shock for you. And if you're from a big city, you may find smaller college towns like Bloomington (home of Indiana University) or Santa Barbara (home of the University of California at Santa Barbara) too slow paced. On the other hand, you may relish the excitement of going to school in an environment completely different from the one you're used to.

If you're part of an ethnic minority, you may want to find out how diverse the student body is. Are most of the minorities on campus part of the athletic program? If so, would you prefer a school with more diversity throughout the entire student body?

If you aren't a big partier, you may want to make sure the school you're considering isn't known for being a party school. *Remember:* Even at the big party schools, you can find a niche of people who are hitting the books more than the bars.

You can find out all kinds of information about the schools you're considering by visiting www.princetonreview.com/college/ or by buying the latest edition of *The Best 361 Colleges: The Smart Student's Guide to Colleges* (Princeton Review).

Is the School Right for You Athletically?

When you're considering a particular school, be realistic about your chances of playing. Will you really enjoy your collegiate career if you go to a top program and don't get the opportunity to play?

We've heard countless stories of athletes who could have gone to a bigger, more prestigious school but understood that their playtime would be limited. Instead, they followed the heart of a true athlete and chose playtime over status. Never have we heard an athlete object to playing the field rather than riding the bench.

Co-author Pat Britz was offered a scholarship to play at Wake Forest but understood he would be riding the bench for at least two years and possibly four. If he played with the University of North Carolina at Asheville, however, he knew he would be able to play. Britz went on to play as a starter and left as the top scorer in UNC's school history as a Division I program.

If you play basketball or football, playtime as well as team style could be major factors in your decision. If you're a three-point shooter, and you like to play in a "run-and-gun" offense, going to a school where the coach focuses on a more controlled game that tries to pound it inside may not be in your best interest. Likewise, if you're an option quarterback who likes to run a lot, you may not want to go to a college where the team passes the ball 40 to 50 times a game. In both cases, you may want to consider other options. Research the college you're looking at to ensure that the team's style matches your style of play.

Is the Coach the Best One for You?

This topic is a hot one for many athletes and their families. Although many student-athletes sign with a school for the opportunity to play for a specific coach, that coach may not be with them for their entire college career.

Ask the coach during your campus visit or interview how long his contract lasts and if he's looking elsewhere. Although asking the question doesn't guarantee a happy ending for you, it improves your chances of knowing the truth and being able to make an informed decision based on that information.

The National Letter of Intent states that you sign with a school, not with a coach, so make sure the school is the right fit first. That said, when you're choosing a school, consider whether you like and respect the coach. You're going to spend a lot of time the next four or five years with this person, and he can contribute to making your life miserable or very happy. Your coach is definitely going to mold you as an athlete, but ideally and more important, your coach also will help you grow as a person and prepare you for life beyond college.

If your coach leaves your college or university just a semester after you arrive, don't jump ship just yet. *Remember:* You signed with the school for the school — not just because of the coach. Give the new coach and your team a chance before chasing a coach who has his own agenda.

How Much Time Will You Spend in School versus Playing Your Sport?

Time management is a big part of being a successful student-athlete. If your sport monopolizes your time, one of two things is very likely to happen:

- ✔ **You'll get burned out or lose interest and quit the team.** Playing a sport is fun, but having to wake up at 6 a.m. for practice or weights, go to class for three or four hours, and then go for more practice or weights is more demanding than most incoming freshmen realize.

- ✔ **You'll start to struggle academically.** Many student-athletes don't appreciate the lack of free time they may have when they play a sport in college. If you don't prioritize going to class and keeping up with schoolwork, you could find yourself not only off the team, but also out of school.

Make sure you know the normal, day-to-day schedule of student-athletes at the school you're considering.

Going to class is a necessity. Many people go to school as athletes and think going to class is a nuisance. These are the ones who likely won't be around more than one or two years!

What Kind of Academic Services Are Offered to Student-Athletes?

Most Division I programs have a department devoted solely to assisting student-athletes with their class schedules, arranging tutors, and helping out with other academic issues.

Playing a sport in college can mean a lot of travel, which also can mean a lot of missed class time. If you aren't an exceptional student, or you don't have a lot of self-discipline, you may end up falling behind academically fairly quickly. With the assistance of the academic counselors, you can find a tutor and make sure you take the right classes.

The athletic department's academic counselors don't take the place of the counselor you'll have within the department in which you choose to major. The academic department's counselor will help you make sure you meet the requirements to graduate in that particular major; the athletic department's counselor will help you with studying and keeping your grades up.

Don't expect counselors or tutors to do your schoolwork for you! The athletic department's academic counselors are there to assist you, not to take tests and write papers for you. In fact, if they did, it would be considered academic fraud and would get both you and the counselor in a lot of hot water.

What Is the Graduation Rate of Student-Athletes at the School?

Are you serious about getting a degree? If a school has a low graduation rate for its student-athletes, it may mean the focus for that athletic department is strictly athletic, not academic. Although some sports may have better graduation rates than others, if the overall student-athlete graduation rate is on par with that of the regular student body, this is a good indicator that the athletic program's priority is for the student-athletes to succeed academically and earn a degree.

The NCAA requires its schools to provide you with a copy of the school's official graduation rates prior to your signing a National Letter of Intent, so finding out what the school's graduate rate is easy. If you don't receive a copy of it, you can contact the NCAA for this information — it's a matter of public record.

An incentive for Division I schools is called the Academic Progress Rate (APR), which is the percentage of student-athletes who remain eligible and/or leave school (transfer, go pro). For each student-athlete who becomes ineligible and/or leaves, the school could potentially lose a point, which will negatively impact its (APR). If a school has a low enough APR, it could suffer penalties, such as loss of scholarships or the ability to participate in postseason play. The bottom line: The APR rules motivate schools to graduate their student-athletes, in case the schools aren't motivated to do so on their own.

How Many of the School's Athletes Have Transferred Recently

If a program seems to have a new roster almost every year, try to figure out why. Are student-athletes leaving to play elsewhere or simply not returning to the team? If so, why?

Student-athletes may transfer for several reasons. They may feel they're not getting enough playtime, or personal problems at home may require that they move closer to home and family. Sometimes athletes are unhappy with their teammates or even a coach.

Whatever the reason, if transferring seems to be a common occurrence in a school you're considering, find out why. You don't want to go to a school where the team seems to start from scratch every year.

What Kind of Medical Treatment Will You Have if You're Injured?

Injuries are part of the life of an athlete, so expect them when you play at a higher level. The type of medical treatment available to athletes should be a factor in your decision. If you're planning to attend a major Division I school, chances are that the school will have at least one certified trainer at each practice and more than one at games. In sports that have more contact (for example, football), this is usually a no-brainer. But even for noncontact sports (such as swimming or cross country), you want a certified trainer to be present at practices and games in case you injure yourself or become ill.

If having medical personnel present at noncontact activities is not a priority for the school you're looking at, you probably want to consider going elsewhere.

Also consider the number of team doctors who work for the school. Local doctors usually volunteer their time to help the school; in return for their service, they get season tickets and other perks. If a school has 500 student-athletes and only one team doctor, chances are that the doctor's time will be monopolized by the major sports (football and basketball), so all the other athletes may not get the same kind of care. You need to decide if you're willing to put up with that type of inequity.

Make sure you visit the training room and talk to the head trainer so you're comfortable with how you'll be taken care of in case of an injury.

What's the Game and Practice Schedule during the Holidays?

If you play basketball or football, you can pretty much kiss your Thanksgiving and Christmas breaks goodbye. Most teams have games scheduled during these breaks, and if there are no games scheduled, you'll be expected to stay on campus for practices. The coach will usually allow to you to go home for two or three days between the end of the fall semester and the beginning of the spring semester, but you won't have three or four weeks off like the rest of the student body.

The same is true of spring vacations if you play a spring sport (golf, baseball, and so on). While your friends are planning their Easter holidays and their spring-break trips to Cancun or Daytona Beach, you'll be on campus practicing with the team or traveling to away games. Your spring break may be little more than competitions and extended road trips with the team.

If you're planning on going to school several hundred (or even several thousand) miles away from home, keep in mind that your trips back to see your parents will be few and far between if you play a sport. Sometimes, you may not know you're going to have a few days off until the day before, so planning a trip home may be impossible. Feel free to talk to other players about how this works so you can prepare your family and high school friends for how little you'll see them.

The important things to consider are these: How much time and energy are you willing to give to your sport? And how much is required at the school you're considering?

Appendix A

College Scholarship Web Sites and Resources

*E*ven if you don't get an athletic scholarship (or you get a partial scholarship), you have many options that can assist you with paying for college. In this appendix, we fill you in on some helpful resources.

Free $ For College For Dummies

Free $ For College For Dummies, by David Rosen and Caryn Mladen (Wiley), is a guide on how to find scholarships, grants, and other "free" money to use for your college expenses. Here, you can get advice on how to apply for federal grants, participate in state tuition plans, and compete for scholarships from private organizations. In addition, you discover how to avoid scams, how to complete applications on time, and how to find financial aid from unlikely sources.

Free Application for Federal Student Aid

If you want to be eligible for financial aid, you'll need to fill out the Free Application for Federal Student Aid (FAFSA), which will be sent to six schools to which you're applying to determine your financial-aid eligibility. You can complete a FAFSA online at www.fafsa.ed.gov. (If you're applying to more than six schools, go to the FAQs page on the Web site to find out your options for sending the FAFSA to schools beyond your initial six.) The kinds of aid you might receive include Pell Grants, Stafford Loans, PLUS Loans, Perkins Loans, and work-study. The Web site offers detailed information on all these possibilities and more.

Scholarships.com

This Web site (www.scholarships.com) offers free college-scholarship searches and financial-aid information resources. You can create a personal profile, and the service will present you with information on the most relevant and attainable college scholarship awards. You can sort scholarships by deadline, dollar amount, and relevancy. You also get tips on how to spot fraudulent scholarships. The scholarship database is updated regularly, so it pays to check the Web site often.

College Connection

College Connection (www.collegescholarships.com) offers free information on various scholarships. If you want to join the scholarship search service, it'll cost you $39.95 ($49.95 if you're an international student). The scholarship search service will search a large database of scholarships for you. Keep in mind you can do this work yourself, using this Web site and the others we list in this appendix, although doing so is time consuming. If you have more money than time, you may find this service worthwhile.

FreeGovMoney.net

According to this Web site (www.freegovmoney.net), the federal government gives away $10 billion in government grants every month. From FreeGovMoney.net, you can buy their Grant Information System ($39.99 if you download it directly from the site), which has information not only on how to receive a scholarship for college, but also on how to receive a grant to start a business or buy a home, as well as grants for minorities.

ScholarshipCoach.com

Ben Kaplan, a Harvard graduate who (by researching and applying for more than three dozen scholarships) amassed nearly $90,000 in scholarships and financial aid to pay for his tuition, is the Scholarship Coach (www.scholarshipcoach.com), and his Web site has a plethora of products to assist you in finding financial resources to attend college. Most of these are in a CD-ROM format or printed book. Some of the more popular ones are *Honey,*

I Shrunk the Tuition; How to Go to College for Almost Free: 10 Days to Scholarship Success; Essay Boot Camp; and *The Scholarship Scouting Report.* These range in price from $19.95 to $49.95, but some can be downloaded directly from the Web site for less.

ScholarshipCoach.com even has a Sports Scholarships link, which offers basic information about myths regarding athletic scholarships; general facts about the NCAA, NAIA, and NJCAA; information about campus visits; and more.

GuaranteedScholarships.com

This Web site (www.guaranteed-scholarships.com) is simply a listing of scholarships that are "guaranteed" as long as you meet the minimum requirements of the scholarship. For example, if you want to attend Albright College in Pennsylvania and you're a member of the National Honor Society, you can get a $1,000 scholarship. You're not in competition with other students for the scholarship — as long as you meet the minimum requirements, you've got it.

To be safe, always check with the college offering the scholarship to see what the requirements are.

CollegeBoard.org

Even the Internet home of the SAT test, the College Board, offers advice on how to find college scholarships (www.collegeboard.org/pay). This simple format offers a scholarship search of more than 2,300 sources for college funding totaling nearly $3 billion in available aid. In addition to information on how to apply for a loan, this site offers a college financing calculator that estimates how much it will cost you to attend college and how much you should be saving each year to pay for it all. You'll also find a financial-aid calendar, which is helpful when you're deciding when and where to start the process of applying for financial aid.

Appendix B

Resources for College Recruiting and Selecting Colleges and Coaches

● ●

*T*he research tools in this appendix will help you select the college that is best for you, as well as the best scholarship or financial-aid options available to you. Throughout this book, we suggest that you research individual colleges' athletic programs, their coaches, their graduation rates, and their individual academic and athletic requirements before you commit to one school. If practice makes perfect, research certainly offers more security.

The following is a list of excellent resources that can help you find the information you need:

✔ **At First Glance Corp:** A college athletic recruiting firm designed to help student-athletes and parents with the college recruiting process through a CD-ROM that contains a complete list of academic and athletic accomplishments as well as live video of individual athletes, allowing them to showcase their skills to college coaches even if they can't play in front of a particular coach. Services range from $599 to $2,499. (20 Pleasant St., Newburyport, MA 01952; phone: 978-465-3931; Web: www.atfirstglancecorp.com; e-mail: info@at firstglancecorp.com)

✔ **Athletes Advance:** Unlike other services that send out personal profiles by bulk mail but "do not guarantee that a student-athlete's profile is ever seen by a college coach," Athletes Advance claims that college coaches actively search its database looking for athletes who meet their specific criteria. This free information service helps student-athletes get noticed specifically by Division II and III colleges. (35 Salutation St., Suite 3, Boston, MA 02109; Web: www.athletesadvance.com; e-mail: info@athletesadvance.com)

✔ **Athletic Recruiters Service or MVP Services:** Calling itself the "paramount scouting and recruiting company," MVP connects

23,000 coaches at more than 2,000 colleges and universities listed with MVP Services to athletes in the United States, Canada, Australia, England, Italy, Germany, and Romania. Among the services offered are a personal athletic Web-site profile for each athlete and a "mentorship" established between student-athletes and coaches. Contact the company for fees. (Web: www.athleticrecruiters.com or www.mvp-recruits.com; e-mail: contact@mvprecruits.com)

✔ **Athletic Scholarship Connection (ASC):** This free Web site claims to be "the most complete . . . site available to assist you in the search for an athletic scholarship" and the one source you will need to obtain a scholarship. Its services include assisting you in building your own academic and athletic résumé and enabling you to see the postings of coaches from around the country looking for athletes. The site also gives you direct links to every college team's Web site; to every college's main page; to athletic-conference Web sites around the country; to the NCAA, NAIA, and NJCAA Web sites; and more. (Web: www.theasconline.com)

✔ **beRecruited.com:** This free college recruiting service claims to be the "largest college recruiting service on the Web," reaching more than 20,000 NCAA coaches (3,500 of whom are registered users of the service) in 16 NCAA sports. It also boasts making more than 350 college recruiting connections each day and more than 300,000 each year. Students can search any college in the country by location, size, major, and so on. (Web: www.berecruited.com; e-mail: info@berecruited.com)

✔ **CampusChamps.com:** Sponsored by American Education Services (AES), this free Web site offers "a one-stop shopping solution" for student-athletes' college planning and financial-aid needs — whether you're looking for colleges, applying for admission, or searching for financial aid. Services include a Campus Finder Web site; DynamiteSports.com, an educational program for student-athletes preparing for the recruiting process; SportsCamper.com, a directory of sports camps for more than 50 sports in every state; and more. (Web: www.campuschamps.com; e-mail: info@campuschamps.com)

✔ **College Admission Services:** This specialized service — geared toward 150 top undergraduate schools and the top 50 business schools in the United States — helps students decide what schools to apply to by calculating (with 98 percent accuracy) their chances of getting into those schools. The service matches your background, test scores, and achievements to the schools' admission requirements and helps you narrow your school search and focus on the ones where you have the best chance of getting in. The fee is $12 to $16 per school. (641 W. Willow St., Suite 107, Chicago, IL

60614; phone: 312-498-2823; fax: 312-951-8260; Web: www.go4ivy.com; e-mail: comments@go4ivy.com)

✔ **College Athletic Placement Service (CAPS):** The first service to place a student-athlete with an athletic scholarship in the United States, as well as the first to place a woman with an athletic scholarship, CAPS assesses a student-athlete's academic and athletic abilities and matches that student to specifically targeted schools. One-time retainer fee of $500. (P.O. Box 28849, Rancho Bernardo, CA 92198; phone: 888-860-2277 or 858-451-3300; fax: 858-451-3357; Web: www.capsplacement.com; e-mail: info@caps1971.com)

✔ **College Athletic Scholarships:** This free site helps you find and contact college coaches with information such as "what college coaches need to know about you" and "what you need to know to get an athletic scholarship," as well as with links to other helpful Web sites and information. (Web: www.college-athletic-scholarships.com)

✔ **College Coaches Online:** This search site endorses the do-it-yourself approach to college selection but makes the process much easier for you by helping narrow the search for coaches at any college in the country. You can find the names, addresses, e-mail addresses, and phone numbers of 20,000 current NCAA and NAIA coaches in seconds. Narrow your search by individual categories such as location, size, tuition cost, sport, division, academics, and so on. The fee is $19.95. You also can order a College Coaches Online CD for $29.95. (2205 S. Hoyt Ct., Lakewood, CO 80227; Web: www.collegecoachesonline.com; e-mail: administrator@collegecoachesonline.com)

✔ **College Partnership, Inc.:** This is a comprehensive "full-service" college planning and preparation company that helps college-bound students and student-athletes prepare for standardized tests such as the PSAT, SAT, and ACT; apply for scholarships and financial aid; contact coaches through scouts; and so on. Contact the company for fees. (333 S. Alison Parkway, Suite 100, Lakewood, CO 80226; Web: www.collegepartnerships.com; e-mail: info@collegepartnership.com)

✔ **College Prospects of America, Inc.:** This marketing service for athletes — which claims to be the largest marketing service for athletes in the world — helps athletes from the United States and many other countries find schools where they can play their sports. You can find the name of your local sports representative by visiting the Contact Zone at the Web site. Contact the company for its fee. (P.O. Box 269, Logan, OH 43138-0269; phone: 740-385-6624; fax: 740-385-9065; Web: www.cpoa.com; e-mail: homeoffice@cpoa.com)

✔ **College Sports Scholarships:** This sports recruiting service covers all NCAA and NAIA sports. Its services include preparing a college athletic scholarship résumé for each student-athlete and having it individually addressed and delivered to the head coach of your sport at every school in the NCAA and NAIA system. The company also provides scholarship, recruiting, and financial-aid information for your specific sport. (phone: 831-582-0333; Web: www.athleticscholarships.net; e-mail: mike@athleticscholarships.net)

✔ **Collegiate Sports of America (CSAPrepStar):** Claiming to be the first and largest recruiting service for college-bound student-athletes seeking athletic scholarships, CSA matches student-athletes with 15,000 college coaches (at 2,000 colleges) registered in the CSA database using 78 registered scouts. Contact the company regarding other services and the fees. (22900 Ventura Blvd., Suite 100, Woodland Hills, CA 91364; phone: 818-225-7300; fax: 818-225-1098; Web: www.csaprepstar.com; e-mail: info@csaprepstar.com)

✔ **FastWeb:** This free scholarship search site — which claims to be the largest, most accurate, and most frequently updated scholarship database — matches your background with eligibility requirements for scholarships around the nation and advises you about scholarship opportunities tailored to you. It boasts a database containing more than 400,000 listings; an extensive directory of more than 4,000 schools; accessible information from national experts on admissions, financial aid, college searches; and more. (phone: 800-214-5656; Web: www.fastweb.monster.com or www.finaid.org/scholarships)

✔ **FindTuition:** This subscription-based scholarship search service allows subscribers to search scholarship opportunities through specific college, athletic, and scholarship searches based on individual needs and abilities. FindTuition — which claims to be the only place that has all the scholarships offered by all the colleges and universities in the United States — lists all the athletic awards available for student-athletes and will give you detailed advice on how to locate and apply for athletic scholarships. Contact the company for fee information. (Web: www.findtuition.com)

✔ **JUCO Sports Recruiting:** A junior-college or community-college scholarship is a very real alternative for student-athletes who want to continue their sporting careers at the college level but don't want to pursue a four-year degree, or for those who have been overlooked by NCAA schools but hope to compete at the junior-college level for a year or two and then be offered athletic scholarships at NCAA Division I schools. The NJCAA has more than 45,000 students competing in 15 men's sports and 12 women's sports (covering three divisions). And

JUCO successfully markets athletes to more than 500 schools in 43 states. (Web: www.athletic-scholarships.net; e-mail: ken@athletic-scholarships.net)

✔ **National Recruiting Network:** This hands-on service helps market you and connect you directly with college coaches (whether NCAA Division I or NJCAA) with a personal profile you create and they distribute. Your profile (which can be updated at any time) includes your academic and athletic accomplishments and statistics, test scores (such as SAT), press clippings, letters of recommendation, and so on. This profile is marketed to coaches at up to 50 colleges of your choice. The one-time fee, which includes other services, is $995. (1901 Harrison St., Hollywood, FL 33020l; phone: 954-725-8880; fax: 561-988-2073; Web: www.national recruits.com; e-mail: info@nationalrecruits.com)

✔ **National Scouting Report:** NSR claims to be the top professional recruiting organization in the world, the oldest and most successful high school athletic scouting and promotional company in America, and the largest and most frequently visited Internet site in the United States for scouting and promoting prospects. It promises to help you stand out among the 400,000 student-athletes who vie each year for 4,000 roster spots — if you're a good-enough athlete and student to meet NSR standards. Contact the company for its fees. (128 Total Solutions Way, Alabaster, AL 35007; phone: 800-354-0072 or 205-216-0080; Web: www.nsr-inc.com)

✔ **Recruit-Me Athletic Scholarship System:** The Recruit-Me system promises to teach you to search for and find an athletic scholarship "like a pro" for a "fraction of the cost" that a recruiting service or consultant would charge you. But the service requires that you meet three conditions: (1) You must be an excellent athlete; (2) You must be a good-enough student to be admitted to college; and (3) You must be willing to "work the system." (P.O. Box 928, Pismo Beach, CA 93448; phone: 805-481-0144 for orders and 805-550-7566 for consulting; fax: 805-481-5037; Web: www.recruit-me-now.com; e-mail: support@recruit-me-now.com)

✔ **ScoutUSA.com:** This program claims not only to be "the nation's top-rated college sports recruiting and scholarship service," but also to be the only recruiting service that uses scouts. You work with local scouts to create your online player profile, which you can update for free at any time so recruiters and coaches can follow your athletic career week to week; the profile is faxed to your top school choices. The one-time fee ranges from $99 to $549, depending on which program you select. (1505 Villanova, Austin, TX 78757; phone: 512-454-9062 or 877-202-8605; fax: 512- 454-0798; Web: www.scoutusa.com; e-mail: scout@scoutusa.com)

✔ **Sending Your Child to College: The Internet Guide for Parents:** This free informational site is geared primarily to parents and was developed by a librarian after years of his answering questions about colleges, the admissions process, and financial aid. Its format is straightforward and simple, with no fancy graphics. It simply points you in the right directions — to the Web sites (or other addresses) you need to contact depending on the topic (for example, financial aid, college applications, college admissions essays, and so on). It is, in effect, a "pathfinder" to the Internet and to all the information you need to find the right college and the right scholarships/financial aid for your college-bound child. (Web: www.guideforparents.com)

✔ **Sport-Scholarships.com:** This international service helps students who want to study in the United States obtain athletic scholarships and the opportunity to play in the United States. The service arranges scholarships in all 29 NCAA or NAIA sports and promotes athletes to 8,000 college coaches in the United States. Contact the company for the fee. (Philipp Liedgens, Center for International Education and Careers, Geiststr. 49, 48151 Muenster, Germany; phone: 49-251-2872424; fax: 49-251-53959525; Web: www.sport-scholarships.com; e-mail: pliedgens@sport-scholarships.com)

✔ **University Prospects (UP):** This international sports-recruitment service connects student-athletes with coaches at every college and university in the United States and Canada. UP walks each student through the recruitment process; promotes athletes by mailing student profiles to coaches, Internet marketing, and editing student-athletes' videos; assists students with SAT counseling and financial aid; and more. Established in 2000, the company had a 95 percent success rate with students enrolled in 2001. Contact the company for its fees. (*United States:* 1133 Broadway, Suite 706, New York, NY 10010; phone 888-208-9882; Fax: 888-208-9882; Web: www.university prospects.com; e-mail: usa@universityprospects.com. *Canada:* 70 E. Beaver Creek Rd., Richmond Hill, Ontario, Canada, L4B 3B2; phone: 905-882-7068; fax: 905-882-7078; e-mail: brian@universityprospects.com)

✔ **Varsityedge.com:** This free site provides student-athletes, their parents, and coaches information about the college recruiting process (information about athletic scholarships, recruiting, financial aid, recruiting rules, college applications, visiting schools, NCAA rules, and more). In addition to information about these topics, the site provides links to other helpful sites, relevant news articles, and application forms. (New England Interactive, 3 Sunset Ridge, Lexington, MA 02421; phone: 871-862-3180; Web: www.varsityedge.com; e-mail: info@varsityedge.com)

Beware scholarship scams

Every year, hundreds of thousands of students and parents are defrauded by scholarship scams, to the tune of more than $100 million a year. Here are some general guidelines to avoid becoming the victim of a scholarship scam:

✔ **If you must pay money to get the scholarship, it may be a scam.** Beware of application fees (even for as little as $2) or any fee you have to pay before getting a loan — such as "guarantee fee," "insurance fee," or "processing fee."

✔ **If the scholarship sponsor guarantees winnings or makes unreasonable predictions about success, it's probably a scam.** No legitimate scholarship sponsor will guarantee you'll win an award. And when "guarantees" are made, there usually are hidden conditions. If it sounds too good to be true, it probably is.

✔ **If everyone is eligible, something is amiss.** No scholarship sponsor gives money to students simply for breathing.

✔ **If the sponsors claim that they will apply on your behalf, be wary.** To win any scholarship, you must submit your own applications, write your own essays, and get your own letters of recommendation. You must do your own work — no exceptions.

✔ **If the sponsor requests personal information, such as bank-account numbers, credit-card numbers, or Social Security numbers, it's probably a scam.**

✔ **If the offer comes from an organization with an official-sounding name, check whether there is really a federal agency with that name.** And if the organization claims to be endorsed by a federal agency, beware — the federal government, the U.S. Department of Education, and the U.S. Chamber of Commerce do *not* endorse private businesses.

✔ **If the application has spelling and typing errors or looks unprofessional, be careful.** Legitimate sites pay attention to spelling.

✔ **If there is no telephone number or return address other than a post-office box, it may be a scam.** A legitimate scholarship will have both a phone number and an address.

✔ **If you're notified by phone, it's probably a scam.** You'll be notified of a legitimate scholarship in writing.

Because many of these sites offer — or claim to offer — the same services, you must do your homework to find the best deal. Research each site to find out what services it really offers, contact the local representatives, and ask questions. Find out which one offers the most bang for your buck.

Don't forget, during your scholarship search, to look into less-popular or lesser-known scholarships (such as those offered by smaller companies), unusual scholarships (such as the Student for Organ Donation Youth Leadership Award, for students who have made a commitment to raising awareness of organ donation and transplantation), and scholarships for average students (such as the Duck Brand Duct Tape Stuck at Prom Contest for students over 14 who are attending a high school prom in the spring). See more of these scholarships at `www.finaid.org/scholarships/unusual.phtml` and `www.finaid.org/scholarships/average.phtml`. And remember that many companies —such as Coca-Cola, Sears, Nike, and Balance Bars — offer yearly scholarships or grants.

Index

• D •

• *S* •

BUSINESS, CAREERS & PERSONAL FINANCE

0-7645-5307-0 0-7645-5331-3 *†

Also available:

✔Accounting For Dummies †
0-7645-5314-3
✔Business Plans Kit For Dummies †
0-7645-5365-8
✔Cover Letters For Dummies
0-7645-5224-4
✔Frugal Living For Dummies
0-7645-5403-4
✔Leadership For Dummies
0-7645-5176-0
✔Managing For Dummies
0-7645-1771-6

✔Marketing For Dummies
0-7645-5600-2
✔Personal Finance For Dummies *
0-7645-2590-5
✔Project Management
For Dummies
0-7645-5283-X
✔Resumes For Dummies †
0-7645-5471-9
✔Selling For Dummies
0-7645-5363-1
✔Small Business Kit For Dummies *†
0-7645-5093-4

HOME & BUSINESS COMPUTER BASICS

0-7645-4074-2 0-7645-3758-X

Also available:

✔ACT! 6 For Dummies
0-7645-2645-6
✔iLife '04 All-in-One Desk Reference
For Dummies
0-7645-7347-0
✔iPAQ For Dummies
0-7645-6769-1
✔Mac OS X Panther Timesaving
Techniques For Dummies
0-7645-5812-9
✔Macs For Dummies
0-7645-5656-8
✔Microsoft Money 2004 For Dummies
0-7645-4195-1

✔Office 2003 All-in-One Desk
Reference For Dummies
0-7645-3883-7
✔Outlook 2003 For Dummies
0-7645-3759-8
✔PCs For Dummies
0-7645-4074-2
✔TiVo For Dummies
0-7645-6923-6
✔Upgrading and Fixing PCs
For Dummies
0-7645-1665-5
✔Windows XP Timesaving
Techniques For Dummies
0-7645-3748-2

FOOD, HOME, GARDEN, HOBBIES, MUSIC & PETS

0-7645-5295-3 0-7645-5232-5

Also available:

✔Bass Guitar For Dummies
0-7645-2487-9
✔Diabetes Cookbook For Dummies
0-7645-5230-9
✔Gardening For Dummies *
0-7645-5130-2
✔Guitar For Dummies
0-7645-5106-X
✔Holiday Decorating For Dummies
0-7645-2570-0
✔Home Improvement All-in-One
For Dummies
0-7645-5680-0

✔Knitting For Dummies
0-7645-5395-X
✔Piano For Dummies
0-7645-5105-1
✔Puppies For Dummies
0-7645-5255-4
✔Scrapbooking For Dummies
0-7645-7208-3
✔Senior Dogs For Dummies
0-7645-5818-8
✔Singing For Dummies
0-7645-2475-5
✔30-Minute Meals For Dummies
0-7645-2589-1

INTERNET & DIGITAL MEDIA

0-7645-1664-7 0-7645-6924-4

Also available:

✔2005 Online Shopping Directory
For Dummies
0-7645-7495-7
✔CD & DVD Recording For Dummies
0-7645-5956-7
✔eBay For Dummies
0-7645-5654-1
✔Fighting Spam For Dummies
0-7645-5965-6
✔Genealogy Online For Dummies
0-7645-5964-8
✔Google For Dummies
0-7645-4420-9

✔Home Recording For Musicians
For Dummies
0-7645-1634-5
✔The Internet For Dummies
0-7645-4173-0
✔iPod & iTunes For Dummies
0-7645-7772-7
✔Preventing Identity Theft
For Dummies
0-7645-7336-5
✔Pro Tools All-in-One Desk
Reference For Dummies
0-7645-5714-9
✔Roxio Easy Media Creator
For Dummies
0-7645-7131-1

SPORTS, FITNESS, PARENTING, RELIGION & SPIRITUALITY

0-7645-5146-9

0-7645-5418-2

Also available:
- Adoption For Dummies
  0-7645-5488-3
- Basketball For Dummies
  0-7645-5248-1
- The Bible For Dummies
  0-7645-5296-1
- Buddhism For Dummies
  0-7645-5359-3
- Catholicism For Dummies
  0-7645-5391-7
- Hockey For Dummies
  0-7645-5228-7

- Judaism For Dummies
  0-7645-5299-6
- Martial Arts For Dummies
  0-7645-5358-5
- Pilates For Dummies
  0-7645-5397-6
- Religion For Dummies
  0-7645-5264-3
- Teaching Kids to Read
  For Dummies
  0-7645-4043-2
- Weight Training For Dummies
  0-7645-5168-X
- Yoga For Dummies
  0-7645-5117-5

TRAVEL

0-7645-5438-7

0-7645-5453-0

Also available:
- Alaska For Dummies
  0-7645-1761-9
- Arizona For Dummies
  0-7645-6938-4
- Cancún and the Yucatán
  For Dummies
  0-7645-2437-2
- Cruise Vacations For Dummies
  0-7645-6941-4
- Europe For Dummies
  0-7645-5456-5
- Ireland For Dummies
  0-7645-5455-7

- Las Vegas For Dummies
  0-7645-5448-4
- London For Dummies
  0-7645-4277-X
- New York City For Dummies
  0-7645-6945-7
- Paris For Dummies
  0-7645-5494-8
- RV Vacations For Dummies
  0-7645-5443-3
- Walt Disney World & Orlando
  For Dummies
  0-7645-6943-0

GRAPHICS, DESIGN & WEB DEVELOPMENT

0-7645-4345-8

0-7645-5589-8

Also available:
- Adobe Acrobat 6 PDF
  For Dummies
  0-7645-3760-1
- Building a Web Site For Dummies
  0-7645-7144-3
- Dreamweaver MX 2004
  For Dummies
  0-7645-4342-3
- FrontPage 2003 For Dummies
  0-7645-3882-9
- HTML 4 For Dummies
  0-7645-1995-6
- Illustrator CS For Dummies
  0-7645-4084-X

- Macromedia Flash MX 2004
  For Dummies
  0-7645-4358-X
- Photoshop 7 All-in-One Desk
  Reference For Dummies
  0-7645-1667-1
- Photoshop CS Timesaving
  Techniques For Dummies
  0-7645-6782-9
- PHP 5 For Dummies
  0-7645-4166-8
- PowerPoint 2003 For Dummies
  0-7645-3908-6
- QuarkXPress 6 For Dummies
  0-7645-2593-X

NETWORKING, SECURITY, PROGRAMMING & DATABASES

0-7645-6852-3

0-7645-5784-X

Also available:
- A+ Certification For Dummies
  0-7645-4187-0
- Access 2003 All-in-One Desk
  Reference For Dummies
  0-7645-3988-4
- Beginning Programming
  For Dummies
  0-7645-4997-9
- C For Dummies
  0-7645-7068-4
- Firewalls For Dummies
  0-7645-4048-3
- Home Networking For Dummies
  0-7645-42796

- Network Security For Dummies
  0-7645-1679-5
- Networking For Dummies
  0-7645-1677-9
- TCP/IP For Dummies
  0-7645-1760-0
- VBA For Dummies
  0-7645-3989-2
- Wireless All In-One Desk Reference
  For Dummies
  0-7645-7496-5
- Wireless Home Networking
  For Dummies
  0-7645-3910-8

HEALTH & SELF-HELP

0-7645-6820-5 *†   0-7645-2566-2

Also available:
- Alzheimer's For Dummies
  0-7645-3899-3
- Asthma For Dummies
  0-7645-4233-8
- Controlling Cholesterol For
  Dummies
  0-7645-5440-9
- Depression For Dummies
  0-7645-3900-0
- Dieting For Dummies
  0-7645-4149-8
- Fertility For Dummies
  0-7645-2549-2

- Fibromyalgia For Dummies
  0-7645-5441-7
- Improving Your Memory
  For Dummies
  0-7645-5435-2
- Pregnancy For Dummies †
  0-7645-4483-7
- Quitting Smoking For Dummies
  0-7645-2629-4
- Relationships For Dummies
  0-7645-5384-4
- Thyroid For Dummies
  0-7645-5385-2

EDUCATION, HISTORY, REFERENCE & TEST PREPARATION

0-7645-5194-9   0-7645-4186-2

Also available:
- Algebra For Dummies
  0-7645-5325-9
- British History For Dummies
  0-7645-7021-8
- Calculus For Dummies
  0-7645-2498-4
- English Grammar For Dummies
  0-7645-5322-4
- Forensics For Dummies
  0-7645-5580-4
- The GMAT For Dummies
  0-7645-5251-1
- Inglés Para Dummies
  0-7645-5427-1

- Italian For Dummies
  0-7645-5196-5
- Latin For Dummies
  0-7645-5431-X
- Lewis & Clark For Dummies
  0-7645-2545-X
- Research Papers For Dummies
  0-7645-5426-3
- The SAT I For Dummies
  0-7645-7193-1
- Science Fair Projects For Dummies
  0-7645-5460-3
- U.S. History For Dummies
  0-7645-5249-X

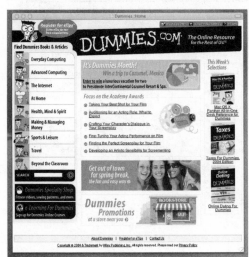

Get smart @ dummies.com®

- **Find a full list of Dummies titles**
- **Look into loads of FREE on-site articles**
- **Sign up for FREE eTips e-mailed to you weekly**
- **See what other products carry the Dummies name**
- **Shop directly from the Dummies bookstore**
- **Enter to win new prizes every month!**